每天读一篇
美丽 英文

Everyday English Snack

每一次跌倒，都是最好的成长
Think Positive II

［美］
杰克·坎菲尔德（Jack Canfield）
马克·维克托·汉森（Mark Victor Hansen）
艾米·纽马克（Amy Newmark）/编

李娴/译

湖南文艺出版社
HUNAN LITERATURE AND ART PUBLISHING HOUSE

博集天卷
CS-BOOKY

图书在版编目（CIP）数据

每一次跌倒，都是最好的成长：汉英对照/（美）坎菲尔德（Canfield, J.），（美）汉森（Hansen, M.V.），（美）纽马克（Newmark, A.）编；李娴译 .—长沙：湖南文艺出版社，2015.1
书名原文：Chicken soup for the soul:think positive

ISBN 978-7-5404-7022-7

Ⅰ.①每… Ⅱ.①坎… ②汉… ③纽… ④李… Ⅲ.英语—汉语—对照读物②人生哲学—通俗读物 Ⅳ.① H319.4：B

中国版本图书馆 CIP 数据核字（2014）第 270833 号

著作权合同登记号：图字 18-2012-42

上架建议：心灵励志·英语学习

CHICKEN SOUP FOR THE SOUL: Think Positive
101 Inspirational Stories about Counting Your Blessings and Having a Positive Attitude
By Jack Canfield, Mark Victor Hansen, Amy Newmark. Foreword by Deborah Norville
Published by Chicken Soup for the Soul Publishing, LLC www.chickensoup.com

Chicken Soup for the Soul, P.O. Box 700, Cos Cob, CT 06807–0700, Fax 203–861–7194

每一次跌倒，都是最好的成长

编　　者：（美）坎菲尔德 等
译　　者：李　娴
出 版 人：刘清华
责任编辑：薛　健　刘诗哲
监　　制：蔡明菲　潘　良
特约编辑：苗方琴
版权支持：辛　艳
版式设计：崔振江
封面设计：壹诺设计
内文排版：百朗文化
出版发行：湖南文艺出版社
　　　　　（长沙市雨花区东二环一段 508 号　邮编：410014）
网　　址：www.hnwy.net
印　　刷：北京嘉业印刷厂
经　　销：新华书店
开　　本：880mm×1230mm　1/32
字　　数：332 千字
印　　张：12
版　　次：2015 年 1 月第 1 版
印　　次：2016 年 8 月第 2 次印刷
书　　号：ISBN 978-7-5404-7022-7
定　　价：36.00 元

质量监督电话：010-59096394
团购电话：010-59320018

目录
Contents

Chapter 2   Health Challenges
第二部分   健康挑战

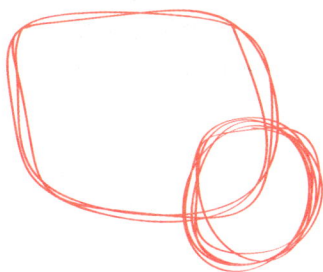

前言
Foreword

Change your thoughts and you change your world.

—Norman Vincent Peale

I can't remember how long it's been since I first heard those words. "Change your thoughts and you change your world." It's a simple enough phrase, but wow—those words are packed with power. They have been something of a lifelong mantra for me. Change your thoughts and you change your world. When times are tough, when I feel so frustrated by disappointments and not reaching my goals, I repeat those words in my head and make a conscious, almost physical effort to change course, recalibrate, and steer my little ship of self in a fresh, more positive direction.

The other day I was speaking to a group of

women in the financial industry and one woman asked to what I credited my long television career. I had to think for a moment. I have been blessed in the television business. I started working at the CBS station in Atlanta when I was still in college and interviewed then-President Jimmy Carter on live TV when I was only nineteen years old. (I don't know which was more exciting: Interviewing the President or having ABC's White House Correspondent Sam Donaldson asking me afterward what he said! You could have shot me and my tombstone would have read, "She died happy.")

Even when my career took some unexpected tough turns, I somehow managed to pull myself and my career back together, pick up the pieces and start over. But what was the secret to my long and still successful career? As I pondered the question, I realized there were probably three qualities that have worked in my favor—and the good news is anyone can develop them. I have an extraordinary capacity for hard work, an insatiable curiosity, and a (sometimes) ridiculous ability to look on the bright side. All of us can work hard, put in a few more hours at work, and try a bit harder to master a challenge. Contrary to the old saying, curiosity didn't kill the cat or anyone else. Learning new things, exploring topics about which we know nothing—that's what gives life its zest. But finding the bright side? Well, how does one do that when you've lost a job, gotten a dire diagnosis, or seen your personal life shattered?

For me, finding the silver lining in life's clouds was something of a coping mechanism. As a little girl, my mother battled chronic illness. I remember when school was dismissed, I'd hear other kids see their moms' cars in the pick-up line and complain their playground time was cut short because "Mom is here already." I was thrilled when my family's station wagon was among the cars. It meant Momma was having a "good day." Later when she died (I was twenty at the time), I was able to find gratitude in the knowledge that she was no longer in pain.

When I started my television career before I graduated from the University of Georgia, I had to deal with plenty of naysayers. How would you respond to a woman who said to you, "You have no business being here and are taking away a job from someone who is qualified?" I will never forget that moment in front of the vending machines at Channel 5. I stammered out a reply along the lines of "Well, the boss is giving me this chance and I hope to prove him right." I also resolved to make the most of the opportunity as long as it lasted. Who knows, the boss might be persuaded the female reporter was right!

Later when my career was derailed, I discovered that while I couldn't control what happened in my life, I could control how I let it impact me. The Greek Epictetus said it quite elegantly, "Ask not that events should happen as you will, but let your will be that events should happen and you will have peace." I must confess I only made that discovery after wallowing in depression and self-pity for a time.

It is NOT easy to do. How many times have you not gotten the job? Haven't you felt kicked in the teeth when denied opportunities, been frustrated when someone not nearly qualified enough got the green light instead? Maybe health problems have rearranged your family's life. It just isn't fair! I know I've felt that way. It isn't fair. But here's the thing. I've given birth to three children and at no point was there ever anyone in the delivery room looking at that newborn and saying, "Kid, from here on out, it's all fair." Life just doesn't work that way.

Some people don't seem to be affected by that. Just as there are those who can walk through a field of poison ivy and never have the slightest discomfort, there are some people who can be hammered by all of life's negatives and still remain unscathed. I am not one of them. Deny me entry to the club, and part of me wants to sob in the corner wondering why I'm not good enough. But the bigger part of me has realized it's no fun going to a pity party. The better I get at resisting the temptation to give in to sorrow, frustration, or stress, the more successful I seem to be both personally and professionally.

Was this real—or was this something I was imagining? I have spent the last several years researching these kinds of values: gratitude, respect, resilience, and faith. What is it that makes some people more resilient? How are some people able to let the difficulties of life roll off them like water off a duck's back? Why do some people just seem stronger? The answer is—think positive. Recent scientific studies have proven that a positive attitude actually has measurable benefits. Grateful, positive people report they have better lives and more positive memories. People who can recall positive events have been proven to be more resilient, even in the most difficult of situations. People who keep track of the "good things" in their lives are healthier, more active, more productive—and held in higher regard by those around them. There's peer-reviewed proof of this!

What's more, people who are able to "accentuate the positive" are smarter, better able to make cognitive associations and connections. They solve problems faster and more correctly. Kids who summon up positive memories do better on tests.

But how do you summon up positive memories when you're in a really tough spot? Plenty of people are right now. The collapse of financial markets wiped out jobs and life savings. Retirements have been postponed and homes foreclosed upon. Terror scares have changed the way we travel and the way we look at people from other countries.

Change your thoughts and you change your world.

Let's face it. It isn't always easy. When things aren't going your way, those peppy little sayings—Count your blessings instead of sheep, When life gives you lemons, make lemonade, and If you see it, you can be it —are just plain annoying. Maybe they make good needlepoint pillows for the family room couch, but somehow when you're in the midst of a really difficult situation in life, trite sayings just don't help much. But this book will.

This wonderful new volume of 44 inspirational stories, *Chicken Soup for the Soul* is filled with the experiences of real people living everyday lives with real problems—yet they've found the inner strength to overcome those challenges or just ways to make their lives more meaningful. Their examples can help you find the keys to think positively, enhance your own life, and provide that little bit of motivation that will help you get over the speed bumps of life.

In fact, the tale of the *Chicken Soup for the Soul* series is a great example of thinking positively. I fell in love with the series when it debuted years ago—but I love the story of how it came into existence even more. I cite it often in speeches as a great example of perseverance. Jack Canfield and Mark Victor Hansen were convinced their little collection of inspirational stories had the power to make a meaningful difference in the lives of readers. Trouble was—they couldn't find a publisher who agreed with them. They took their book to publishing conferences and literally hundreds of publishers ignored them. Finally they found a small publisher who would print a few thousand books for them and they started selling *Chicken Soup for the Soul* from the backs of their cars as they drove around making speeches and doing book signings. Eventually the book, that wonderful "little engine that could," turned into a worldwide bestseller and *Chicken Soup for the Soul* became a publishing phenomenon, one of the most successful lines of books in history.

You just gotta believe. Like JB, the foster kid in the movie *Angels in the Outfield*. Every night the little boy went to bed with the hope that tomorrow would be the day he found a family. "It could happen," JB would say as he snuggled under the covers. In true Hollywood form, the movie ends with JB being adopted by the baseball coach George Knox, played by Danny Glover.

JB never gave up hoping that "it could happen." The founders of *Chicken Soup for the Soul* never gave up on their dream of changing lives through inspiring stories. George Patton said "Courage is fear hanging on one second longer." I like to paraphrase General Patton by saying "Success is failure trying one more time." Most of us don't succeed because we give up too soon. Did you know the average customer has to be pitched five to seven times before he will make a purchase? The average salesman gives up after two or three attempts. Want to read the ultimate tale of persistence? Pull out your kid's copy of *Green Eggs and Ham*. Count up how many times Sam I Am offers up that plate of green eggs and ham. Sixteen tries! As we all know, when he finally gave it a taste, he liked it after all!

It could happen for you too. You just gotta believe. The stories that follow will help you summon up that extra bit of energy and positive attitude that you need to help you reach your potential. They already have for me.

Change your thoughts and you change your world. I didn't know until I did a computer search that those were the words of Dr. Norman Vincent Peale. Did you know he too suffered from self-doubt? After his manuscript for *The Power of Positive Thinking* was rejected for the umpteenth time, he tossed it in a wastebasket, where it was retrieved by his wife Ruth. It went on to publish 20 million copies in 42 languages. Ruth Peale, who died in 2008, was quoted as saying of her husband, "I don't have as much self-doubt as he did."

You'll love James Scott Bell's story of how the now-bestselling author first met the "father" of positive thinking. Bell tells how meeting Norman Vincent Peale influenced his life and helped him get through the anxiety of being a lawyer turned author.

Got a dream you want to pursue but afraid to give it a shot? Just do it. When unemployment hit both her and her husband, Debbie Acklin was terrified to start a new business but circumstance had backed her into a corner. Starting from scratch, she made up flyers advertising computer training, rented out a space, and fielded enough clients to launch a successful new business. Her example has made me strategizing how I can extend my own fledgling yarn business into something more.

Health issues are something every family must confront but it's not always easy to see the blessing in such unfair adversity. The chapter "Health Challenges" is filled with stories in which unforeseen medical misfortunes changed lives but also offered opportunities. People like Shawn Decker, a hemophiliac who contracted HIV from a childhood blood transfusion. Instead of turning bitter, Shawn is upbeat and grateful for life. Now a leader in the HIV community, he's coined the term "positoid" for people in his situation.

Sometimes the magic is in the moment. Surveys show nine out of ten of us say we are "extremely pressed" for time (and the other ten percent were too busy to talk to the pollster, I bet!) The stories in the "Every Day Is Special" chapter remind us that sometimes there's nothing better than an average mundane day. Elaine L.Bridge used to treat herself to a special coffee on Fridays and always had an upbeat attitude on those days. Then she realized she could have that fancy coffee and that positive attitude any day of the week. Why not make every day a special day?

Heather Gallegos had gone to the local track a bit reluctantly for her morning run when she was confronted with an incident that underscored how an ordinary day can turn out to be anything but. When a man collapsed on the track in front of her, she administered CPR compressions for eleven minutes until paramedics arrived. As she put it, it was "Enough time to save his life. Enough time to change mine."

They say God never gives you more than you can handle, but you have to marvel at the strength and resilience of the people who share their stories in the chapter called "Role Models." You all know the emphasis I put on gratitude and giving thanks. In the "Counting Your

Blessings" chapter, Jane McBride Choate's story on how a gratitude journal helped when her husband's business hit on hard times will probably encourage many of you to try the technique. As I've written in my own books, weaving gratitude into our daily lives empowers us to lead happier more productive lives. This powerful book ends with a chapter on "Gratitude," with inspiring examples of how the power of "thank you" can make an incredible impact.

As you read along, dog ear the stories that particularly resonate for you. You'll want to refer back to them on those days when you're feeling like "life" is getting the better of you. I also suggest you keep a pencil and paper handy to jot down the questions you might find yourself asking of you. Each of these 44 stories has a lesson of unique benefit. What you take from the stories might be different from what I learn or what a friend might discover from the story. As you go through the book, you'll begin to see a pattern to your scribbles. The questions you write—and the answers you offer to them—can provide a template to help you live your own life more authentically and more fully.

Are you living the way you feel you are meant to?

What are the benefits that come from your own adversities?

What blessings have happened this day, this week?

Who serves as a role model for you? Have you told them?

How can you celebrate the mundane and the ordinary?

What is it your life lacks that would give it greater meaning?

Share this book with family and friends. Give a copy to someone who needs a boost. And when you need a reminder that life is filled with blessings, benefits, opportunities, and joy return to this book. You'll find you're looking ahead with grateful, positive happy eyes that recognize all the good in your life now—and to come. I'm just positive of it!

—*Deborah Norville*

• • • • • • • •

改变你的想法，你也改变了你的世界。

——诺曼·文森特·皮尔

　　我已经记不清距离自己第一次听到这句话有多长时间了："改变你的想法，你也改变了你的世界。"就是这样一句简单的话语，却充满了无穷的力量。它就是我的人生格言。改变你的想法，你也改变了你的世界。在遇到困难时，在没有实现自己的目标而失望沮丧时，我就会在头脑中不断重复这句话，并且从精神和体力上努力去逆转局势，重新定位，用一种全新的更加积极的态度来调整自己的方向。

　　一天，我与一群从事金融业的女士交谈，其中一位询问我怎样评价自己长期从事的电视行业。我思考了一会儿，我享受着电视行业。当我还在上大学时，就开始在亚特兰大的哥伦比亚电视台工作，十九岁时就现场采访了时任总统吉米·卡特。（我不知道哪件事更加让我激动：采访总统先生还是之后美国广播公司白宫记者萨姆·唐纳森问我他说了些什么。你可以用枪击毙我，然后看到我的墓志铭写着"她幸福地死去了"。）

　　即使在我的事业遇到意想不到的困难的时候，我也努力地使自己和事业振作起来，整装待发，重新开始。但是，什么是我取得事业长期稳定成功的秘诀呢？当仔细考虑这个问题时，我意识到或许有三个对我有利的因素起到了作用——而令人高兴的是每个人都能够做到这三点。我有非凡的勤奋工作的能力，永不满足的好奇心，还有偶尔看似滑稽可笑的乐观处事的能力。我们所有人都可以勤奋工作，多花一些时间投入到工作中，更加努力地去征服新挑战。恰恰与老话相反，好奇心不会害死猫或者任何人。学习新事物，探究我们未知的主题——会让生活别有一番趣味。但是要如何乐观处事？好吧，当你失去了工作，收到可怕的诊断结果或是发现自己的生活支离破碎时，你又怎么能做到？

　　对我来说，在生活的愁云中找到一线希望本来就是一种应对机制。童年时，我的母亲长期与疾病抗争。我记得每当放学时，我听到其他孩子抱怨，因为看到母亲的车已经在排队等候而缩短了他们在操场上玩耍的时间，因为"妈妈已经在那儿等着了"。每当家里的旅行车也在其中时，我会兴奋不已，这说明妈妈"这一天状况不错"。后来她离开了人世（那时我二十岁），当明白她不必再遭受痛苦时，我的内心充满感激。

　　在我从佐治亚大学毕业前，刚开始从事电视工作时，我不得不与很多唱反调的人打交道。你该如何回应一位女士对你说："你无权待在这里，你剥夺了一个称职的员工的工作权利！"我永远不会忘记在第五频道办公楼内自动售货机前的那一幕。我结结巴巴地说："哦，老板给了我这个机会，我希望证明他的决定是对的。"与此同时，我下定决心竭尽全力地把握住这一次机会。谁知道，老板会不会被说服相信这位女士是对的！

　　之后当事业偏离轨道时，我发现虽然我无法控制人生中发生的事情，但是我可以控制它们对我的影响。希腊人爱比克泰德曾从容地说过："不要指望事情如你所愿，而是当事情发生时，心存平静。"我必须坦白，沉浸在沮丧与自怜中一段时间后我才意识到这一点。

这做起来并不容易。有多少次你被工作拒之门外？难道你没有在错失机遇时倍感受伤，在一个勉强合格的人却能顺利过关时万分沮丧吗？而或许因为健康问题，你的家庭生活发生了改变。这是多么不公平啊！我知道我会这样想，这不公平。重要的是，我已经生了三个孩子，而每次都有人在产房里对着刚出生的婴儿说："孩子，从现在开始，一切都是公平的。"只是生活从来不会按照他们所说的那样进行。

有些人似乎并不受影响。就像一些人穿过长着毒藤的原野，却并没有感到任何不适，有些人饱受生活的磨砺，但仍旧安然无恙。我并不是他们中的一员。当我被俱乐部拒之门外时，其中一个自己便想要躲在角落里哭泣，想知道为什么自己不够优秀。但是那个更强大的自己意识到自怨自艾毫无意义。我越是抑制住这种悲伤、沮丧、沉重的情绪，越能感觉到自己在个人成长以及职业上的成功。

这是真的吗？——或者只是我臆想的东西？我花了好几年的时间来寻找这几种价值：感激、尊重、豁达和信仰。是什么让这些人如此乐观？他们怎么能够对生活中的困难不屑一顾地一扫而过，就像水流过鸭子的后背？为什么他们会变得更加强大？答案就是——积极思考。最新的科学研究证明积极的态度可以让人受益匪浅。感恩、乐观的人表现出拥有更加美好的人生和更多积极的记忆。那些拥有美好的记忆的人被证实即使在最困难的境况下，也会表现得非常豁达。那些在人生中留下"美好事物"的人更加健康、积极、多产——并且得到身边人更多的青睐。对此的评论证明屡见不鲜！

除此之外，能够"强化积极因素"的人更加聪明，更容易产生认知联想、建立事物的联系。他们能更加准确快速地解决问题。那些能唤起积极记忆的孩子在考试中也表现得更好。

但是如何能在艰难的时刻唤起积极的记忆呢？现在许多人正处于这种境况里。金融市场的崩溃让人们失去了工作和毕生的积蓄，退休时间被推迟，家庭开支不断缩减，对恐怖主义的恐慌改变了我们旅行的方式及看待来自其他国家民众的眼光。

改变你的想法，你也改变了你的世界。

让我们来面对一切，虽然并不总是那么容易。当事情没有按你预计进行，那些令人振奋的语句——细数你的幸福而不是绵羊；当生活抛给你柠檬，那就来做柠檬汁；还有你能想到，就能做到——只会让人厌烦。它们就像家里沙发上的绣花枕头，而当你真正身处人生困境时，那些陈词滥调根本不起作用。但是这本书却能做到。

新的一卷《心灵鸡汤》包含了四十四个精彩纷呈、鼓舞人心的故事。它们都是生活中的真实的人物和他们所遇到真实的困难，然而他们都找到了内心的力量去跨越挑战或让生活更加富有意义。他们的实例会帮助我们找到积极思考的关键，改善你的生活，为你走出人生的低谷提供一些动力。

事实上，《心灵鸡汤》故事系列是一些积极思考的极好实例。当它几年前刚刚问世的时候，我就喜欢上了这个系列——但是我更喜欢这些故事产生的方式。在演讲中，我经常引用它作为坚持不懈的典范。杰克·坎菲尔德和马克·维克托·汉森确信他们收集的这些振奋人心的故事能够给读者的生活带来不同凡响的变化。问题是——他们没法找到与自己意见一致的出版商。他们把自己的书带到图书出版洽谈会，众多的出版商对他们的存在不屑一顾。最终，他们找到一个愿意为他们印刷几千册的小出版商，并开始开车四处宣讲，在汽车后备厢那里签名销售《心灵鸡汤》。最终，这个不可思议的"小小引擎"变成了一部遍布世界的畅销书籍，《心灵鸡汤》成了一个出版业的奇迹，是图书史上最成功的系列书籍之一。

你不得不去相信。就像在电影《棒球天使》中那个被收养的孩子 JB 一样。每天夜晚，小男孩儿都满怀着明天就能找到家人的希望入眠。"这有可能发生。"他蜷缩在被子下面说道。在真实的好莱坞模式中，影片以 JB 被由丹尼·格洛弗饰演的棒球教练乔治·诺克斯收养而结束。

JB 从未放弃"这有可能发生"的希望。《心灵鸡汤》的创立者们也从未放弃用鼓舞人心的故事改变人们生活的梦想。乔治·巴顿将军说过："勇气就是在害怕时再坚持一秒。"我想把巴顿将军的话改写一下："成功就是在失败时再尝试一次。"我们多数人没有成功是因为过早地选择了放弃。你们知道一个普通顾客在被推销五到七次后才会决定购买吗？大多数推销员尝试两到三次后就选择放弃了。你想要读到坚持不懈的故事吗？拿出你的儿童画本《绿鸡蛋和火腿》，数一数萨姆做了多少份绿鸡蛋和火腿。十六份！正如我们所知，他最终做成了美味佳肴，这至少让他欣喜若狂。

这也可能发生在你的身上。只要你愿意相信。随后的故事会帮助你激发更多的力量和积极的态度，帮助你发挥自己的潜能。它们已经为我准备好了。

改变你的想法，你也改变了你的世界。直到我用电脑搜索，才知道这是诺曼·文森特·皮尔博士的话。你们知道他同样也受到自我怀疑的折磨吗？当他的《积极思考出奇效》的手稿被无数次退稿时，他把它扔进了垃圾箱，又被他的妻子露丝拾了回来。这本书之后被翻译成四十二种语言出版了两千多万册。露丝·皮尔在 2008 年去世前谈及她的丈夫时说："我不像他那么自我怀疑。"

你会喜欢上现在的畅销书作者詹姆斯·斯科特·贝尔第一次与这位"积极思考"的创始人相遇的故事。贝尔会告诉我们遇见诺曼·文森特·皮尔怎样影响他的人生，帮助他摆脱作为律师的不安，并成为了一名作家。

你有了想要追求的梦想但不敢去尝试？想做就做吧。当黛比·爱克林和丈夫共同遭遇失业，她胆怯于开始一份新的事业，但是现状让她没有退路。她从零开始，自己制作宣传单为电脑培训课程做广告，租用场地，招来足够多的客户，开始经营一项新的事业。她的例子帮助我为自己刚刚起步的纱线事业制定了进一步拓展的策略。

健康问题每个家庭都会遇到，而在这样的厄运中人们总是很难看到希望。"健康挑战"这一部分包含了一些因意外患病的不幸遭遇而改变了生活，但同时也带来了机会的故事。像肖恩·德克尔，一名因儿时输血而感染上艾滋病病毒的血友病患者，他并没有变得愤世嫉俗，而是乐观感恩地面对生活。现在作为一名艾滋病社团的领袖，他为与自己处于同样境况的人创造了一个新的词语"乐观细胞"。

有时候奇迹就在眼前。根据调查，有十分之九的人感觉时间"十分紧迫"（另外那十分之一的人或许太忙了，没有时间停下来跟民意测验员对话，我确信！）。在"每一天都是特别的"这一部分中的故事提醒我们有时没有什么比平凡而普通的一天更美好。伊莱恩·L.布里奇过去习惯在星期五的时候为自己买一杯特别的咖啡，之后的那些天她便会精神抖擞。现在她意识到自己可以在每个星期的任何一天为自己准备一杯神奇的咖啡和积极乐观的态度。为什么不让每一天都成为特别的一天呢？

希瑟·加利西亚斯为了晨跑不得不有点儿不情愿地去了当地的跑道，

在那里偶遇了一次意外，让她深深感悟到普通的一天可以多么不同凡响。一位男士在她前方的跑道上跌倒在地，她对他进行了十一分钟的心脏复苏按压，直到医护人员到场。就像她所说的，十一分钟"足够拯救他的生命，足够改变我的人生"。

人们说上帝绝不会安排给你超过你能力的事情，但是不得不为在"榜样"这部分中的人物所表现出的力量与达观而惊叹。你们或许都知道我对感恩和感谢的重视。在"细数幸福"这一部分，简·麦克布莱德·乔特的故事讲述了感恩日记如何在她丈夫事业受挫时帮助他们渡过难关，或许这种方法能激励你们当中的许多人。就像我在自己的书中写到的一样，把感恩编织进我们每天的生活中，就能让我们的生活更加幸福快乐、丰富多彩。这本具有强大力量的书以"感恩"作为结尾篇章，用振奋人心的实例告诉我们"感谢"的力量如何产生不可思议的影响。

在阅读的时候，你会翻烂那些讲述了让你产生共鸣的故事的书页书角。你会想要回到那些让你感觉变得越来越好的生活中的时光。我还要建议你准备好纸笔，记录下那些你想要问自己的问题。这四十四个故事中的每一篇都会让你得到特别的收获。你从这些故事中所获得的或许不同于我所学到的或另一位朋友从中而得的发现。在你阅读的过程中，会开始看到自己随意书写的模式。你所写下的问题——以及你所给出的答案——会帮助你为活出更加真实而充实的自我提供一个参考的范本。

你现在过着自己想要的生活吗？

你在自己所遭遇的逆境中收获了什么？

每一天、每一个星期有哪些幸运的事发生？

谁为你扮演了榜样的角色？你告诉过他们吗？

你怎样庆祝平凡而普通的日子？

你生活中缺少哪些可以赋予它更大意义的东西？

与你的家人和朋友分享这本书吧。为那些需要动力的人递上一本。当你需要提醒自己生活中充满幸福、收获、机会与欢乐时，就回到这本书中来。你会发现你在用感恩、积极、快乐的眼睛展望未来，它能帮助你关注生活中所有的美好事物——无论现在还是将来。我对此确信不已！

——德博拉·诺维尔

心灵鸡汤：
每一次跌倒，
都是最好的成长

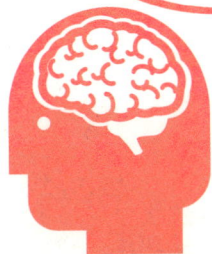

第一部分　改变我一生的话

Chapter 1
Words that Changed My Life

Words have the power to both destroy and heal. When words are both true and kind, they can change our world.

—Buddha

话语同时具有毁灭和治愈的能力。真实而善意的话语能改变我们的世界。

——佛陀

The Day I Met Norman Vincent Peale
遇到诺曼·文森特·皮尔的那一天

Four things for success: work and pray, think and believe.
—Norman Vincent Peale

"Why are things so bad now?" Cindy, my wife of twenty-eight years said. "Why does it have to be so hard?"

I didn't have an answer because I felt exactly the same way.

We were sitting in our family room that morning, sipping our coffee. Cindy had just suffered a major setback in her real estate work. Another agent had done something unethical, cutting her out of a commission she'd earned. It looked like things were heading toward litigation, with all the attendant stress.

And I, a writer of thrillers, was facing the biggest hurdle of my career—a jump to a new market that was anything but guaranteed.

So we sat there for a moment in silence, and then this popped out of my mouth. "We have to be more Norman Vincent Peale-ish."

I hadn't mentioned his name in a while, but now it seemed exactly right. Because once, some thirty years before, his words delivered me from a very dark time in my life.

I was acting then, living in Hollywood, working sporadically, auditioning, going through the rounds. If there's any profession that is full of defeats, it's acting. Rejection is your constant companion, doubt your chatty next-door neighbor.

One dismal summer day in 1979 I was standing on the corner of Hollywood and Vine. I'd just come from an audition and was heading back to my apartment. I paused on the most famous crossroads in Hollywood as a bus drove by and spewed a stream of black exhaust my way. A wave of despair washed over me. What was the point of all this? Like in the old Peggy Lee song, I wondered, "Is that all there is?"

Feeling more than a little desperate, I walked down to Pickwick Bookshop on Hollywood Boulevard. I went to the religion section, thinking maybe what I needed was a recovery of my faith.

After high school, I'd gone on to college. It wasn't long before I was into many of the things I'd heard happen at "party schools." Sundays were not for church, but sitting at the beach drinking beer. Now, three years removed from graduation, I was hoping that I could find in a book some relief for the darkness I felt crushing my spirit.

As I scanned the titles I saw the name Norman Vincent Peale featured prominently. I'd seen the movie *One Man's Way*, the biopic about Dr. Peale. Well, I reasoned, they made a movie about the guy; he must have something going on.

So I bought *The Power of Positive Thinking*, went back to my apartment, and started to read. I followed the steps Dr. Peale laid out at the end of each chapter. Some months later I moved to New York to study acting and work in the theatre. I found lodging at a rooming house on West 23rd Street, took a job as a temporary typist, volunteered to move scenery at an Off Broadway theater, and generally fell into the pattern of the city. Which meant a lot of hurrying around and more than a little urban anxiety.

At some point I remembered that Dr. Norman Vincent Peale had been a preacher in New York at Marble Collegiate Church. I wondered if he was still alive. (This was in the days before the Internet and Google!) I looked up the church's address in a phonebook and went by to inquire about Dr. Peale. They told me he was not only still alive, but preaching every Sunday—at nearly eighty-two years of age.

The next Sunday I was there. It was March 9, 1980. I was in the balcony as Dr. Peale delivered his sermon entitled "You Can Win Over All Defeats." I remember being struck by how deep and resonant and expressive his voice was. Especially when he said, "There's an invulnerability that flows out of faith. I love that word. Invulnerability! And undefeatable! That's what you are! You think I'm building you up too much? I do it on the basis of the *Bible* that says, 'This is the victory that overcometh the world'—that means anything in the world."

I purchased a tape of the sermon. I still have it. On the label is a note I scribbled in ink: "The day I met him."

After the sermon I'd gone to his office, hoping I could shake his hand. A nice secretary said if I'd wait, Dr. Peale would be happy to meet me. I could hear his dynamic voice booming as he spoke to someone on the phone.

Presently, Dr. Peale marched out with a smile as his secretary brought him over to me. I introduced myself and he pumped my hand. "Well I am certainly glad to meet you!" he said.

We conversed for a few minutes. He asked me about my interests and work. It struck me that Dr. Peale was the living proof of the value of his philosophy. He had the energy and enthusiasm of a man half his age. When he spoke, he looked me in the eye and for that moment I felt he was treating me as the most important person in the world.

Life took its twists and turns. I got married, moved back to Los Angeles, went to law school, started raising a family. I also began to write. Through those years I'd occasionally re-read Dr. Peale's books and remember fondly his voice resonating from the pulpit.

Now Cindy and I were in this long period of challenge. During those weeks and months we would constantly remind each other to "stay Peale-ish." It wasn't always easy to be positive, but being Peale-ish got us through many a dark day.

And then our prayers were answered.

After many weeks of uncertainty, Cindy's controversy was settled with a simple conference call. She received just and fair compensation and the prospect of protracted litigation lifted off her shoulders.

My waiting stretched into months. And more months. The publishing industry was going through a challenging time. No one in the business seemed to know how it was all going to shake out.

It took a lot of reminding for me to stay Peale-ish during this time.

The day finally came when my agent called with the good news. The multiple-book contract I'd been waiting for had come through, and it was everything I'd hoped for.

After Cindy and I celebrated with a little jig around the family room, it struck me how crucially important that day was years ago when I walked into Pickwick Bookshop and found Dr. Peale's book. Also the day I met him and heard him speak.

Whenever I need them, his words are right there waiting for me: "Invulnerability! And undefeatable! That's what you are!"

—James Scott Bell

成功的四个要素：工作、祈祷、思考、信念。

——诺曼·文森特·皮尔

"事情怎么会像现在这样糟糕？"我二十八岁的妻子辛迪说道，"为什么会这么难啊？"

我没有回应她，因为事实上我也有这样的困惑。

那天早上，我们坐在屋子里喝着咖啡。辛迪刚刚在她的房地产工作中遭受了挫折：另一个地产中介做了一些不道德的事，使她本已到手的佣金流失了。这就像是即将提起公诉的案件一样，正处于众目睽睽的压力之下。

我，作为一名惊险小说作家，正面临着事业上最大的一道坎儿——跳到一个根本没有保障的新市场。

我们坐在那里沉默了片刻，然后我蹦出来一句话："我们应该像诺曼·文森特·皮尔那样。"

我有一段时间没有提及他的名字了，但现在似乎正是时候。因为曾经，大约三十年前，就是他的话让我走出了人生中最黑暗的一段时光。

那时我住在好莱坞，演戏，试音，跑场，做些零星的工作。在这些职业里，让人饱受挫折的要数演戏了。被拒是家常便饭，就像你那说起话来喋喋不休的邻居那样熟悉。

那是 1979 年的夏天，一个令人忧郁的日子，我站在好莱坞藤街的转角。刚刚试音回来，正要返回我的公寓。我驻足在好莱坞最著名的十字路口，一辆公共汽车驶过，喷出的一股黑乎乎的废气挡住了我的去路，一股绝望之感油然而生。所有这些的关键是什么？我想，就像佩姬·李的老歌："那是全部吗？"

极度绝望之下，我走向了好莱坞大道的匹克威克书店。我走到了宗教书区，心想我可能需要重获信念。

高中毕业后，我上了大学。不久，我就沉浸在了早有耳闻的"派对学校"的生活中。星期日不去做礼拜，而是坐在沙滩上喝啤酒。现在，毕业已经有三年了，我希望能从一本书中找到一些安慰，让我从精神折磨的阴暗中解脱。

当我在浏览书目时，看到诺曼·文森特·皮尔的名字醒目地标注在那里。我看过一部叫作《一个人的路》的电影，是关于皮尔博士的传记电影。我推断了一下，既然他们拍了关于这个人的电影，那他一定有些值得称道的事。

就这样，我买了《积极思考出奇效》这本书，回到我的公寓，开始阅读。我按照皮尔博士在每章结尾设计的步骤去做。几个月后，我搬到了纽约，开始学习表演，并在一家剧院工作。我在二十三号西街租了一间房子，做临时打字员的工作，在外百老汇剧院义务给人拉布景，我基本适应了这个城市的生活模式。这就是匆匆忙忙的生活的意义所在，而那一点儿都市焦虑就不足一提了。

有时我会想起诺曼·文森特·皮尔博士曾经是纽约大理石教堂的传教士，我会想他那时候还健在。（这是在出现互联网和谷歌之前的日子！）

我在电话簿中查找教堂的地址，去那里打听皮尔博士的情况。他们告诉我，他不仅活着，而且每个星期日都会布道——那时他已经八十二岁了。

之后的那个星期日我也出现在那里。那是 1980 年 3 月 9 日。我在楼厅中听到了皮尔博士题为《你能战胜一切失败》的布道。我仍然记得自己沉迷在他那深厚洪亮、极富表现力的嗓音里，特别当他说道："信念会形成一种无懈可击的东西，我喜欢这个词。无懈可击！不可战胜！那就是你！你会觉得我把你说得太高了吗？按《圣经》里说的，确实如此，'就是这胜利，使我们战胜了世界'——世界上的一切。"

我把这段布道录了音，现在我仍然保存着它。在标签上我用墨水写着"我遇到他的那一天"。

布道结束后，我去了他的办公室，希望能够与他握一下手。一位亲切的秘书告诉我，如果我愿意等候，皮尔博士很乐意与我见面。我能够听到他正在电话中与人交谈的强劲有力的声音。

不久，秘书引导他到我这里，他面带微笑。我做了自我介绍，他热情有力地与我握手。"我十分高兴认识你！"他说道。

我们交谈了几分钟，他询问了我的兴趣及工作。令我惊讶的是，皮尔博士就是他自己哲学观的活生生的见证。他有着只有他一半年龄的人所拥有的精力和激情。当他讲话时，他会注视着我的眼睛，在那个时刻，我会感觉他把我作为这个世界上最重要的人对待。

生活中充满曲折。我结了婚，搬到了洛杉矶，去了法学院，开始养家糊口。我也开始了写作生涯。这些年来，我偶尔还会重温皮尔博士的书，深情地回顾他从讲坛上传来的洪亮的嗓音。

现在辛迪和我正处在漫长的挑战时期。在那几个星期以及后来的数月中，我们彼此提醒对方要"像皮尔一样"。要想积极乐观并不容易，然而像皮尔一样却可以帮我们走出无数阴暗的日子。

Chapter 1 Words that Changed My Life
第一部分　改变我一生的话

那么我们的祷告就得到了回应。

在经历了几个星期的不确定后，辛迪的争议在一个简单的电话会议中得到解决。她得到了合理的佣金，旷日持久的诉讼也不复存在了。

我的等待又持续了数月。几个月后，出版业经历了一段极富挑战的时期，在这个行业里似乎没有人知道到底会发生什么。

在这个时期，我不断提醒自己，要像皮尔一样。

最终，我接到了我的经纪人带来好消息的电话。我所期待的一套全集的合同成功签约了，这就是我所期盼的一切。

我和辛迪在房间里跳了一小段吉格舞来庆祝，我突然意识到多年前我走进匹克威克书店找到皮尔博士那本书的那天是多么至关重要，还有我遇到他、听他讲话的那一天。

每当我需要鼓励时，他的话就会浮现在我的脑海中："无懈可击！不可战胜！那就是你！"

——詹姆斯·斯科特·贝尔

Dancing in the Rain
雨中的舞蹈

Anyone who says sunshine brings happiness has never danced in the rain.

—Author Unknown

My husband and I had just finished having dinner at a local restaurant and were enjoying strolling through the stores in an adjacent shopping center. We went into a shop that sold handcrafted items in hopes of finding a few last-minute Christmas gifts. The scent of handmade soaps and potpourri teased our noses as we walked through the door.

There was a lot to see. Every shelf and wall was loaded with different crafters' handiwork. As I walked through the store, I noticed a wooden plaque hanging unceremoniously on a wall. I turned to take a second look and remember shaking my head "yes" at the message printed on the plaque. Moving on, I enjoyed looking at other items in the store, but found myself being drawn back to the plaque.

Standing in front of the plaque, I felt a little like a child who, when digging through the sandbox, finds some unexpected treasure—a shiny quarter or a lost toy. Here among the other handmade items, I found a very simple, yet profound treasure hidden in a message. A message I needed.

"Life isn't about waiting for the storm to pass," the plaque proclaimed. "It's about learning to dance in the rain."

As I pulled my husband over and directed his attention to the plaque, I could see that he too appreciated the simple lesson the plaque shared. How often in our daily lives had we put conditions on our happiness? When we get the house paid off, then we can be happy. When things settle down with the kids, then we'll be able to do more together. There is so little joy for the here and now in the uncertainties of the whens and thens.

Looking at the plaque, I found myself thinking back to a hot and muggy day the summer before, when I unknowingly lived the plaque's message. Dark clouds had rolled in along the foothills of the Rockies, heavy with their burden of moisture. Rain began falling lightly by mid-afternoon, building to a downpour that filled the gutters with rushing water and then moved on as quickly as it had come.

Light rain continued to fall as I walked out to get my mail. Water was still running high through the gutters. I don't know what came over me, but I suddenly felt compelled to do something a little crazy for my fifty-plus years.

I slipped off my shoes and stockings and began walking barefoot through the water. It was deliciously warm, heated by the pavement that had been baked by the summer heat.

I'm sure my neighbors thought that I had lost my last vestige of sanity, but I didn't care. For in that moment, I was alive. I wasn't worried about bills, the future or any other day-to-day cares. I was experiencing a gift—a pure and simple moment of joy!

The plaque now hangs in my living room, a Christmas gift from my husband. I walk past it multiple times each day and frequently pause to ask myself, "So, am I dancing in the rain?"

I think I am. I know I try to. I'm definitely more committed to taking time to pause and recognize and be grateful for the immense blessings that are all around me —the joys that were too often going unnoticed in my rush to future happiness. I celebrate more fully my dear blessings, such as a son with special needs learning to drive alone, the love of good friends and the beauty of spring. Yes, one step at a time, I am learning to dance in the rain!

—Jeannie Lancaster

有人说阳光能带来欢乐，那是因为他从未在雨中跳舞。

———逸名

　　我和丈夫刚刚在当地的一家餐馆吃过晚餐，现在正在毗连的购物中心里闲逛。我们走进一家手工艺品商店，希望能在最后的几分钟里找到圣诞礼物。当经过店门口时，手工香皂的气味和百花香气刺激着我们的嗅觉。

　　店里有许多值得一看的东西。架子和墙上都摆放着由工匠们制作的各色手工制品。当我在商店穿行的时候，我注意到一块木质的牌匾随意地悬挂在墙上。我转过头又看了一眼，没忘了朝着牌匾上印刷的字点头说了声"对"。我一边向前走着，一边欣赏着店里的其他工艺品，然而发觉自己仍心系那块牌匾。

　　站在牌匾前面，我感觉自己就像个孩子，挖着大沙箱，找那些意想不到的宝藏——一枚闪闪发光的两角五分硬币抑或一个丢失的玩具。在这里，在一堆其他手工制品中，我发现了一个隐藏在话语中简单而意义深远的宝藏，我所需要的启示。

"生活不是等待着暴风雨快过去，"牌匾上写着，"而是学习在雨中舞蹈。"当我推着我丈夫，把他的注意力引向牌匾的时候，我可以看到他同样也很感激牌匾与我们分享的小小一课。在我们的日常生活中我们是否会经常给快乐设定条件呢？当我们还完了房贷，我们就会快乐；当孩子的问题解决了，我们就能在一起做更多的事情。在对未来的不确定中，此时此地的快乐也那么少。

看着这一块牌匾，我发觉自己回想起从前一个闷热而潮湿的夏天，我不自觉地实践了牌匾上的启示。黑云从落基山山脚下滚滚而来，附着了大量的湿气。午后便下起了小雨，汇聚的水流注满了水槽，又像来时一样迅速流走。

当我去取邮件的时候，小雨还在下着。雨水仍旧在水沟中奔流，我不知道自己是怎么了，突然觉得应该为自己这五十多年做点儿疯狂的事情。

我脱掉了鞋子和长筒袜，开始光着脚在雨中行走。踩在被夏日的阳光烘烤过的路面上，温暖宜人。

我想我的邻居们一定认为我丧失了理智，但是我并不在乎这些。因为在那一刻，我真实地活着。那一刻，我不在乎钱，不在乎未来，也不在乎那些生活琐事。我正在体验一种恩赐——单纯而简单的快乐时光！

牌匾现在就挂在我的客厅里，这是丈夫送我的圣诞礼物。我每天无数次从它前面经过，无数次驻足问自己："那么，你正在雨中跳舞吗？"

我想是的。我知道我在尝试。我更加确定，要花些时间驻足欣赏，感激我身边所有一切赐福——那些为了追寻未来的幸福而常常被忽略的快乐。我为这珍贵的赐福欢腾庆贺，就像一个有特殊需要的孩子学习独自驾驶，我庆祝着真挚的友谊和春天的美好。是的，一步一步，我学习着在雨中跳舞！

——詹妮·兰卡斯特

Each Day a Masterpiece
每天都是一个杰作

Very often a change of self is needed more than a change of scene.

—Arthur Christopher Benson

I never thought I would move back in with my parents after I graduated from college. In fact, all through my senior year, I told myself that moving from the exciting cultural metropolis of Los Angeles back into my childhood bedroom in the sleepy, small beach town where I grew up was out of the question.

So, I applied for fellowships to travel abroad. I poured hours into my applications—revising essays, collecting letters of recommendation, researching programs, practicing interviews. I made it to the final rounds for two prestigious fellowships, but ultimately was not chosen for either.

Refusing to dwell on my disappointment, I applied to graduate schools across the country. Four months later, my mailbox was filled with nothing but rejection slips.

It was now April. I had only a month left before college graduation spit me out into the Real World. I went online and searched for jobs in the Bay Area, where my long-distance boyfriend had one more year left as a student at San Francisco State. I figured I could get a job up there, live close to him, and enjoy the creative stimulus of a new city.

Then, weeks after graduation, my boyfriend and I broke up. My college friends scattered to all corners of the globe. I packed my belongings into my parents' minivan and moved back home, feeling like a complete failure.

Don't get me wrong. I adore my parents, and I understood how generous it was of them to let me move back home and take some time to find my post-grad bearings. When I left for college, they probably shared the same belief I did: that I was moving out for good. But instead of being grateful, all I could focus on was how I felt like a loser. I had a fancy college degree, yet here I was, back where I had started four years before. I was sad about the breakup with my boyfriend. I missed my college friends. I felt like everyone but me was out in the world doing exhilarating, impactful things.

After a few days of wallowing, I came across a popular quote: "Make each day your masterpiece." I realized that I didn't have to be living out on my own in an exciting new city to make my days masterpieces. I could start that moment. I taped up the quote on my bathroom mirror. I typed it into my cell phone background. I added it to the signature line of my e-mails. "Make each day your masterpiece" became my own personal motto.

What did a "masterpiece day" look like? I pondered this question. For me, a day that was truly a "masterpiece" would include time with my loved ones, time spent exercising and taking care of myself, time volunteering to help others, and time devoted to my passion of writing.

I used this knowledge to organize my days.

I shifted my mindset and began to see my time at home as a gift in that I was able to spend a lot of time with my parents. My role in the household no longer felt like that of a child; rather, my parents treated me as an adult, and our relationship matured into one of mutual respect and consideration. Nearly every day I visited my grandfather, who also lived in town, and soaked up his stories. I reconnected with a few close high school friends from whom I had drifted away during the past couple of years.

In college I had often been too busy or stressed to cook healthy meals or exercise very much. Now that I was focused on making each day a masterpiece, I carved out time for nurturing my health. I began waking up early and running every morning at the park nearby my house. I visited local farm stands and bought more fruits and vegetables and scoured the Internet for healthy recipes. Within two weeks, I felt stronger and more energized than I had in years. My morning exercise became my treasured time to think and stay in touch with my inner self.

I volunteered in classrooms, teaching writing exercises and tutoring kids in reading. I spent time at the nursing home visiting with senior citizens. I got in touch with my hometown's volunteer center and helped out at beach clean-ups and fundraising events.

And I began to write for two hours every day. I knew I wanted to make a career as a writer, but my writing schedule in college was erratic—twenty minutes some days, none for weeks, then a whole weekend cooped up in my room with my laptop. Establishing a writing routine helped me more easily shift into the "writing groove." Some days, the words flowed easily. Other days, I spent the better part of my two writing hours staring out the window and scribbling down disjointed notes. But my pages of writing began to add up. I wrote articles, essays, short stories. I even started a novel!

Some days weren't as balanced as others. Tasks and problems popped up unexpectedly; not every day unfurled as planned. But as I lay in bed each night, reflecting on the day, I felt a deep sense of contentment and pride in myself. I really think the cliché is true that "things happen for a reason." Looking back, moving home after graduation was the best thing I could have done. Now, as I prepare to leave for graduate school in a few months, I feel focused, rejuvenated, and happy with who I am.

I was not a failure—I never had been. I realize now that my negative mindset is what held me back more than anything. My "success" is not dependent on what other people think or what my peers are doing or what I feel like I "should" be doing. My life is a success when I am living by my motto and making each day a masterpiece.

—Dallas Woodburn

改变自己往往比改变环境更为重要。

——阿瑟·克里斯托弗·本森

　　我从未想过我会在大学毕业后搬回家与父母同住。事实上，整个大四那年，我告诉自己从洛杉矶这个令人幸福的文化大都市搬回到那个我长大的安静的海边小镇，回到我那童年的卧房是不可能的。

　　因此，我申请了出国留学的奖学金。我投入好几个小时为申请做准备——修改论文，收集推荐信，研究程序，练习面试。我成功地进入了两项享有声望的奖学金的最后一轮竞争中，然而最后都没有被选中。

　　为了摆脱沮丧的情绪，我又申请了国内的研究生院。此后四个月，我的邮箱里除了拒收信件别无他物。

　　那时是四月，我还有一个月的时间就要告别学校真正踏入社会。我上网搜索旧金山湾区的工作，因为我的异地男友还要在旧金山州立大学学习一年。我想我可以在那里找到一份工作，离他近一些，同时享受一座崭新的城市给我带来的充满创造力的刺激。

　　然而，毕业几个星期后，我跟男友分手了。我的大学同窗遍布世界的各个角落，而我把行李打包，搬进我父母的小型货车，然后回到了家里，感觉自己像个彻头彻尾的失败者。不要误会我，我爱我的父母，我很感激他们让我搬回家里，让我可以花些时间寻找自己毕业后的方向。当我离开家上大学时，他们可能和我有着同样的信念：我将永远离开那里了。然而，除了感激之外，我所有的注意力都集中在了自己是个失败者的感受中。我为与男友分手而伤心，我还想念大学里的同窗。我感觉全世界除了我之外，所有的人都正在做着令人愉快、具有影响力的事情。

　　在经历了几天的堕落后，我看到了一句耳熟能详的谚语："让每一天成为你的杰作。"我意识到自己并不一定要在一座新的城市里来让自己的生活成为杰作，此时此刻便可以开始。我用胶带把写着这句话的纸条粘在了我卧室的镜子上，把它输入了手机的背景里，把它添加到了邮箱签名栏里。"让每一天成为你的杰作"成了我的座右铭。

　　"杰作的一天"应该是什么样？我思考着这个问题。对于我来说，真正称之为"杰作"的一天应该包括和挚爱的人在一起的时间，用来锻炼和保养自己的时间，义务帮助他人的时间，还有奉献给我挚爱的写作的时间。

　　我用这些认知来规划我的每一天。

　　我转变了自己的心态，把能在家里并且与父母度过很多时间当作一种恩赐。我在家里的角色不再像个孩子，父母把我当成一个成年人，我们的关系也逐渐成熟起来，变得互相尊重和体谅。我几乎每天都去看望住在同一个小镇的爷爷，听他讲故事。我又和一些前些年关系渐渐疏远的高中密友重新建立了联系。

　　大学时，我常常因为太忙或压力太大而不能烹饪健康饮食和经常锻炼身体。既然我已经专注于让每一天成为杰作，我就要空出时间来呵护健康。我开始早起并每天到家附近的公园跑步。我拜访附近的农场，购买许多水果和蔬菜，在网上收罗健康的食谱。两个星期内，我就感到自己比这几年都要健康而有活力。晨练的时间成为我用来思考和与自己内心对话的宝贵时光。

我在学校义务教学，教授孩子们写作练习和阅读；我花时间到养老院拜访老年人；我和家乡的志愿者中心取得联系，帮助清理海滩和筹集资金。

之后我开始每天写作两小时。我知道我想要把写作作为我的职业，但是大学时的写作计划时间表却很不规律——有时隔几天写二十几分钟，有时几个星期不动，尔后又可能整整一个星期都把自己关在房间里对着笔记本电脑。建立写作秩序，帮助我轻松地养成了写作习惯。有的时候，行云流水；有的时候，用两小时写作时间中的一部分时间来眺望窗外，然后草草写下一些随笔。我写作的纸张越积越多。我为报刊写文章，写随笔、小故事，甚至尝试写小说！

有些时候也会遇到波折，任务和问题总是出乎意料地出现，不是每一天都会按计划进行。但是当我每天晚上躺在床上，回顾一天所发生的事时，就会产生深深的满足感和自豪感。我觉得那句陈词滥调——"事出有因"，不无道理。回想起来，毕业回家是我做的最棒的一件事。现在我正准备在几个月后去攻读研究生，我感觉自己精力集中，再次充满活力，我为这样的自己感到快乐。

我不是一个失败者——从来都不是。我意识到阻挡我的只是自己消极的心态。我的"成功"并不取决于其他人的看法和做法，也不取决于我觉得我"应该"怎么样。当我按照自己的座右铭去生活，去让每一天成为杰作时，我就是成功的。

——达拉斯·伍德伯恩

Words of Wisdom
智慧箴言

I don't like that man. I must get to know him better.
—Abraham Lincoln

It was the first day after I gave up teaching in a classroom to become the high school student assistance coordinator. I asked the woman who was retiring from that job how she tolerated working with a principal who was extremely narrow-minded and negative in his approach to teachers.

Her answer was so amazingly positive and beautiful that I embraced it immediately. It spared me unending hours of frustration and became the solution for conflicts throughout my life.

She said simply: "I pray for him. It's very difficult to dislike someone for whom you are praying."

—Kay Conner Pliszka

我不喜欢那个人。我必须更加了解他。

——亚伯拉罕·林肯

那是我放弃教学工作成为一名中学学生助理协调员的第一天，我向刚刚从这个岗位退休的女士问起她如何能忍受与一个心胸如此狭隘、消极对待老师们的校长一起共事。

她的回答如此正面而美妙，让我立即接受了它。它让我释放了数小时无尽的沮丧，成为我化解人生矛盾的良方。

她坦白地说："我会为他祈祷。你很难讨厌那个你为之祈祷的人。"

——凯·康纳·普利兹卡

Two Strangers
两个陌生人

Good fortune shies away from gloom. Keep your spirits up. Good things will come to you and you will come to good things.

—Glorie Abelhas

My charmed life has been full of humorous moments—tidbits for laughable dinner table conversations with friends. I've noticed that often my life stories begin with the words "Guess what happened to me," followed by stories of horrible dates or embarrassing situations. While comical and entertaining, none of these moments have held great significance or importance. I didn't realize that a truly profound moment was heading my way one humid day in July when my car broke down in St. Joseph, Michigan.

A mere seven weeks before this breakdown, I left Michigan after walking out of a meaningless job, heading to Colorado to begin a new life and career at the age of twenty-six. I felt deeply that this was my chance to make my way in the world—living out a dream working with kids at the YMCA in Colorado Springs.

This dreamed "new life" never happened. Instead, I spent four of the seven weeks sick before facing the fact that the altitude did not agree with my asthma. Forced to leave what I thought was my new, exciting life, I faced the unpleasant reality of returning to my ho-hum existence in Michigan where my life status would read: twenty-six-year-old woman, single, unemployed, living at home with parents and no idea what to do with her life.

Driving 1,400 miles alone, sick and down-in-the-dumps was awful, although the word "awful" doesn't fully describe how bad the reality was. The constant wheezing, shortness of breath, and heavy pain in my lungs caused me extreme discomfort and the medication I consumed made me constantly drowsy.

Relief appeared as I reached the Michigan border at about 10:00 PM. Tired and facing a four-hour drive, I pulled off in the town of St. Joseph, rented a room at a motel, and immediately went to bed. I hadn't noticed the exhaust fan in my car was still running as I walked into the hotel. I definitely noticed when my car wouldn't start the next morning.

At that minute, in the parking lot of the motel, I wanted to cry. I wanted to scream. On top of all of the medical and mental stress heaped on me over the past seven weeks, I now had to tackle not only a physical breakdown, but also a car breakdown. I just wanted to be home. Home. But here I was—stuck, sick, tired of driving, mad at having to leave opportunity behind, and mad at the world. I've grown up listening to people tell me that, "God never gives us more than we can handle." It seems in moments like these that He likes to push the envelope.

After a tow to the nearest dealership, I settled in the waiting room for a two-hour repair. That's when I started talking to an older woman who sat a few chairs away from me. She had a friendly face lined softly with wisdom, and an approachable, motherly look.

"So you're having some repairs done?" she asked with concern in her voice. I guessed she could see the frustration on my face.

"Yes," I said with a sigh. "My car wouldn't start. I have no idea what happened." I leaned back in my seat, put my head back against the blank wall behind me and stared up at the dull, fluorescent lights on the ceiling contemplating how many hours I would be sitting there.

That's when unexpectedly, unknown to me, and at the strangest time, my significant moment began to unfold. It began normally as this kind lady and I started to talk. She asked me to tell her about what happened to my car. I did, and then we settled into comfortable, casual conversation—the stuff you talk about with strangers in waiting rooms like vacations, the history of weather in Michigan, and places to eat. Then our conversation shifted from the obscure to more personal things. She talked about her struggle with feelings of guilt as she contemplated putting her eighty-five-year-old mother in a nursing home. I tried to sympathize and told her how my parents, themselves into their sixties, were talking about getting insurance in case one or both wound up needing nursing home care. We talked about life—real life. We talked about my trip to Colorado, my asthma, her home, her husband retiring, my parents retiring.

"Your car is ready ma'am," said the service manager to the woman.

"Oh, thank you," she said.

She stood up and I smiled at her. She wished me luck as she gathered her purse and car keys from the seat next to her. But then as she was about to walk away, she hesitated and then turned back to me.

"You know, I have to tell you something," she said, and I could see a serious expression color her face. The brightness in her blue eyes dimmed a bit as she glanced at the floor and then looked straight into my eyes. "My daughter died a few years ago. It's so hard even now to do just the simple things." She swallowed hard, exhaled deeply and went on, "But every now and then I meet someone who reminds me of my daughter, and today, you reminded me so much of her." She smiled with tears in her eyes and went on. "I believe that sometimes God puts people in my path to remind me of her and to show me that my daughter is still with me and that I can get through this. I've so enjoyed talking to you today." A genuine smile covered her face. "When you get home I want you to hug your parents. They are very lucky to have you."

I gulped down an enormous lump in my throat. I didn't know how to respond. I felt tears of my own welling up in my eyes, and all I managed was to mumble a lame-sounding, "Oh gosh, thank you." I was dumbfounded, confused, and most of all sad. I felt so moved by what she said, so touched by this revelation about her daughter and the whole-hearted sentiment she put into telling me this. I'm a person who normally hides my emotions, but that day I stood up and hugged her and said, "I enjoyed talking to you too," and I meant it.

A few hours later, I pulled into the driveway at my parents' house. My mom came outside with her usual broad, inviting smile, and she wrapped me in a huge hug—the kind that generates love and warmth that only a mom can give. I was home. I hugged my mom with all my might. Since that day I've never questioned why bad things, crazy things, funny things, or just plain everything sometimes happen to me. And I'll certainly never ask "why me" when I have car trouble again.

—Maggie Koller

好运躲避忧郁。保持愉快的心情，美好的事物会与你相聚。

——格洛里·阿伯哈斯

　　我充满吸引力的生活中有很多幽默的时刻——那些和朋友们在茶余饭后谈论的趣事。我发现我的人生故事是从"猜猜我会发生什么事"这句话开始的，随之而来的，是一些可怕的日期和令人尴尬的场面。然而除了滑稽有趣，这些时刻都无足轻重。我没有意识到真正意义深远的时刻是在七月一个闷热的日子里——我驾车赶路却在密歇根州的圣约瑟夫抛锚的时候。

　　在这次抛锚之前七个星期，我结束了一份毫无意义的工作后离开了密歇根州，准备到科罗拉多州开始我二十六岁的新生活和新事业。我深深地感到这是我在这世界上开创自己道路的机会——在科罗拉多州斯普林斯的基督教青年会和孩子们一起为梦想而工作。

　　梦想的"新生活"从未出现。相反，在这七个星期的时间中，我病了四个星期，最终我不得不面对现实，我的哮喘病不能适应这里的海拔。被迫放弃梦想的令人兴奋的新生活，我得面对让人不悦的现实，回到密歇根州我原来乏味的生活中去。在那里我的生活状态可以解读为：二十六岁未婚女性，无业，与父母同住，对生活还无计划。

独自行驶了一千四百多英里，懊恼和沮丧让我感觉糟透了，虽然"糟透了"这个词也不能描述糟糕的现实。不断的喘息、短促的呼吸、肺部的疼痛，让我极度不适，吃下去的药物让我一直昏昏欲睡。

在晚上十点到达密歇根州边界的时候，终于可以松一口气了。四小时的驾驶让我疲惫不堪，我把车停到了圣约瑟夫镇，在汽车旅馆订了一个房间，立即倒头大睡。我完全没有意识到汽车的排气扇在我进入旅馆后依旧是开着的，直到第二天早晨车已经不能发动了，我才意识到。

那一刻，在汽车旅馆的停车场上，我很想放声大哭，我想尖叫。在过去的七个星期里，我备受药物和精神压力的折磨，而现在我不仅要面对自己被拖垮的身体，还要面对抛锚的车子。我只想回家，回家。但是现在我陷入了困境，我病了，因长时间驾驶而疲惫不堪，因为不得不放弃机会而恼火，对全世界恼火。从小到大，人生总告诉我说："上帝从来不会施加给我们超过我们所能应付的。"这一刻，他似乎要挑战我的极限了。

在把车拖到最近的维修商那里后，我坐在休息室里等了两小时直到车子修好。这期间，我和一个坐在与我隔了几把椅子位置上的年长一些的女人开始交谈。她的面庞线条柔和，透露着睿智、亲切与慈爱。

"这么说，你也有些东西需要修理？"她用关心的语气问道。我想她一定是看到了我脸上的沮丧。

"是的，"我叹气说道，"我的车不能发动了。我不知道该怎么办。"我倚着靠背，把头靠向空空的墙壁，眼睛盯着天花板上昏暗的荧光灯，揣度着我得在那里坐上多久。

就是这时，这个奇妙的时刻，重要的时刻出乎意料地在我毫无意识的时候到来了。我和这位善良的女士的交谈以通常的方式开始，她问我车的情况，我告诉了她，然后我们聊了一些轻松随意的话题——就像你和休息室里陌生人所交谈的内容一样，比如旅游、密歇根州的天气状况、就餐的地方。然后我们的交谈从寒暄转为更加私人的事情。她向我诉说她考虑将八十五岁的母亲送到养老院的内疚与苦恼。我向她表示同情，并告诉她我六十多岁的父母正在讨论要投保以防他们两人中的一个或两个受伤需要家庭护理。我们谈论生活——真实的生活。我们谈论了我在科罗拉多的旅行，我的哮喘病，她的家庭，她退休了的丈夫，我退休了的父母。

"你的车好啦，女士。"维修经理对她说。

"噢，谢谢您。"她说道。

她站在那里，我冲着她微笑。她祝我好运，从旁边的位子上拿起了她的钱包和车钥匙。但当她正准备走时，她犹豫了一下，把头转向了我。

"你知道，我有些事想告诉你。"她说道。我看到了她脸上严肃的表情。她蓝色的眼睛失去了光泽，她扫视了一下地面，然后直直地看着我的眼睛。"我的女儿几年前去世了，即使现在提起这些事也很难。"她努力地忍耐着，深深地呼了一口气，继续说道，"但是时常会遇到让我想起我女儿的人，而今天，你让我想起了她的很多事。"她含泪微笑着，继续说道："我相信上帝有时会在我的人生轨迹中安排一些人，她们使我想起我的女儿，告诉我她依旧和我在一起，我能够度过这一切。我很高兴今天能与你交谈。"她的脸上浮现出真诚的微笑，"当你回到家时，我希望你能拥抱你的父母。他们会因为拥有你而感到幸运。"

我感觉像是被一个巨大的硬块儿塞住了喉咙，我不知道该如何回应。泪水从眼眶中奔涌而出，我唯一能做的就是含糊地说道："哦，天哪，谢谢您。"我目瞪口呆，困惑不堪，尤其是悲伤难耐。我被她的话感动了，被关于她女儿的出乎意料的事情和她真情实感的诉说所触动。我是一个常常会掩饰自己情感的人，但是那一天我伫立在那里，拥抱了她，说"我也很愉快能与你交谈"，我说的是真实的想法。

几小时后，我开车驶进了父母家房子的车道。妈妈迎了出来，带着她那一贯的引人注目的微笑，她给了我一个大大的拥抱——只有妈妈才能给予这样的爱与温暖，我到家了。我一整晚都拥抱着妈妈。从那天起，我再也没有质疑为什么糟糕的疯狂的滑稽的无聊的事情时常发生在我身上。当然当车再次抛锚时，我也不会再问"为什么是我"了。

——玛吉·科勒

Listen to Your Mother
听妈妈的话

The person who is waiting for something to turn up might start with their shirt sleeves.

—Garth Henrichs

My grandmother always said, "Can't never could until he tried." My mother took up the mantra and recited it to me many times during my childhood. She normally used it to try and coerce me into doing something I didn't want to do. It was like waving a red flag in front of a bull. Irritating as it was, it took root.

Many years ago, my husband was downsized out of his job, leaving us with a single income—mine. We were a two-income family with two-income bills and two children to support. He had been given a generous severance, but that money would only last so long. Just when it looked like things couldn't get any worse, they did. I lost my job too.

While my husband was out pounding the pavement, knocking on doors, making calls, and scanning the papers for another job, I stayed home and did my best to figure out how to make the most of every cent. It was often difficult to maintain a hopeful, positive attitude, but we did our best.

One day I took some milk from the refrigerator and noticed that it was lukewarm. We could not afford to call a repairman, so we just turned the refrigerator up as high as it would go and prayed for the best.

Anxious about our situation, I tried to think of something that I could do to earn some money. Even a little would help. Maybe we could at least get the refrigerator repaired. But what could I do? I, too, began searching the want ads, applying for anything for which I was even remotely qualified.

One day I had lunch with a former coworker who insisted that I would be great at teaching computer classes. I had used word processing software extensively at my former job and was definitely an expert, but could I sell that skill? Was it possible that people would actually pay me to teach them? The only teaching I had ever done was in Sunday School. I remembered my mother's mantra—"Can't never could until he tried."

I wasn't sure where to start. Finally formulating a plan, the first thing I did was check on the availability and the cost of a meeting room. After securing a room, I went down to the Chamber of Commerce and got a list of local business addresses. I typed the addresses into my home computer and printed them on labels. I then designed a brochure that could be mailed, advertising my class. I sat on the den floor, folded my brochures and stuck address labels and stamps on them. The next day I sat in my car and prayed outside the post office, then went in and mailed the brochures. We could not really afford to spend the money that all this had cost.

I was filled with self-doubt as I waited for responses. I had absolutely no experience in running a business, even a small endeavor like this one. I had no training experience. I just had a need and I remembered my mother's words, "Can't never could until he tried." Well, "Can't" was trying.

Every day, I waited eagerly for the mail. On the third day, I got my first response. I ran inside to show my husband. "Why haven't you opened it?" he asked. I carefully opened the envelope to find a check and two registrations. I couldn't believe it! I needed ten people to break even on my expenses. Over the next two weeks I got more checks and registrations in the mail. On the day of my first class, I had seventeen students.

I had rented computers, but could not afford for them to be delivered and set up. "Don't worry, honey," my husband said, hugging me. "You've got me. I'll help you out. We can do it." On the day of my class, he and I left early and picked up the computers. It took two trips to get them all to the classroom. We spent the next hour unloading, setting them up and installing the software. Then my husband left and there I stood, alone, waiting for my first student to arrive.

Over the next fifteen minutes, I made two trips to the bathroom, checked my hair and make-up three times, and had a small panic attack. What the heck did I think I was doing? These people were going to want their money back!

The first people walked in. I smiled, introduced myself, and checked them off my attendee list. One by one, my students wandered in and took their seats. I did my best to pretend I was busy getting set up, turning to smile nervously at the class a few times. Once everyone was present, I passed out the course sheets and began. Within minutes I was relaxed, guiding them through, answering all their questions. The hours passed quickly.

When my husband came to help me break down the computers, I ran to him excitedly. "They loved the class! They asked if I was doing others so that their coworkers could attend."

"Great!" he said, a little dazed. I'm not sure that he thought I would succeed, but he had remained supportive.

Over the next months, I did several more classes. I discovered metered mail, set up a business phone line, and got a business license. I made enough money to cover my expenses and have a little left over each time. I wasn't going to get rich, but I was helping keep us afloat, and that felt wonderful!

I will never forget the day that our new refrigerator was delivered. It was much larger than our old one. I paid for it with my training money. I could not have been more proud if I had been paying for a new car. Well, okay, that would have been a pretty big deal. Nevertheless, I had a tremendous satisfaction that I had tried and succeeded!

Eventually both my husband and I found full-time employment. My new boss told me that the two things that made my résumé stand out were my training experience and the fact that I had run my own business, indicating that I could handle projects and work self-directed. I have been with that company for sixteen years.

Whenever I am handed a seemingly overwhelming project or I have to work with something new, I still hear my mother's voice, "Can't never could until he tried." Thanks Mom!

—Debbie Acklin

有所期待的人会首先挽起他们的衣袖。

————加思·亨里奇

　　我的祖母总是说"不去尝试就永远不可能"。童年时，母亲常常向我叨叨这句话。她经常试图用这个去逼迫我做一些不想做的事情。就像是在一头公牛面前挥舞小红旗。即使是愤怒，也都是有原因的。

　　许多年前，我的丈夫因为被裁员而失业，使我们家只剩下我一个经济来源。我们本来是一个有两份账单要付、两个孩子要供养的双收入家庭。他过去有着不错的收入，但只能到那时为止。就在看起来事情不能再糟糕的时候，我也失去了工作。

　　当我的丈夫在街头徘徊、敲门、打电话、浏览报纸找工作的时候，我就待在家里，绞尽脑汁地思考怎么用好每一分钱。保持积极乐观的态度是很困难的，但是我们尽了最大的努力。

　　一天，我从冰箱里拿出牛奶，却发现它是温的。我们请不起修理工，所以我们只能祈祷，看着它继续升温了。面对这样的境况，我焦虑不安，我试图想出些能赚钱的方法。即使能赚一点儿也会有帮助，或许至少可以把我们的电冰箱修好。

但是我可以做什么呢？我也开始看招聘广告，甚至与申请资格相差甚远的工作我也会申请试试。

一天，我与一位以前的同事一起吃午餐，她告诉我教计算机课程对我来说会是个很好的选择。在之前的工作中，我大量地使用文字处理软件，无疑已成了专家，但是我该怎样出售这项技能呢？会有人付给我钱，让我来教他们吗？我唯一做过的教学工作是在主日学校。我想起了妈妈常说的话——"不去尝试就永远不可能"。我不知道该从哪里开始。最终，我做了一个计划，我做的第一件事是确保有一间会议室并有足够的租金。在确认了房子之后，我去商会拿到了当地企业的地址，我把这些地址输入电脑，并把它们打印成标签条。然后，我设计了一个可以邮寄的宣传册，用来宣传我的课程。我坐在房间的地板上，折好宣传册，并把地址标签条和邮票粘贴上去。第二天，我坐在车里，在邮局外祈祷，然后走进去，寄出宣传册。事实上我已经负担不起这些花销了。

等待回复的日子里，我总是自我怀疑。我根本没有做生意的经验，甚至像这样的小买卖也没有做过。我没有培训经验，只是需要这份工作，而我记着我母亲的话——"不去尝试就永远不可能"。"不可能"也是一种尝试。

每天，我都焦急地等待着邮件。第三天，我收到了第一个回复，我跑进房间给我的丈夫看。"你为什么还没打开它？"他问道。我打开了信封，发现了一张支票和两张报名表。我真的不敢相信！我需要十个人报名才能抵销我的花费。在之后的两个星期里，我收到了更多的支票和报名表。在第一堂课的那一天，我有了十七名学生。

我租了电脑，却没有钱让他们运送过来并组装。"别担心，亲爱的，"丈夫拥抱着我说道，"你还有我呢，我会帮助你的，我们一定能做到。"上课的时候，我和他一早就出门去取电脑，来回跑两趟才能把它们都运到教室，我们还要再花一小时来卸载、组装，还要安装软件。之后我的丈夫离开了，我独自站在教室里，等待第一个学生出现。

十五分钟过去了，我去了两趟卫生间，检查了三次头发和妆容，我有点儿惊慌失措。见鬼！我到底在想什么？这些人会把他们的钱要回去的！

第一个学生走了进来。我微笑着跟他做自我介绍，查看我的出勤表。一个一个学生走了进来，找到自己的位子。我努力假装自己正在忙着安装，转过头去紧张地朝学生们笑了几回。所有的人都到齐了，我发下课程讲义，开始上课。几分钟后，我就放松下来了，指导他们操作，解答他们所有的问题，时间很快就过去了。

当我的丈夫来帮我拆分电脑时，我兴奋地跑向他："他们喜欢这堂课！他们问我他们的同事是否可以报名参加。"

"太好了！"他说道，有些无法置信。我不知道他是否确信我可以成功，但是他一直在支持我。

之后的几个月里，我开设了更多的课程。我发现了邮资总付邮件，开设了办公专线，办理了营业执照。我赚到了足够的钱来支付我的开销，而且每次还会有一点儿结余。我没有变得富有，但是让我的生活更好了一些，这种感觉太美妙了！

我永远都不会忘记新冰箱送到的那一天，它比之前的冰箱大了许多。我用培训赚来的钱买了它，这比花钱买一辆新车还要开心。当然，那会是一笔大开销。不过，我对自己的尝试和成功有着极大的满足感。

最后我和丈夫都找到了全职的工作。我的新老板告诉我，我的简历中有两项内容让我脱颖而出，那就是我的培训经历和我创办了自己的事业，这表明我能操作项目并自主工作。我在这家公司工作了十六年。

无论何时，当我接受一项似乎无法完成的任务或者不得不尝试一些新事物时，我仍然会听到妈妈的声音——"不去尝试就永远不可能"。感谢你，妈妈！

——黛比·爱克林

Chapter 1 Words that Changed My Life
第一部分　改变我一生的话

Finding the Real Me
找到真实的自己

He is a wise man who does not grieve for the things which he has not, but rejoices for those which he has.

—Epictetus

　　It started out as one of the best days of my life, and certainly, of my career. My staff and I had been named the number one unit in our company, and I was taking them out for a celebratory lunch. I worked with a wonderful group of people and we were proud of what our hard work and team spirit had accomplished during the prior year.

　　Lunch was fun, the food excellent, and the camaraderie at the table made me smile. I was proud of this group, who laughed, cried, and loved each other, and I felt blessed to be their leader. The weather was crisp, cool, and sunny, and I thought to myself "it just doesn't get any better than this." It was a perfect day.

　　After lunch, we returned to work. As I checked

my e-mail, an urgent message popped up for a mandatory teleconference later that afternoon. We had these types of teleconferences quite a bit to cut costs versus expensive management meetings, so I thought nothing of it and continued to catch up on work and phone calls I had missed during lunch.

Two o'clock came—time for the teleconference. I put my phone on speaker so I could work and listen at the same time—multi-tasking as usual. I heard our associate director's voice, usually so friendly and upbeat, take on a somber tone. He stuttered and stumbled, which was not like him, and finally gave us the bad news.

"You are all being relocated to Ohio, if you are willing to move," he told us with a tremble in his voice, "and if you cannot move, you will be given a severance package, and sixty days notice."

I felt numb. How could this be happening? Most of us had been at the company for years and had been told our jobs were some of the most secure in the organization. None of us, for various reasons, would be able to relocate, and there were no other jobs available within the company in our area, so it appeared my team and I would soon be out of work.

I had the heartbreaking task of sharing the news with my staff. As their leader, I had to be strong, upbeat, and courageous, but inside I was scared to death. While I gave them words of encouragement, I felt my world was slowly coming to an end.

My husband and family consoled me, but I was scared. Really scared. Financially, I knew we would be okay—my husband had a good job, and the severance and other savings I had would keep us going for quite a while, but I had worked full-time my whole life and did not know if I could deal with losing my job. It had become my identity—who I was and how I defined myself. I was a leader, and I felt, a good one. What would I be with that taken from me?

The first few days after my job ended, I didn't want to get out of bed. I kept up a brave front for my children and husband, but moped around the house, not really knowing what to do. After working nonstop for twenty-five years I was lost. I sent out résumés, but due to the economic conditions, job postings in my field were few and far between. It looked like I would be out of work for quite a while, and I didn't know what to do with all my newfound extra time.

One day, after sitting around feeling sorry for myself, I turned on the television and watched a program about a missions group that helped children and hungry people all over the world. I felt guilty knowing that even though I had lost my job, we had plenty of good, healthy food on the table every night. The words spoken by the missionary seemed directed specifically at me— she told viewers that the "best way to be blessed and to forget about your own problems is to help someone else."

Ashamed, I realized that I had been wallowing in self-pity when I had so much to be thankful for—a loving husband, beautiful children, and family and friends who needed me. I could either continue to focus on what I had lost and be miserable, or I could count my blessings and bless others.

I decided to get up, get dressed, and cook a great meal for my family that night. I had always loved to cook, learning at the side of my mom and grandmothers, all wonderful Southern cooks who taught me their secrets. I also thought I could make some extra food to take to our neighbors who were retired, and brighten their day as well.

I began to assemble the ingredients for my dinner, humming to myself a little as I prepared our meal. I was starting to feel like my old self again. Just then one of my daughters walked into the kitchen and asked if she could help me cook dinner. As we stirred and sifted, basted and baked, our dinner came together. We laughed, talked, and shared stories. I told her how my mom and grandmothers had let me help them cook when I was a little girl, and I still used many of their recipes. I forgot about how depressed I had been, and when we put the meal on the table for the rest of the family, we were both proud of the delicious dinner we had made and basked in the compliments we received.

After dinner, as I cleaned up the dishes, it occurred to me that I had never taught my children to cook. I had been so busy being a "career woman" that I had not taken the time to show them how to make the wonderful dishes I had learned to make as a child and young woman. I had always cooked for my family, but had not given them the gift that I had been given—the gift of learning how to prepare a meal for my loved ones. I was saddened by this, and decided that I was going to use my unexpected free time to change all that.

The next morning I announced to my family that I was going to start a cooking school for them. This was met with groans from my kids, who all had busy lives and plans of their own. But I convinced them to give it a try and we decided we would prepare supper the next night. I let each child pick a dish to prepare for the meal, with my guidance. We decided to do this weekly and make extra food to share with friends or neighbors in need in our community.

The next morning, we shopped for our dinner at our grocery store and local farmers market. We unloaded our ingredients, put on our aprons, and started cooking. I shared cooking techniques, short cuts, and the background behind many of the recipes we had decided to prepare. While making my grandmother's famous lemon meringue pie, I remembered the many times I had stood in her kitchen, licking the beaters thick with white, fluffy meringue, sweet and cloudlike, and how much fun those times had been. Now I was sharing them with my own children. I could almost see Grandmother smiling down from heaven, watching my children and I carrying on her traditions. Nothing had made her happier than cooking something wonderful for her family, and now I knew how she felt. Instead of rushing to put something quick on the table between business meetings and reports, I got to take the time to enjoy cooking and eating the beautiful meal we were creating. Plus, I got to share the company of my children—listen to them joke, find out what was going on with each of them, and appreciate the personalities of each one. All four of them were so different, yet so special, and brought so much joy into my life—I had just been too busy to notice that before. I had been so busy providing for my family financially, and basing my worth on my career, that I had forgotten what was really worthwhile, and who I really was—a wife and a mother to these amazing people who deserved my time, my guidance, and affection.

Cooking school continued each week. It became a time we all looked forward to a time of laughter, love and learning. And, of course, some really great meals. Cooking with my kids was just the start—I began doing things with them and for them that they enjoyed—going to the library, movies, playing tennis, or lounging by the pool. For the first time, I was able to really focus on and enjoy my family, without deadlines looming in the background, working on my laptop, or checking my e-mail at the same time. Instead of multi-tasking, I focused on the one task that mattered most—making sure my family knew that they were loved and were number one in my life.

I did eventually go back to work, but I found a job that was more flexible and allowed me to spend much more time with my husband and children. It turned out to be an even better job than my previous one—it paid better, was much less stressful, and gave me the flexibility I needed to be there when my family needed me. My priorities had changed, and I never again wanted to put my loved ones in second place to my career.

I had thought losing my job was the worst thing that had ever happened to me. But, it turned out to be a blessing in disguise. While I had thought that losing my job was the end of who I was, it was really only the beginning of discovering the real me.

—Melanie Adams Hardy

聪明的人不会为自己所没有的东西而哀伤，他会为所拥有的东西而
欣喜。

——爱比克泰德

　　一个我人生事业最美好的日子来临了，我们
部门被公司授予第一名，我正准备带员工们去庆
祝午宴。我和一群很棒的人一起共事，我们为自
己在过去一年的辛勤劳动和所表现出的团队精神
而感到自豪。

　　午餐很愉快，食物很美味，桌上大家互诉友
情，让我感到舒心。我为有这样一个同甘共苦、
互助互爱的团队感到自豪，为成为他们的领导而
感到幸福。天气凉爽，阳光明媚，我心想"没有
比这更好的事情了"，这是完美的一天。

　　午餐后，我们回去工作。我查看电子邮件，
有个当天下午晚些时候召开电话会议的紧急通
知。为了减少高昂的会议开支，节省预算，我们
常常召开这种电话会议。因此，我并没有多想，
继续补上午餐时间落下的工作和错过的电话。

　　下午两点到了——电话会议的时间，我把电
话调到免提以便我可以一边工作一边听电话——
和平时一样多项任务同时进行。我听到了副主任

的声音，他的声音通常都是友善快活的，这次语气却十分严肃。他说话结结巴巴，与平时判若两人，最后说出了一个坏消息。

"如果愿意的话，你们都将被重新分配到俄亥俄，"他用颤抖的声音告诉我们，"如果不愿意搬过去，会得到一笔辞退补偿金和提前六十天的通知。"

我呆住了。怎么会这样？我们中的大多数人已经在公司工作多年，并且被告知我们的工作是在公司中最稳定的。因为各种原因，我们没有人能够接受再分配，然而公司在我们的地区再没有其他空缺的岗位了，我和我的团队似乎马上要失业了。

告诉我的员工们这个消息是一项十分困难的任务。作为他们的领导，我必须坚强、乐观、勇敢，然而我的内心却恐惧得要死。当我鼓励他们的时候，我感到自己的世界正慢慢走向尽头。

我的丈夫和家人安慰我，但是我仍旧害怕，真的害怕。我知道经济上不会有困难——我丈夫有一份不错的工作，还有补偿金和其他积蓄可以让我们支撑很长一段时间，但是我一直做着全职工作，不知道该如何面对失业的问题。它已经成为我的身份了——我是谁，我如何定义我自己。我是一个领导，自我感觉是个不错的领导。如果没有了它，我又该怎么办呢？

失去工作的第一天，我不想起床。我在孩子和丈夫面前假装坚强，但是除了拖地，我不知道还能够做什么。在不间断地工作了二十五年后，我失业了。我发送简历，但是受到经济形势的影响，我所在的行业所能提供的职位寥寥无几。看起来我似乎要失业很长一段时间了，但是我不知道该如何应对这新的空闲时间。

一天，在我无所事事、伤心难过了一番后，我打开了电视机，看到了关于一个任务组在全球帮助儿童和饥饿人群的电视节目。虽然我失去了工作，但是每晚餐桌上还有丰盛健康的食物，我为此感到内疚。传教士的话似乎直指向我——她告诉观众"活得幸福和忘记烦恼的最好的方式就是帮助别人"。

我感到很惭愧，意识到自己一直沉浸在自怜的情绪中，忽视了有那么多值得感恩的事情——我忠诚的丈夫、可爱的孩子，还有需要我的家人和朋友。我可以选择关注那些已失去的东西而一直痛苦下去，或者去细数自己的幸福，同时祝福别人。

我决定起床梳妆打扮，在晚上为家人献上丰盛的晚餐。我一直喜欢烹饪，曾在母亲和祖母旁边学习，她们都是绝佳的南方厨师，教给了我她们的厨艺秘诀。我想我可以多做些食物，送给已经退休的邻居，让他们也一起高兴起来。

我一边自娱自乐地哼着小曲儿，一边准备晚餐的材料。我感觉找到了原来的自己。就在这时，我的一个女儿走进了厨房，询问是否需要帮忙做晚饭。我们搅拌、过筛、涂油、烘烤，晚餐最终大功告成了。我们欢笑着、交谈着、分享各自的故事。我告诉她童年时我母亲和祖母让我帮她们做饭，我现在仍在使用她们的许多食谱。我忘记了之前的沮丧与忧郁。当我们把晚餐呈现在家人面前时，大家连连称赞，我们为自己制作和烘烤的美食而感到自豪。

晚饭过后，清洗餐具时，我突然意识到从未教过孩子们如何烹饪。我过去一直是一名忙碌的"职业女性"，从来没有向他们展示我在童年和少年时代学到的精湛厨艺。我常常为他们做饭，却没有送给他们一样礼物——学习如何为心爱的人烧菜做饭。我为此感到有些悲伤，决定用我这些意料之外的空余时间来挑战一下。

第二天早上，我对家人宣布，我要为他们开设烹饪学校。这遭到了孩子们的抱怨，他们都生活忙碌，有自己的计划。但是我说服了他们尝试一下，我们决定一起准备第二天的晚餐，我让孩子们在我的指导下每人为晚餐做一道菜。我们决定像这样每个星期进行一次，并多做些食物与朋友和社区的邻居分享。

第二天，我们去食品杂货店和农贸市场为晚餐采购了食材，之后卸下原料，系上围裙，开始烹饪。我给他们讲授我们所要准备的菜品相关的烹饪技艺、快捷方法和经验知识。制作祖母最拿手的柠檬酥皮派时，我想起了多少次我站在她的厨房里，舔着沾满白色松软酥皮的搅拌器，甜甜的，像白云一样，那些时光多美好啊。现在我把它们与自己的孩子一起分享，我似乎看到祖母在天堂朝我们微笑，看到我和孩子们继承了她的传统。对她而言，没有什么比为家人烹饪美食更开心的事了，我现在体会到了她的感受。不再是在商务会议和汇报空当儿匆匆忙忙将东西放回桌上，而是与孩子们一起享受烹调和食用我们制作的美好的食物。另外，我开始珍惜孩子们的陪伴——听他们讲笑话，发现每个人身上的事情，理解他们每个人的个性。他们四个性格迥异，每个人都是那么独特，给我的生活带来了如此多的欢乐——我之前太忙了以至于都没有留意。我忙着赚钱养家，在事业上寻找人生价值，忘记了真正有价值的事情，忘记了真正的自己——我是这些了不起的人的妻子和母亲，他们需要我花些时间去关心和爱护。

每个星期的烹饪学校在持续，它成了我们共同的期待——一段传递欢笑、表达爱意、学习知识的时光。当然，还有真真正正的美食大餐。和孩子们一起烹饪只是个开端——我开始和他们一起做很多事情，也做些他们喜欢的事情——去图书馆、看电影、打网球、懒洋洋地躺在泳池旁。第一次，我感到自己能完全沉浸在家庭的欢乐里，不用担心着渐渐逼近的截止日期，同时还要伏在笔记本电脑前工作或查看电子邮件。我不再同时处理多项任务，我只关注一项最重要的任务——让家人知道他们被爱着，他们在我的生命中最重要。

　　我最终回到了工作中，但是找了一份时间更加灵活的工作，以便让自己有更多的精力和丈夫孩子在一起。事实证明这份工作比之前的更加适合我——收入多了，压力小了，在家人需要我时我可以更加自由地安排时间。我改变了优先考虑的事情，再也不想把挚爱的人排在事业的后面。

　　我原本以为失去工作是我至今遭遇的最不幸的事情，结果却因祸得福。原本以为失去工作就永远失去了自我，但事实上我才刚刚开始发现一个真实的自己。

——梅勒妮·亚当斯·哈迪

License to Smile
微笑通行证

A cloudy day is no match for a sunny disposition.

—William Arthur Ward

Anyone who knows me well would almost certainly label me an optimist. I believe in embracing hope and finding something positive even in the most difficult circumstances. My own optimism stems from a strong, personal faith in a loving God who I believe is very interested in the personal details of our lives, not just the "big stuff." I also believe that things happen for a reason and that if we keep our minds and spirits open, our invisible God often becomes visible, sometimes in ways that are quite humorous!

With that being said, even optimists can temporarily lose hope. This was the case for me on a particularly cold and gloomy January day. I felt overwhelmed by the painful challenges I was dealing with in my personal life. Marital, health, and financial struggles had joined forces to create a tornado of emotion that threatened to crush my spirit. I felt angry, frustrated, burdened, and distanced from the presence of God. The weather seemed to reflect my mood—the gray sky blocked even a single ray of sunlight. As I drudged through my workday, I just couldn't shake a sense of hopelessness and despair.

About midway through the day, I left work to get some lunch. Still feeling pessimistic and negative, I noticed that the sun had come out for a brief moment. I began to think about my negative attitude and reminded myself that I was responsible for choosing my state of mind. While I could not ignore the pain I was going through, I could choose to dwell on the negative or I could choose to shift my thinking to a more positive focus. Even as I consciously reminded myself of this truth, I felt incapable of making the shift. So I gripped the steering wheel and prayed an honest, heartfelt prayer. "God," I cried, my tears ready to spill out, "where are you? I don't want to feel this way but I am miserable and hopeless today. Please lift me out of this dark, gloomy place!"

As I stopped at a red light, I looked at the car directly in front of mine. The personalized license plate caught my eye—it read "SUNZOUT." This brought an immediate smile to my face. It felt like a reminder from God that the sun was shining after all, and in the midst of the longest, darkest, coldest winter in years, this in itself was a blessing. But then my eyes moved to the car that was perfectly parallel to the SUNZOUT vehicle. The license plate on that car read "GROUCH." So as I read these two license plates side by side, I said out loud "SUNZOUT, GROUCH." This brought more than a smile to my face as I laughed out loud! Seeing the two very opposite license plates right next to each other at that exact moment in time also strengthened my previous recognition of my ability to choose my outlook despite my circumstances. I felt my spirits and mood lift as I made the conscious decision to choose a positive attitude.

I returned to work and shared my story with several co-workers who responded with warm laughter at what I referred to as my "message from beyond." I learned that day that when we are feeling too discouraged to bring ourselves out of a state of negativity, relief is only a prayer away!

—Julie A. Havener

阴天也无法对抗好心情。

——威廉·阿瑟·沃德

　　每个熟悉我的人几乎都会理所当然地给我贴上乐观主义者的标签。我坚信在最困难的境况下也要怀有希望，去发现事物积极的方面。我的乐观主义来自对慈爱的上帝坚定的个人信仰，我认为他非常在乎我们生活的点点滴滴，而不仅仅是"大事件"。我也相信事出有因，如果我们能打开我们的思想和精神世界，无形的上帝就会变得清晰，有时甚至是以十分诙谐幽默的方式存在。

　　话虽如此，但即使是乐观主义者也偶尔会失去信心。在一月寒冷阴郁的某一天，情况就是这样。我为处理私人生活里各种痛苦的挑战而疲惫不堪。婚姻、健康和经济上的挣扎一齐袭来，就像龙卷风一样几乎要把我的精神摧毁。我感到愤怒，沮丧，不堪重负，慢慢远离了上帝的存在。天气也如同我的心情一样——阴云阻挡住了唯一一缕阳光。我辛苦地工作着，无法摆脱沮丧与失望的心情。

　　到了中途休息的时候，我放下工作去拿午

餐。心情依旧悲观消极，我注意到太阳突然出来了。我开始反思自己消极的态度，提醒自己应该对选择的心态负责。虽然我不能忘记现在所遭受的痛苦，但是我可以选择是消极思考还是转换为一种更加积极的方式。即使我有意识地提醒自己这一事实，我仍不能做出改变。我握紧方向盘，虔诚地祷告。"上帝，"我哭喊道，我的眼泪要流出来了，"你在哪里？我不想这样难受，但是今天就是这样悲惨无望。请带我离开这个黑暗阴郁的地方吧！"

当我在红灯时停下来，看到了前面的那辆车，个性化的车牌吸引了我的眼睛——上面写着"SUNZOUT"（太阳出来了）。我的脸上立刻露出了笑容，它就像来自上帝的暗示，一下提醒我在经历过漫长、黑暗而阴冷的冬天后，阳光终究会灿烂明媚，这本身就是一种祝福。然后我又看了看正好与挂着 SUNZOUT 的车并排的车辆，它的车牌上写着"GROUCH"（发牢骚）。因此当我一起看这两个车牌的时候，我大声说道："太阳出来了，发发牢骚。"这让我不只是微笑，而是哈哈大笑起来。就在那一刻，看着这两个极端的车牌并排在一起，又让我加深了无论在何种情况下对选择态度和看法的能力的认识。当我有意识地决定积极应对时，我的精神和心情都好了起来。

回到工作的地方，和几个同事分享了我的故事，他们对我所说的"话外之意"用温暖的笑声报以回应。那一天我学会了：当我们太过沮丧而无法摆脱消极情绪的时候，放松心情就是一种祷告！

——朱莉·A. 哈夫纳

Hearing the Worst
听到最糟糕的事

If you don't like something, change it; if you can't change it, change the way you think about it.

—Mary Engelbreit

Sue and I sped along the highway at seventy-five miles per hour as we began our climb up the curving mountainous roadway where North Carolina intersects with the southern border of Virginia. Sue, my youngest daughter, also a mother and grandmother, is a young-at-heart fifty-year-old widow. I suppose she could be identified as a "tweener"—between me and her younger family— since I've often asked her to drive me long distances or to do other things I can't or don't want to do for myself.

The more politically correct term, I suppose, is that Sue is now a member of "The Sandwich Generation." These young to middle-age men and women are still raising their families, even if they are mostly grown, and suddenly they find themselves also responsible for their aging parents and must add additional responsibilities to an already busy lifestyle.

I leaned back in my seat and enjoyed the luxury of the comfortable ride, while taking in the sunshine and scenery so different from that in Florida. I had to admit there were times when I longed to see the mountains and rolling hills, and missed the colors of the changing seasons. Still, Florida had been a good place for me to live after retirement and while caring for my aging mother—except in situations such as this when my son developed a potentially serious medical problem. I was happy that my daughter had been willing and able to transport me to see him through surgery. It was a free trip for her, too, a chance to visit with old friends and other family members.

As we entered Virginia, the trees and valleys glistened ever more brightly with deepening shades of green reflecting the sunlight of late spring. One of the most beautiful spots along the ascending highway featured a vertical drop to picturesque valleys on the right, looking over many miles of neatly manicured farmland dotted with white buildings of civilization. On our left were even steeper cliffs rising skyward with trickles of running water, jutting rocks with mossy patches and scattered growth of new plant life highlighting the incline of the mountain. Occasionally, small piles of rock and dirt had broken loose from their moorings and lay as evidence of man's failed attempt to conquer the hilly terrain.

I twisted my body to the right in my seat, trying to find the mountain with the "bite" taken out of the top. I assumed it was a "man-made" bite to make way for utilities and other signs of civilization, but it had become a game for my family, looking for the sign that we were approaching the area where Uncle Charlie used to live.

It was April 28, 2009, a day I should not forget—but for how long would I truly be able to remember it?

My cell phone rang, breaking the tranquility of the pleasant scene. I glanced at the caller ID and answered with a degree of trepidation. I had been waiting for this particular call.

"Hello, Ms. Bennett," the cheery voice said. "This is Annette in Dr. Jay's office. He wants you to know that your PET scan results are in. They're consistent with Alzheimer's disease."

I gasped! No friendly word foreplay to break the ice or soften the blow—just the dreaded diagnosis—one which I expected but dreaded nonetheless. I had even asked to have the PET scan (an imaging technique—positron emission tomography—producing three-dimensional images of a body process) done.

"He wants you to start taking Aricept right away," the caller added. "I'll call in a prescription for you. You have a good day now, you hear." And just as quickly, she was gone.

I closed the cell phone, put it back in my purse, and said nothing, just stared at the scenery, which had lost some of its magical luster.

"Who was that?" Sue questioned.

"Just someone at the doctor's office," I replied, trying to show at least a half-smile. "She's calling the pharmacy with a prescription for some of my memory problems."

Sue turned her head toward me and started to speak.

I placed my hand on my daughter's arm, stopping her before she could question me further.

"Better keep your eyes on the road, sweetie. This road is really curvy—and steep. Looks like those clouds are dropping right on top of us."

I was not ready to share my diagnosis with family or anyone else at this time even though nothing had really changed—it had just become formal—no longer a suspicion, but now a reality.

Had I been driving, my thoughts could easily have led me down a dangerous path. The callousness and lack of empathy with which the news was delivered sent chills racing up and down my spine as my eyes strayed to the steep descent to the valley below. For a split second I wondered if I'd be better off just to leave the highway and sail through the air and trees and brush to my ultimate fate, rather than spending years dependent on others and living in the foggy mental state that surely lay before me.

But reason prevailed and in that instant, I made a major decision.

I will not become a victim. I will take each day as it comes and deal with it. Beyond that, it's out of my hands. But, I will never consider myself just a number or a victim—I'll do what I can to try to slow the process down, but never, ever will I be a victim.

—Lois Wilmoth-Bennett

如果是你不喜欢的东西，改变它；如果你不能改变它，那就改变你
的想法。

——玛丽·恩格尔布莱特

　　休和我以七十五英里的时速行驶在公路上，
我们将要攀爬北卡罗来纳州与弗吉尼亚南部边界
交会处那崎岖的山路。我的小女儿休，既是母亲
又是祖母，是个心态年轻的五十岁的寡妇。我把
她当作在我和她年轻的家庭间的一个"游离人"，
因为我常常让她带我驾车远行或做一些我一个人
不能做和不想做的事情。

　　用政治上更加准确的术语来说，我想休是
"三明治一代"中的一员。这些接近中年的男人
女人仍在供养家庭，虽然他们的孩子大部分已经
长大，而突然间发现还要照顾年迈的父母，不得
不为本已忙碌不堪的生活再添负担。

　　我倚靠着车座的后背，享受着舒适旅途的奢
侈和不同于佛罗里达的阳光和景致。我必须承认
我时常渴望看到连绵起伏的山脉和季节变化的色
彩。佛罗里达对我来说，是退休后的宜居良所，
可以照看我年长的母亲——除了我的儿子出现了
严重的疾病征兆。我很高兴女儿愿意并且能载我

Chapter 1 Words that Changed My Life
第一部分　改变我一生的话

去看他进行手术。对她来说，这是一次自由的旅行，也是一个拜访老友和家人的机会。

当我们到达弗吉尼亚时，树木和山谷在深绿色的荫翳中与暮春的阳光交相辉映，熠熠生辉。沿着公路上行，最美的景色要数右侧那风景如画的山谷，俯视便是绵延数里整齐的农田和星星点点的白色房屋；在我们的左边是陡峭入云的山崖、潺潺的溪流、苔痕斑驳的岩石和零散分布在山坡上的引人注目的新生植物。偶尔会有小块的岩石和尘土纷落，作为人类企图征服低山丘陵失利的证明。

我在座位里把身体蜷缩向右侧，试图找到那座山顶被"咬"掉的山峰。我想这"人为"的一口应该是为了提供便捷，或是其他人类文明的标志，但它也成为我们家的一个游戏，寻找查利叔叔原先住处的一个标志。

那是 2009 年 4 月 28 日，一个我永远不该忘记的日子——但是我能够记住多久呢？

我的手机铃声响了，打破了这令人愉悦的美景与安宁。我看了一下来电地址，有些惊慌地接起电话。我一直在等这个特别的电话。

"贝内特太太，您好，"一个轻快的声音传来，"我是杰伊博士诊所的安妮特。他要我通知您正电子扫描的结果已经出来了，与老年痴呆症的症状吻合。"

我深吸一口气。没有任何友善的话语做铺垫，来打破坚冰或减轻打击——就是这种可怕的症状——虽然我有所预料但仍令人恐惧。我甚至要求做了正电子扫描（一种影像技术，通过正电子发射断层显像造影术生成人体三维立体影像）。

"他想让您现在就采取安全措施，"打电话的人补充道，"我会为您开处方，祝您今天愉快。"她迅速挂断了电话。

我关掉了手机，把它放回口袋里，什么都没有说。我凝望着美景，然而它们却已经失去了一些神奇的光彩。

"是谁？"休问道。

"医生诊所里的人，"我回答道，试图露出哪怕是半个微笑。"她让药房给我开些治疗我的记忆问题的处方。"

休把头转向了我，开始讲话。

我把手放在女儿的胳膊上，阻止了她继续向我提问。

"最好仔细看路，宝贝儿。这条路真是又曲折又陡峭。就像那些云彩，好像掉在我们头顶上一样。"

我还没有准备好和家人或任何其他人坦白我的病情，即使任何事都没有真正改变——但它已经变得严肃了——不再是怀疑，而是事实。

如果是我在开车，或许我的思想会很容易让我走上危险的道路。坏消息如此残酷无情地传来，让我浑身上下不寒而栗，我的眼睛不经意地向陡峭的悬崖下望去。那一瞬间，我想如果我离开公路，翱翔在天空和树丛里，到达我生命的终点，是不是比终年依赖别人活着或生活在我必定要面对的精神混沌状态里要好得多。

但是理性最终获胜，在那一刻，我做了一个重要的决定。

我不会成为受害者，我会把握和珍惜每一天。除此之外，我无法掌控。但是，我绝不会让自己成为一个数字或是一名受害者——我会尽可能地减缓这个过程，但就是不会做一名受害者。

——洛伊丝·维尔莫斯 – 贝内特

心灵鸡汤：
每一次跌倒，
都是最好的成长

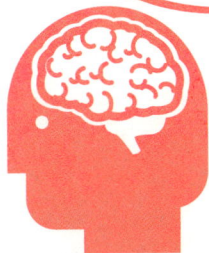

第二部分 ｜ 健康挑战

Chapter 2
Health Challenges

Being in a good frame of mind helps keep one in the picture of health.

—Author Unknown

良好的心态有助于保持身心健康。

——逸名

I'm Positive... Really
我很乐观……真的

Positive anything is better than negative thinking.
—Elbert Hubbard

The second son of a middle-class family, I presented more challenges for my parents than did my big brother, two years my elder. I was born with the bleeding disorder, hemophilia, meaning that each move I made, from crawling to learning how to walk, was closely monitored for fear that the most insignificant fall could result in a serious bleeding issue. In those early years one physician told my parents that I might not survive childhood.

Being born in the mid-1970s meant that I got to sport the latest in red bell-bottoms made specifically for toddlers. More importantly than that, I was the beneficiary of advances in the treatment of hemophilia. If I got a bump, bruise or nosebleed, I could get an injection of concentrated blood plasma that would help control the bleeding. Often times, I was back on the playground with friends within hours of taking a health-related delay of game.

A more normal life for those with hemophilia had started to set in, and I enjoyed all the perks of growing up in small-town America, from neighborhood reenactments of my favorite movies with friends to farm league baseball, playing right alongside my brother.

Over time, the trips to the hospital stopped being stressful and traumatic. Instead of resenting the unexpected bleeds that took me away from the neighborhood games, I grew to enjoy the opportunities to hang out with my "grown-up" friends, the nurses and doctors who patched me up. In the hospital, I'd see people who were really having health problems. My mother made a special point of teaching me about spirituality, that nobody knows for sure what happens after we pass, but that she felt our spirit lives on. Based on the love I received at home and in the care of my grown-up friends at the hospital, I couldn't find a reason to doubt that belief.

That conviction came in handy when, just before I hit puberty, another medical drama rocked my family. At age eleven I tested positive for HIV— infected by tainted blood products used to treat my hemophilia.

Unlike hemophilia, there weren't any treatments for HIV at the time of my diagnosis. Worse still, HIV was viewed much differently than hemophilia. Many of the parents of my best friends wouldn't let their children spend the night with me. I was expelled from my sixth grade class two months before the end of the school year. There was so much fear and misinformation.

Once the initial shock wore off, I went about life as usual by making new friends, dating and worrying about my complexion. In other words, I became a "normal" teenager. Admittedly, I used my HIV status on more than one occasion to stay home from school to sleep in and play video games. (I'm sorry, Mom and Dad. I wasn't sick most of those times!)

Though I enjoyed that particular perk, one thing I didn't like anymore were the trips to the hospital to see my new doctor, an HIV specialist. Though the appointments were only four times a year, I'd argue against them so hard that my mom had to pretend that she was taking me to school—then hop on the interstate for the hour-long drive to the big city. Instead of leaving the hospital with a medical problem fixed, I left with the cruel reminder that I was HIV positive and might have one Chuck Taylor in the grave.

Still, with each year that passed I gained more confidence that I might just survive this thing, and though I slacked on my responsibilities in school, I managed to graduate with my classmates right on schedule. Not only that, my peers gave me the greatest honor of my life up to that point when they anointed me as their Homecoming King. Even though I never openly admitted that I had HIV, most of my peers had heard the rumors. The moment was surreal for my family, who weren't sure I'd live to see graduation, much less a quite literal crowning moment.

Often times when people hear my story, I am the object of sympathy because of how I contracted HIV, or that it happened when I was a child. In actuality, I'm quite fortunate in how the timing played out. Hemophilia taught me that life is to be enjoyed on a daily basis, and that friends could be peers as well as mentors. And with HIV, I learned about discrimination based on fear of someone who is perceived to be different. When I came to terms with the fact that everyone has challenges, and mine happen to be medical, I felt lucky that mine were so painfully obvious to identify.

By the age of twenty I'd lived half my life with HIV, and I was finally comfortable with the idea of not only talking about my status, but doing what I could to help others cope with the virus or stay safe from contracting it to begin with. When I put up a website and started a blog, I was surprised to discover that I had a knack for writing. A word that I made up for those living with HIV—

"positoid"—started to get used by people in the HIV/AIDS community. I was totally comfortable with HIV's role in my life, and figured that if others weren't, then that was their problem and not mine.

One of the questions I've been asked over and over is: "Would you trade your life for someone's who didn't have HIV?" For me, the answer is no. Why spend all these years learning the lessons I've been taught to trade in my adversity for a whole new, unknown batch of problems? Plus, if I wasn't born with hemophilia and didn't have HIV, I wouldn't have met Gwenn, an HIV educator who was looking for someone with HIV for an educational project, and ended up finding me.

That was ten years ago, and we've been together ever since.

I strongly believe that the toughest parts of our lives provide us with the best opportunities to grow, and as a result of my medical conditions I have been the recipient of a tremendous amount of love, support and compassion, all of which has outweighed the negativity I've encountered. As a happily married man in my mid-thirties, I take my health very seriously because I know there are a lot of people who have not been as fortunate. Those who didn't live to see the advent of HIV medications, or who currently live where there is no access to such treatment.

To live my life without a deep appreciation for that would be an insult to their memories, and an insult to everyone who provided their help in making my happiness a reality. I love my positoid life.

—Shawn Decker

任何积极的东西都好过消极思想。

——埃尔伯特·哈伯德

　　我出生于一个中产阶级家庭，排行老二。与大我两岁的哥哥相比，父母对我更操心。我从出生那天起就患有出血性疾病，也就是血友病。正因为如此，我成长过程中的每一步，从爬行到学习走路，都受到密切的关注，以免小小的跌跤造成严重的出血后果。在我很小的时候，一位医生就曾告诉我的父母说我活不过童年。

　　因为出生在 20 世纪 70 年代，我有机会穿着专为初学走路的小孩子设计的红色喇叭裤炫耀，但比这更重要的是，我还是一名血友病治疗技术进步的受益者。如果身上有肿包、瘀伤或者鼻出血，注射一针浓缩血浆就可以了。常常，我得以回到操场，和小伙伴们一起玩儿几个小时的健康延迟游戏。

　　血友病患者也已经开始更加正常地生活。我在美国一个小城镇里长大，很享受在这里成长的乐趣。观看附近经常放映的我最喜爱的电影，还有和小伙伴们打农场联盟棒球比赛，这些都是和哥哥一起。

　　时间久了，去医院不再是一件压抑痛苦的事情，我不再埋怨因为意外出血而不能继续和伙伴们玩耍，反而渐渐地喜欢上和那些"成年"朋友待在一起，他们是照顾我的护士和给我治病的医生。在医院里，我看到了很多真正有健康问题的人。妈妈特别注意培养我对于精神的信仰。她说，没有人确切地知道死后会发生什么，但是，她觉得人死后，精神还继续存在。从家人和那些医治我的年长朋友那里，我得到了太多的关爱，我没有理由不去相信精神在人死后依然存在。就在我刚刚步入青春期时，又一次病痛的悲剧带给家人巨大的冲击。这个时候，也正是这一坚定信仰给予我们支撑的力量。十一岁时，我的艾滋病检测呈阳性——原因是，治疗血友病时，输入了感染有艾滋病病毒的血液。

　　艾滋病不同于血友病。在我被确诊患有艾滋病的时候，还没有针对它的有效治疗手段。更糟糕的是，比起血友病，艾滋病更被常人用异样的眼光区别对待。很多好伙伴的父母都不允许他们陪我过夜，距六年级学年结束还有两个月的时候，我就被开除了。因为对于艾滋病，常人有深深的恐惧，也有太多关于它的误传。

　　当最初的恐惧慢慢退去，我像往常一样生活——结交新朋友、约会以及担心自己的气色。换句话讲，我是个"正常的"青少年。不敢否认，我曾经不止一次以艾滋病为由逃课，待在家里睡觉、玩儿电子游戏。（对不起，妈妈爸爸，大多数时候我并没有生病！）

　　我享受那种特殊待遇，但我不再愿意去医院看医生，去见给我治疗艾滋病的专家。尽管一年只去四次，但我还是非常抵触。因此，妈妈必须装作是送我去学校——然后转到开往大城市的州际公路，需要一小时才能到医院。我并不是病愈出院，而是带着一个残酷的预言——我身体的艾滋病病毒检验呈阳性反应，一只脚很可能已经踏入了坟墓。

　　然而，随着一年又一年过去，我愈发有信心我可以活得更久。在学业上，虽然我有些怠慢，但还是按照学年计划与同龄人一起毕业。不仅如此，同龄人还给予我有生以来最大的荣誉——我当选为校友代表。我从未公开承认自己患有艾滋病，但大多数同龄人都已经听过一些传言。对于我的家人来说，获得荣誉的时刻有些不真实，他们曾不确定到毕业的时候，我是否还活着，更不曾想过这一最荣耀的时刻。

　　通常，人们听到我的故事，了解到我是如何感染艾滋病的，或者因为我还是个孩子就遭受这些病痛，而表示同情。事实上，我很感激命运的安排。血友病让我明白要活在当下，明白朋友不仅仅是同龄人，还可以是值得信赖的人。艾滋病让我体会到了被歧视的滋味。因为常人对艾滋病的恐惧，患者常被人们区别看待。我慢慢地认识到，每个人都可能承受磨难，而我所面临的是身体上的病痛。我觉得自己很幸运，因为这些病痛是显而易见，可以被人察觉到的。

　　二十岁的时候，我已经携带艾滋病病毒度过之前生命的一半。我已经可以很淡然地谈论自己的身体状况，并且努力地尽我所能去帮助他人一起面对艾滋病病毒，或帮助他人预防感染艾滋病病毒。当我开通网站，并开始写博客后，我惊讶地发现自己很擅长写作。我为艾滋病患者创造的一个词——"positoid"（自造词，可以理解为"乐观细胞"）——开始被很多患者使用。我已经接受艾滋病，承认它在生命中所扮演的角色；也明白了如果其他人不能够接受它，那是他们的问题，不是我的。

　　我经常被问到："你是否愿意和没有艾滋病的人交换生命？"当然不愿意。这么多年来，在逆境中成长，我学到了很多东西。我为什么要以这些为代价换得新生命，面对一些新的未知问题呢？再者，如果没得血友病，也不曾感染艾滋病，我就不会遇到格温。格温是位艾滋病教育家，他当时在为了一个教育项目寻找艾滋病患者的时候，最终找到了我。

Chapter 2 Health Challenges
第二部分　健康挑战

那是十年前的事情了。从那时开始，我们一直是朋友。

我深信，正是生命中那些最为艰难的时刻让我们成长。也正是由于疾病，我得到很多的关爱、支持和同情，这些感情远胜过我所产生的负面情绪。三十多岁的时候，我拥有了一个幸福的家庭。我很重视身体健康，因为我知道有很多人并不像我一样幸运，比如那些没有看到有效治疗艾滋病手段诞生的人，还有那些无法获得有效治疗机会的人。

如果生命如我，而没有深深的感激之心，那伤害的是他们自己，也伤害了那些帮助他人把幸福变为现实的人。我热爱生活，纵然有艾滋病相伴。

——肖恩·德克尔

A Wink from God Himself
来自上帝的眷顾

Oh, my friend, it's not what they take away from you that counts—it's what you do with what you have left.

—Hubert Humphrey

My Irish grandmother, who raised me, could find a blessing in the direst of circumstances. She proclaimed our poverty a gift from God, because the Lord had a special place in His heart for the poor. Whenever I bemoaned the fact that my clothes came from church rummage sales, Gran directed my eyes to one of her favorite Irish blessings which she'd painstakingly stitched and hung over the kitchen table in our tiny apartment:

"May you enjoy the four greatest blessings:

Honest work for your hands to do.

A hearty appetite to nourish you.

A good man or woman to give you love,

And a wink from God himself above."

Shortly after my twenty-third birthday,

Chapter 2 Health Challenges
第二部分　健康挑战

however, I encountered a situation that I believed even Gran would have found impossible to consider a blessing. The sudden onset of an autoimmune disease caused a systemic inflammation in my blood vessels and gangrene in my lower legs. Neither surgery nor chemotherapy halted its spread, leading to the eventual amputation of my right leg and leaving my left leg with nerve damage and encased in a brace.

Gran had died two years earlier, but even her legacy of faith couldn't pull me out of the self-induced isolation in which I put myself when I was discharged from the hospital. The chemotherapy had left me bald, and the enormous steroid dosing bloated my body so that I went from a size eight to a size twenty. I no longer recognized myself and did not want to be seen in public. I hung pillowcases over both mirrors in my apartment so I wouldn't see myself, and my new prosthesis gathered dust in the closet. I think my friends were glad that I no longer communicated with them; their visits to me in the hospital had been painfully awkward. What could they say?

I allowed myself to wallow in self-pity for a few weeks before I got sick of my own company. I had turned down the opportunity for outpatient physical therapy when I left the hospital, but now I began a self-designed program, wearing the prosthesis and hobbling around the apartment for longer periods each day. Amazingly, the pain in my stump began to lessen. I took the pillowcase off the closet mirror and watched myself walk, keeping my eyes on my legs and off my bloated torso.

Then one day I did study my body. Could I do without the cortisone pills that had assailed it? I called my doctor, and he agreed to wean me off the pills. It would take the better part of a year, cutting me down a half tablet every two weeks. I felt a surge of hope as the pounds slowly melted off with my decreasing medication and increased exercise.

I began to believe that I could work, but not at the nursing aide work

I'd done previously. I remembered that at some point in the hospital a social worker had told me of a job-training program for which I qualified. I called her, and soon I was taking a special van back and forth each day, learning office skills that would qualify me for work as a secretary.

During my van rides, I made friends with some of the riders. One told me about a social group for adults with disabilities. I attended one of their get-togethers, and within six months I was an officer in their group. I'd also begun dating a handsome fellow amputee I met there.

A week after I graduated from the business school, their administrator called me. Their secretary was moving out of state. He offered me the job and I accepted. When the school closed two years later, I got an administrative job at a local university, where I went to school at night and majored in journalism, a career I'd never considered but discovered I was good at.

Not too long ago, I was packing to move from Pennsylvania to Texas when I came across the sampler Gran had stitched. It was yellowed and frayed, but its words still spoke volumes. I closed my eyes and pictured Gran, her eyes full of faith, pointing at the blessing. I knew just what she'd say about that awful day I lost my leg. Had that not happened, I would not have met the man I love, nor have a career as a writer—honest work indeed, which brought me food for nourishment and, most decidedly, "a wink from God himself above."

—Kathleen M. Muldoon

朋友，重要的不是别人可以从你身边拿走的，重要的是你如何看待你所拥有的。

　　我是由祖母抚养长大的，祖母是爱尔兰人，她信仰上帝，纵然在悲惨的境遇中也能找到来自上帝的祝福。她说贫穷是上帝赐予我们的礼物，因为在上帝心中，穷人占据着特殊的位置。每当我抱怨自己的衣服都是些教堂义卖的东西时，祖母就会指给我看那幅爱尔兰祝福语的绣品，那是祖母最珍爱的东西。也是祖母亲手辛辛苦苦绣好的，悬挂在厨房的饭桌之上。

　　"愿你拥有四大祝福：

　　双手换取诚实的劳动，

　　健康的饮食滋养着你，

　　温柔的异性深爱着你，

　　还有来自上帝的眷顾。"

　　然而，二十三岁生日过后不久，我的悲惨遭遇，相信即使是祖母也不会把它看作福分。我的自身免疫能力急剧变差，导致血管发生系统性炎症以及小腿坏疽。手术和化疗都不能阻止坏疽扩散。最后，不得不对右腿进行截肢，只留下神经损坏了的左腿，还要戴着假肢。

祖母两年前就去世了。即使是她那坚定的信仰也没能把我从自我孤立的状态中解救出来。自出院以来，我一直都是这种状态。因为化疗，我的头发已经掉光；因为大量服用类固醇药物，身体变得臃肿，体形从八号变成二十号。甚至连我自己也认不出自己，更不想在公共场合被别人看到自己现在的样子。因此，我用枕套蒙住公寓里所有的镜子，这样就看不到自己。抽屉里的新假肢上已满是灰尘。我想，朋友们都应该很高兴吧，因为我不再与他们联系。生病住院时，他们去医院探望我，我们都感到难过又尴尬，他们又能说些什么呢？

我放纵自己，沉浸在自怨自艾中好几个星期，直到厌倦了自己。离开医院后，我拒绝进行门诊理疗。之后，我开始自己设计治疗方案，戴上假肢，每天在公寓里练习走路，每天都增加练习量。令人惊奇的是，残肢的疼痛感逐步缓解。从此，我摘下蒙在镜子上的枕套，开始看着自己走路，把注意力集中在腿上，避开臃肿的身体。

一天，我注意到自己的身体。心里想，我可以不再服用折磨人的可的松药片吗？咨询了医生后，他同意我停止服用，所以大半年之后，我可以每两个星期减少一半的药量。随着药物用量的减少和运动量的增加，体重慢慢下降，我心中充满希望。

我相信自己可以工作了，但不是做之前的护理工作。记得在医院的时候，有一位社会工作者告诉过我，有一个工作培训项目很适合我。之后，我给她打电话，很快，为了使自己成为一名合格的秘书，我开始每天坐着专车去参加培训，学习一些办公室技能。

就在去上课培训的途中，我和一些乘客成了朋友。其中一位朋友告诉我，有一个专为成年残障人士成立的社会团体，我参加了一次他们的社交聚会，六个月之后，我成为小团体里的干部。此外，我也开始与一位截了肢的帅小伙约会，他也是我在这个团体里认识的。

从商学院毕业一个星期之后，学院行政人员给我打了通电话，因为他们学院的秘书要辞职，他向我发出工作邀请，我接受了这份工作。两年后，学校关闭，我又在当地的一所大学找到一份行政工作，在那里，我晚上去学习新闻与传播专业，一份我从未考虑过却很擅长的职业。

不久前，我打算搬离宾夕法尼亚到得克萨斯，在收拾行装时，无意中发现祖母绣的那件东西，虽已泛黄、磨损，但那些话依然在耳边回荡。我闭上眼，在脑海里刻画出祖母的样子，她的眼睛里充满虔诚的信仰，手指着这些祝福的话。对于那天的痛苦遭遇，我知道祖母会对我说些什么。如果没有发生这一切，我不会遇到我爱的那个人，也不会成为职业作家——依靠这份诚实的劳动，获取滋养我的食物。可以说，这是一份"来自上帝的眷顾"。

——凯瑟琳·M.马尔登

Walking Through My Paralysis
走过瘫痪的岁月

Some see a hopeless end, while others see an endless hope.

It has taken me seven years to consciously relive the events of January 22nd, 2003. It's not that I've developed courage to face what happened. I relive it in my dreams. Many nights my husband, Bob, wakes me because I'm screaming. I should have stopped repressing the memories years ago. It is time to tell my story.

Many concerned people have asked me the specifics of what happened, yet apologize for prying. Nobody's prying. It has been my fear of facing as well as telling the truth. As Christopher Reeve said, "Living in fear is not living at all."

Cape Cod, where I live, is a kayaker's dream. For years, Bob and I were four-season kayakers. We planned our work schedules around the tides. Two days before my breakdown, Bob and I had taken a beautiful winter excursion in Cape Cod Bay, where curious harbor seals escorted our boat.

That night, weird symptoms began. In bed, I couldn't keep my legs still. Until dawn, I sat watching TV while continuously needing to swing my legs back and forth.

The next night it became hellish. I needed to stand up and sit down constantly. Then it felt like electrical impulses gone haywire. My legs, seemingly on their own, were flinging up as far as legs could go. I couldn't stop them.

Bob called our friend, Judy, who's a chief doctor at a Boston hospital about two hours from our home. I could tell Bob was trying to control his panic.

"What did she say?" I said.

"It's not good."

"Just tell me!"

"She said, 'Take Saralee to my hospital's emergency room right now. I'll meet you there.'"

"What does she think is wrong?"

"She thinks it's your spinal cord."

I was shocked. "I didn't have an accident! And I don't have pain!"

"I told her that. But she said, 'Something's happening very fast.'"

When I was wheeled into the hospital, I couldn't walk and had no feeling in my hands. I was petrified.

Three neurologists tested me. I looked away as they touched sharp instruments to my body. I felt nothing. Bob saw the startling abnormalities. For my sake, he never showed his terror on his face.

A CAT scan ruled out a brain tumor. Nearly everything was ruled out: multiple sclerosis, bone disease, rheumatoid arthritis.

I needed an MRI but their machine was down. Now I had no feeling in my legs and arms. Since I was losing precious function so fast, we decided to go to another hospital.

A neurologist rushed to stop us. "If you leave here," he said, "you could become a quadriplegic and permanently on a vent." So of course we stayed.

By the time of my MRI, I had no feeling in my torso.

The chief neurologist of several Boston hospitals had been called in. My medical team observed as we looked at my MRI images.

Two vertebrae in my neck had completely disengaged and were rapidly crossing over each other, choking off my spinal cord. Without immediate surgery, the cord would be severed entirely and I'd be completely paralyzed.

Why did this happen? Nobody knew.

It happened spontaneously.

"Can you fix it?"

"No." He was a straight shooter. "What's done is done. We can hopefully stop the progression surgically."

"Hopefully?"

"There's no guarantee of improvement. There's a fifty percent chance that even with surgery you will never walk again."

I slung my arms over the ledge of the nurses' station. I was in an advanced state of spasticity. Everything was moving on its own. My arms and legs were uncontrollably swinging widely through the air. "Are you telling me that even if surgery stopped the progression, I could spend the rest of my life like this?"

"Yes."

The surgery did stop the progression.

My neurologist said, "If there's any improvement, ninety percent will occur in the first three days. The only other variable that could help is time. Whatever state your body is in two years from now, you will always be."

Bob asked if occupational therapy, physical therapy, or medication would help. He shook his head no. My doctor's words felt as authoritative as an edict from God.

I'd rather not name my doctors. They did terrific surgery. I love them all and we get along beautifully. However I'm disappointed in myself that I initially took their words as gospel. Christopher Reeve didn't listen to his doctors. He said, "It's pretty irrefutable that you can help yourself. I just don't believe in ultimatums."

I wish I had been prepared for the psychological and physiological aftereffects. Bob was angry. "They sent you into a whole new world without telling you one thing to expect."

There was no improvement in those three days.

I kept falling. My brain was sending incorrect signals, such as how high to lift my foot over a two-inch obstacle. Had the medical professionals told me two words—"look down"—many dangerous falls would never have happened.

Christopher Reeve said, "Gratitude, like love, needs to be active." When I regained use of my typing fingers, I started using them with gusto.

I'm privileged to help others by writing for the Christopher and Dana Reeve Foundation, though I'm still surprised every time I see myself described on their website as a "woman living with paralysis." Paralysis is defined by the foundation as a central nervous system disorder resulting in difficulty or inability to move the upper or lower extremities. As Christopher said, "Living a life with meaning means spreading the word. Even if you can't move, you can have a powerful effect with what you say." Using my writing to help other people with disabilities has become a mission for me. After all, Christopher also said, "Even if your body doesn't work the way it used to, the heart and the mind and the spirit are not diminished."

In these seven years, I haven't been able to change some malfunctions… yet. Walking feels like I'm on a tightrope while moving through molasses. Though I can walk, I can't climb one step. With no balance, I can't stand still.

But I've become determined to help myself. Again I take inspiration from Christopher Reeve, who said, "I gradually stopped wondering, 'What life do I have?' and began to consider, 'What life can I build?'"

I learned that there's no greater antidepressant than helping others. It is dramatically gratifying to make a difference in others' lives through my writing. The countless readers' responses I receive have without a doubt brought meaning to what happened in 2003. I am eternally grateful for all who have helped me by telling me my words are important to them.

My wish is that those who read this story might re-think the words "try" and "hope."

Before my spinal cord collapse, I spent nearly every day kayaking in the magical world of Cape Cod Bay. I assumed those days were gone for good, but now I know they are not. Bob and I have taken five small excursions back to the bay. The curious seals are still there, probably wondering where we've been all these years. I tell them, from my strongest heart and resounding voice, what Christopher Reeve said: "I refuse to allow a disability to determine how I live my life. There is only one way to go in life and that is forward."

At that two-year mark, which is when my neurologist said that whatever I was, I would always be, I could walk no further than twenty feet. This year, which is seven years later, I made it ten miles.

—Saralee Perel

Chapter 2 Health Challenges
第二部分　健康挑战

有些人看到的是无望的尽头，而有些人看到的是无尽的希望。

——逸名

七年来，我一直在重温那件事，发生在 2003 年 1 月 22 日那一天的事。其实，并不是我已经鼓足勇气去面对那时所发生的一切，我每天在噩梦中重温这一切。多少个夜晚，我的丈夫——鲍勃——把我从恐惧的尖叫声中喊醒。我知道自己不应该再埋藏这多年前的记忆了，是时候说出我的故事了。

很多人都曾关切地问我到底发生了什么，之后又为他们的爱打听感到抱歉。没有人再去探究，我一直害怕面对，害怕诉说这件事情。克里斯托弗·里弗曾经说过，"在恐惧中的生活不是生活本身"。

我家住在科德角，那里是皮划艇运动员的理想之地，多年来，鲍勃和我一直是全年度皮艇划手，我们会根据潮汐变化安排工作。就在身体垮掉前两天，鲍勃和我还在科德角海湾享受着我们的冬季短足旅行。在那里，有海湾里生性好奇的海豹为我们的船保驾护航。

那天晚上，我的身体开始出现奇怪的症状。躺在床上，我却不能把腿伸直。到黎明时分，我一边看电视，同时要不断地来回摆动着腿。

到了第二天晚上，情况变得更加糟糕。我必须不断地站起来，再坐下，然后感觉就像是电子脉冲失去控制了一样，我的腿好像不听使唤，自己就往上踢。

鲍勃给我们的朋友——朱迪——打去电话，询问情况，朱迪在波士顿的一家医院当主治医生，医院距离我们家有两小时的车程。我能感觉得到鲍勃在努力控制自己的情绪，不让自己显得恐慌。

"她说了些什么？"我问。

"情况不太好。"

"告诉我！"

"她说：'马上送萨拉莉到我们医院急诊室。我同你在那里见面。'"

"她说哪里不对劲儿？"

"她觉得是你的脊髓出了问题。"

我很震惊："我没碰到过意外啊！我也没感到任何疼痛啊！"

"我跟她讲了。但是她说：'有些状况变化得很快。'"

我被推进医院时，既不能下地走动，双手也没有知觉。那时，我变得茫然不知所措。三位神经科专家一同给我会诊，给我做检查。当他们用锐利的器械轻触我的身体时，我转过脸看别处。我没有任何感觉。鲍勃看到我的异常反应，很是惊讶。但为了稳定我的情绪，他没有露出丝毫恐慌的表情。

计算机断层摄影扫描检查后，医生排除了脑瘤的可能性。除此之外，多发性硬化症、骨骼病和风湿性关节炎也都被排除了。

本来需要进行核磁共振成像检查，但机器坏了。而现在我的四肢已经没有感觉了，鉴于我身体重要机能衰竭的速度如此之快，我们决定转院。

Chapter 2 Health Challenges
第二部分 健康挑战

一位神经科医生匆忙过来阻止我们。"如果现在离开这里,"他说,"将来可能四肢都会永久瘫痪。"为此,我们选择留了下来。

核磁共振检测时,我的身体毫无感觉,多家波士顿医院的神经科主治医生都已经为此被召集了过来。我们边观察核磁共振图像,医疗团队边帮我做检查。他们发现我的颈部有两块椎骨已经完全失去联结,发生交错,导致脊髓阻断。如果不及时治疗,脊髓将会完全被切断,从而导致彻底瘫痪。

为什么会发生这样的事?没有人知道。

自然而然地就发生了吧。

"可以调整椎骨吗?"

"我调整不了。"他是个坦白直言的人,"该做的都已经做了。我们能做的就是希望能够通过外科手术控制病情恶化。"

"希望?"

"我们不能保证一定会好转。有百分之五十的可能性是即使做了手术,你也不可以再下地走路。"我的手臂在护士值班处的窗台上悬吊着。现在已是痉挛晚期,病情持续恶化,而我却无能为力,四肢不受控制地在空中大幅度摇摆着。"您的意思是,即使手术遏制住病情恶化,我以后也只能像这样?"

"是的。"

手术的确遏制住了病情的恶化。

神经科医生说:"如果病情有任何改观,有百分之九十的可能性会发生在手术后的前三天,能帮助我们的也就只有时间了。两年之内,无论你状态如何,你的后半生都将会是这样。"

鲍勃又询问专业治疗、物理治疗或者药物治疗是否会有效,医生摇了摇头。在那时,医生的话就像是上帝的命令一样权威。

我真希望自己没有指责过为我治疗的这些医生,手术很成功,我爱他们，我们相处得很好。但是，我对自己很失望，我刚开始的时候把他们的话竟当作准则，克里斯托弗·里弗曾经并没有完全盲从医生的建议。他说过："毫无疑问，你可以帮助自己。我只是不相信类似最后通牒之类的话。"

我希望自己已准备好承受任何副作用，不管是心理上的还是身体上的，鲍勃却非常生气，他说，"他们把你送往一个全新的世界，却不给你任何期待。"

在那三天里，病情并没有任何好转。

我的身体状况持续恶化，脑部发出错误指示，例如需要抬多高才可以越过两英寸高的障碍物。其实，只要医护人员告诉我——"向下看"——就可以避免很多次跌跤。

克里斯托弗·里弗说过："感恩，就像爱一样，需要主动。"当我又可以活动手指打字时，我怀着极大的热忱积极地活动手指。

我感到非常荣幸，自己可以通过为克里斯托弗和达纳·里弗瘫痪基金会撰稿来帮助其他的人。虽然，我每次在他们的网站上看到自己被称为"与瘫痪共生活的女人"都会有些惊讶。基金会把瘫痪定义为中枢神经系统紊乱病症，瘫痪导致患者很难或不能做到身体活动的最低或最高限。就像克里斯托弗说的："有意义的生活能够传达出这句话——即使你不能活动，你所说的对他人也会产生有力的影响。"对于我来讲，通过写作来帮助其他肢体障碍的人已成为使命。总之，克里斯托弗还说："即使你的身体功能不能正常运转，你的心、思想还有精神没有丝毫改变。"

七年来，我仍然没能改变身体的机能障碍……走路感觉像在走钢丝。我可以走路，但不可以登阶梯，因为没有平衡感，我不能站着静止不动。但我已下定决心帮助自己，又一次从克里斯托弗那里获得启发，他曾说："我渐渐地不再去想'我有着怎样的生活？'而是开始思考'我自己可以创造怎样的生活？'"

我发现没有什么能像助人为乐一样，可以帮助自己抵抗抑郁情绪。我也感到满足，我能够通过写作影响他人的生活。毫无疑问，无数读者的回复让发生在 2003 年的那件事变得有意义。我永远感激这些曾经激励过我的人，因为他们告诉我，我说的话对他们很重要。

希望那些读过这则故事的人能重新思考这两个词："努力"和"希望"。

在脊髓出现问题之前，我几乎每天都在科德角划皮艇，那里是个有魔力的地方。我曾想那样的日子永远地结束了，但是，现在我明白没有结束，鲍勃和我五次回到海湾短暂旅行。那些好奇的海豹依然在，或许在想这些年我们去了哪里。我从坚强的心底，以响亮的声音告诉它们，正如克里斯托弗·里弗曾说过的："我不允许肢体障碍决定我应该怎样生活。生命只有一条路可以走，那就是向前。"

神经科医生告诉过我，手术之后情况如何，以后就会一直是怎样。手术两年之后，我走路超不过二十步。而今，也就是七年之后，我却可以走十英里。

——萨拉莉·佩莱尔

Down But Not Out
击倒，却不曾被击败

The human spirit is stronger than anything that can happen to it.

— C.C. Scott

It was nearing spring in my second year of graduate school that I discovered what I was really made of. I had been writing my Comprehensive Exams for two weeks, primarily seated in front of the computer and taking very few breaks. As I neared completion of my first draft, I realized that I needed to do further research. Tired and hungry but wanting to finish, I trudged off to the library. Once there, I flung my knapsack on a comfortable chair and headed to the stacks with a large leather bag. I filled the bag with books, then leaned to the side to pick it up. As I straightened with the load, I felt a strange sensation that ran from the base of my spine to the top of my scalp. I shrugged it off, hefted the sack to my chair downstairs, and set out to read what I'd found.

Chapter 2 Health Challenges
第二部分　健康挑战

Hours later, I stood to go home, only to feel the sensation again. Once again, I shook it off and headed home. By evening, I'd become so nauseous that I headed to bed.

I woke the next morning feeling even more uncomfortable than I had the previous day. I made it to work, but by lunch I was driving to the University Health Services. I was assessed by a young med student who was quite impressed that I could touch my toes (I was an aerobics instructor after all), but thought little of my achy back and flu-like symptoms. He sent me on my way with a bottle of 800 mg Motrin and wished me well.

That evening, I hosted a work party that had been scheduled for weeks. After the guests left, I fell apart. I called the After Hours Healthcare line and expressed my concern about my growing back pain and general malaise. They told me to lie down on a hard surface and hope that my back would sort itself out. Unfortunately, once on the ground, not only did the pain increase, but I couldn't get up. My husband lifted me to the bed, gave me my Motrin and turned out the light.

I awoke the next morning to sun streaming in the window and the birds chirping. I tried to roll onto my side to get up, but nothing happened. It took a few moments for me to realize that I no longer felt any pain in my back, then only a few more seconds to comprehend that while I no longer felt pain, I no longer felt anything. I began to panic when I realized that I couldn't move at all and woke my husband. He telephoned for an ambulance and the paramedics arrived shortly thereafter, backboard in tow so that they could transport me to hospital. They gingerly wedged the board beneath me, then cinched the first strap down. I heard a high-pitched scream, but confused, didn't realize that it was coming from my own mouth. As the paramedics cinched the second strap, everything went dark.

I came to a few times during the ambulance ride to the hospital, but each time only long enough to know that consciousness was not a good plan. When I was finally alert, I found myself in a hospital bed. Confused, I rang for the nurse and was told that I had herniated three of the discs in my lower back and that the spinal column was impinged. The rupturing had caused the paralysis, and the doctors were evaluating the options for me.

I lay in the hospital bed, waiting for the doctors to decide what to do with me. After three days, the Chief of Orthopedics informed me that in his professional opinion I would never walk again without surgery. I lay there, twenty-two years old, graduate student and athlete, trying to contemplate what that meant. I had always been active and learned most things by doing. I couldn't grasp what it would mean to be unable to do so. I was also deathly afraid of having surgery on my back, and really unable to even consider the option. My husband had gone to work, my family lived 2,500 miles away, and my dear friend Jen could offer little to soothe me. When the doctor left and I started sobbing, Jen stroked my face and spoke softly to me until I drifted off to sleep, then, unbeknownst to me, made the most amazing set of phone calls.

Jen contacted our Department Director, who promptly called his wife, who just happened to be the Director of Sports Medicine. She then called her team, who committed to providing round-the-clock integrative medical care for me until I was walking again. Jen then contacted my husband, who contacted my family (three of them physicians), who then called the hospital and demanded that the new team be allowed to treat me.

A day later, I was being hoisted into a Hubbard tank to begin my hydrotherapy (three times per day). I was fitted for a whalebone and steel corset that was designed to keep my spine straight, whether or not I could stand. The massage therapist came next, and after her, a physical therapist. Even the hospital dietician played a part as she designed a diet that would enhance healing and enable my body to function better. Jen just sat at the side of my bed smiling as each new cast member popped into the room.

I fell the first time they lifted me to my feet. I fell the second and third times, too, but eventually, as the compression eased, I began to regain feeling in my feet, and I was able to stand with a walker. When I was discharged from the hospital, my gait was so bizarre that most people thought I had cerebral palsy. But with a lot of assistance from dear, committed friends, I forced myself to swim two miles per day in the campus pool, went to physical therapy five times per week, and engaged my body to do the unthinkable. Armed with a mind set on full recuperation, after six months I walked into an aerobics class with my physical therapist at my side. The students clapped and my teacher wept.

Twenty years later, as a mother of five, I ran the La Jolla Half Marathon. Those who raced with me will never forget my primal yodeling as we ascended each hill —urging on those at my side to celebrate every step as we made them.

You never know what you've got till you think it's gone.

—Sage de Beixedon Breslin, Ph.D.

人类灵魂的力量是最强大的。

——C.C.斯科特

　　直到研究生二年级春季学期的时候，我才了解到自己身体的真实状况。两个星期以来，我一直在写综合调查研究报告，基本上就坐在电脑前，很少休息。初稿几近完成的时候，我感觉还需要做进一步研究。虽然又疲惫又饥饿，但一心想要完成研究，我还是拖着疲惫的身体到了图书馆。一到图书馆，我就把书包扔到了一个舒服的位置上，拿着一个大皮袋子，往书架走去。塞满皮袋子之后，我斜靠到旁边准备整理一下。就在那时，我感觉从脊椎尾部到头皮有种奇怪的感觉。当时我没有在意，拿起袋子回到楼下的座位上，开始看书。

　　几小时后，我准备起身回家，这时又一次出现那种奇怪的感觉。又一次，我没有重视，就径直回家了。到了晚上，因为感到有些恶心，就去休息了。

　　第二天早上醒来，感觉比前一天更加糟糕。我还是去工作，但是到了中午，我不得不去大学健康服务中心看一下。一位年轻的医学院学生给我做了检查，他只是对我可以下腰触到脚趾印象深刻（我毕竟曾是个健美操教练），却没有考虑到我隐隐作痛的背和类似流感的症状。最后，他给我开了一瓶八百毫克的布洛芬，把我送走，并祝我好运。

就在那天晚上，我办了一个工作派对，之前已经筹划了好几个星期。客人离开后，我感觉像散了架一样。我打通早晚健康咨询电话，咨询越来越严重的背痛和身体不适让我很担心，该怎么办才好。他们告诉我睡硬板床，希望背部能够自动调整不适。不幸的是，刚一着地，不但疼痛更加剧烈，连起身都不行。后来，是老公把我抱到床上，递给我布洛芬药，缓解了疼痛，然后关灯睡觉了。

第二天早上，伴着一缕阳光和鸟叫声，我醒来。我试图翻身起床，但是没有任何动作反应。过了一会儿，我才意识到自己感觉不到背痛了，之后过了几秒钟，我才知道自己不仅感觉不到疼痛，也没有任何其他感觉。当我发现自己动弹不得时，我害怕得叫醒老公。他立即打电话叫了救护车，医护人员很快赶到。随后，医护人员拿来脊椎矫正板，以方便把我运送到医院。他们小心翼翼地把板子放到我身体下面，而后系上第一条固定带。随即，我听到一声尖锐的叫声，但很疑惑，并没有意识到那是自己的尖叫声。当医护人员系第二条固定带时，我感觉眼前一片漆黑。

在车开往医院的途中，我几次恢复意识，但是每次都很短暂，仅仅知道自己长时间处于无意识的状态。等到我再一次恢复意识，发现自己躺在医院的床上。不知所措中，我打电话问护士，护士告诉我说下背部有三块椎间盘已经突出，并已经影响到脊椎。椎间骨断裂已经导致麻痹，医生在筛选最佳治疗方案。

我躺在病床上，等待医生的决定。三天后，骨科主治医生说，从专业角度来看，如果不动手术，恐怕以后都不可能下地走路了。躺在那里，我心想，二十二岁的我还是一名研究生，同时是名运动员，这一切将意味着什么。一直以来，我都很活跃，从亲身实践中学习。我不知道，如果以后不能做这些将会意味着什么。我非常害怕在背部动手术，甚至不敢考虑手术的建议。老公已经去上班，而我家距离医院有二千五百英里。珍，我的好友，也给不了太多的安慰使我平静下来。医生离开后，我开始抽泣。珍轻抚我的脸，在我耳边轻轻说话，直到我在不知不觉中睡着。之后，在我不知情的状况下，珍打了很多通重要的电话。

她联系了我们系主任，主任立刻又打电话给他妻子，她正好是运动医学部主任。她随后又打电话给她的团队，他们答应为我提供二十四小时综合医疗护理，一直到我能够下地走路为止。在此之后，珍又打电话给我丈夫，他又联系了我的家人（其中三位是内科医生），我的家人又打电话到医院，要求让新团队给我治疗。

一天以后，我首先被送到哈伯德水槽治疗室，开始接受水疗（每天三次）。我被放入一个鲸骨钢束里，这是为了保持我的脊柱挺直而专门设计的，不论我能否站立。接着，一位按摩师进来为我按摩，在她之后，又来了一位理疗师。医院的营养学医生也参与到治疗团队当中，她为我设计饮食结构，来巩固治疗，帮助恢复身体功能。珍就坐在我的床边上，对每一个进来的人都报以微笑。

他们帮我试着站起来，第一次我摔倒了，第二次、第三次，依然摔倒，但最后，随着压迫感的减缓，我的脚又重新有了知觉，我能在助步车的帮助下站立起来。出院的时候，我走路的样子看起来很奇怪，以至于很多人以为我得了大脑性麻痹。但是在至亲好友的帮助下，我逼自己每天在校园泳池游两英里；每个星期接受五次物理治疗，并且试着做些超出能力范围的事。因为一心想着康复，就在六个月后，我走进了健美操课堂，理疗医生陪在我身边。看到这样的我，学生给以热烈的掌声，老师也热泪盈眶。

二十年后，我已经是五个孩子的妈妈，也参加了拉霍亚半马拉松比赛。每攀登一座山，我都会高歌以鼓舞士气——一起庆祝成功踏出的每一步，相信那些和我一起参赛的人不会忘记。

你永远不知道你曾经拥有过什么，直到失去它的那天。

——塞奇·德·贝克斯顿·布雷斯林博士

Just One More
再一次

Toughness is in the soul and spirit, not in muscles.

—Alex Karras

"Okay Beth, one more, that's it, just one more."

I huffed and puffed my way through another sit-up, red-faced and exhausted, then collapsed back onto the mat and stared up at the ceiling. My physical therapist leaned over me, a smile on her face and her hand outstretched, waiting for me to lift my arm and slap her five.

"I can't," I said. "Give me a minute."

As I gazed up at the peeling paint of the physical therapy room's ceiling I wondered again how I'd gotten to this point. Five sit-ups? I could barely make it through five sit-ups without having to stop and rest? What had happened to the girl who could swim five kilometers at a time? What happened to the woman who did yoga several times a week? What had even happened to the peppy lady

098_

who would walk an hour to work just because the sun was out?

"She's gone," the physical therapist said gently, sympathy radiating from her kind face. "Whoever you were, she's gone. You have to concentrate on being who are you now."

Squeezing my eyes shut against sudden tears, I inhaled deeply and the smell of stale sweat and antiseptic filled my nostrils. I exhaled slowly, shakily, my diaphragm protesting under even that much use.

I didn't want to be who I am now. I didn't want to have myasthenia gravis (MG), a rare form of muscular dystrophy that causes great muscle weakness. In my case it started with a droopy eyelid, then affected my arms until I could no longer wash my hair without weakness and eventually attacked my legs until walking up stairs became a problem. Physical activity just for the fun of it became a thing of the past and "fitness" became a measure of what tiny fraction of my past routine I could get through in any given day.

With a sigh, I rolled over to my side, pushed up with one arm and eventually drew myself into a seated position. I reached out and gave the PT a high five. She smiled at the evidence that at least I was still trying.

"It sounds so pathetic, but I don't want to be who I am now," I said, admitting it for the first time since my diagnosis.

"I know," she said simply. "If it helps, remember that fitness isn't a competition. From here on out you have to measure yourself against yourself and that's it. If you could do five sit-ups today you have try to do six tomorrow. If you could walk for ten minutes today you have to try for eleven tomorrow."

I nodded, knowing that what she said was important. But deep inside there was a small child who wanted to clap her hands over her ears and sing, "I can't hear you! I can't hear you!"

We got on with the session that day and I took her advice to heart in the coming months, particularly after I had to have a full sternotomy in order to

Chicken Soup 每天读一篇美丽英文
心灵鸡汤 Soul 每一次跌倒，都是最好的成长

take out my enlarged thymus gland in an attempt to alleviate the MG. After the surgery I chanted "just one more, just one more" as I fought to put one foot in front of the other, feed myself, cut my own food and finally climb stairs. When the surgery didn't bring about the results for which we'd hoped, I chanted "just one more, just one more" as I learned to walk with a cane, then a crutch. These weren't things I wanted to do, in fact I downright resented that simply walking could make my legs weak and on hot days a short stroll to the corner could make me sweat as if I'd gone for a long jog. Yet every time I wanted to stop I promised myself I'd do just one more and, most of the time, I'd do a lot more than that before I finally finished.

Now that I've adjusted to life at this slower pace there are few days I still get caught up with how much I can't do. But every now and then I'll watch someone dance or run or swim or even carry a baby and I can't help but compare myself to her. Then I'll hear the PT's voice in my head telling me that fitness isn't a competition and I only need to think about myself. I can still walk and even dance a little, I can swim in my own way and I can carry a baby for short amounts of time. I may not be as healthy or physically fit as others, but I'm still committed to being as healthy as I can be, to doing just one more of whatever I need to do.

Just one more. It's not so much, but there's little more important.

—Beth Morrissey

韧性存在于灵魂和精神里，而不显示在肌肉上。

——亚历克斯·凯拉斯

"好，贝丝，再做一个，就再做一个。"

我气喘吁吁地又做了一个仰卧起坐，累得满脸通红，筋疲力尽；紧接着向后倒在垫子上，眼睛盯着天花板。理疗医生向我俯身过来，面带微笑，张开双手，等着我举起上臂，和她击掌庆祝。

"不行了，"我说，"给我一分钟时间。"

我盯着治疗室天花板上剥落的油漆，在心里又一次感叹自己怎么变成现在这个样子。五个仰卧起坐？我竟不能一口气做完五个仰卧起坐？那个一次可以游五千米的小女孩儿哪里去了？在她身上发生了什么？每个星期练习多次瑜伽的女人哪里去了？她身上发生了什么？只因为太阳出来了，就算需要一小时，也会选择步行的那个活力无限的姑娘哪里去了？她身上发生了什么？

"她已经消失了。"理疗医生温柔地说，友善的脸庞流露出同情，"不管你以前是怎样，但已经逝去。你现在需要关注的是如今的你。"

我闭上眼睛，不让突然到来的眼泪流下来。

我深深地吸了一口气，鼻腔里满是汗臭和防腐剂的味道，又颤抖着慢慢呼出，可膈膜并不那么合作。

我不想像现在这个样子。我不要得重症肌无力。重症肌无力是一种极为罕见的肌肉萎缩症，会导致严重的肌肉无力。我刚开始只是眼皮下垂，后来发展到无法抬起双臂洗头发，最后到无法登台阶。为乐趣而进行体育锻炼已成为过去，"健康"是衡量运动的标准也已成为过去。

随着一声叹息，我侧翻身至一边，用一条胳膊撑着坐起来。我伸出手，同医生击掌。看到我仍在努力，她回我以微笑。

"这听起来让人感到怜悯，但我不想像这个样子。"我说。自确诊以来，这是我第一次接受这个事实。

"我知道。"她简单地回应，"请记住健康不是一场比赛，如果这样有效的话，从现在开始，你只需要与自己较量。如果今天能做五个仰卧起坐，明天试着做六个；如果今天可以走十分钟，明天就试着走十一分钟。"我点头，心里明白她说的很重要。但是，在内心深处，有个小孩儿用手捂着耳朵大声说："我听不到！我听不到！"

那天之后，我继续锻炼身体。在接下来的几个月里，我一直把她的话谨记在心，特别是在做了胸骨切开手术之后。手术切除了肿大了的胸腺，以此来缓解肌无力症状。手术之后，我一边反复地说着"再一次，再一次"，一边努力地向前迈开每一步：自己吃饭、自己动手切食物，到最后自己爬楼梯。虽然手术没有达到我们预想的效果，我依然边说着"再一次，再一次"，边借助手杖练习走路，后来用拐杖走路。我不想做这些事情，实际上，我心里依然在埋怨，埋怨简单的走路就使双腿无力。大热天，小走片刻就使我汗流浃背，好像慢跑了很长时间一样。然而，每次想放弃的时候，我都会告诉自己再一次。而大多数情况下，我会做得更多，才算结束。

现在，我已经适应这样慢节奏的生活，也就不会把自己束缚在我办不到的事情上。但是，每当看到别人在跳着、跑着、游泳或者抱着孩子，我还是会不禁拿自己和她们较量。然后，脑海里会回响起医生的话——健康不是一场比赛，我只需要和自己较量。我仍然可以走路，甚至小跳一会儿舞蹈；我可以以自己的方式游泳；可以抱一会儿孩子。我也许不像其他人一样健康，但我会始终努力保持最健康的状态，再一次做需要做的事情。

再一次，并不多，但是至关重要。

——贝丝·莫里西

Walking Forward
继续前行

The only disability in life is a bad attitude.

—Scott Hamilton

As I sat facing the doctor, I posed the usual question, "What is the prognosis, Doctor?" He said, "It is going to be necessary to amputate your leg just below the knee."

A sudden wave of nausea swept over me. I felt like I was going to faint. Looking back, I can never remember having anything shock me quite as much as those words from the doctor.

Gaining my composure, I asked more questions. It became apparent that it had to be done. Although the amputation was considered elective surgery, the choice wasn't if, it was when. I was twenty-eight years old and out of options.

The doctor explained. If I waited, I would risk gangrene setting in. Then, the amputation site would be dictated by the line of demarcation (a puffy, red

Chapter 2 Health Challenges
第二部分　健康挑战

line that forms between the healthy and gangrenous tissue). I was familiar with gangrene, as I had already lost two of my toes. My chances of having a well-fitting limb, afterwards, would be more favorable if the doctor determined the site.

On the drive home, between bouts of tears, I thought of all the ways an amputation would affect my life. The picture seemed pretty grim. I was terrified.

I had already suffered for four years. My bone grafting surgery had developed complications, followed by residual infections that literally destroyed my whole foot. It had been a tough four years, but I had never expected it to end this way. Wearing an artificial limb wasn't what I anticipated. However, there was nothing more anyone could do to restore my foot and leg. The damage had been far too extensive.

The doctor had made it clear I needed the surgery, and soon. I dreaded telling my husband. We had suffered financial devastation during those four years of numerous surgeries, hospital stays, and treatment. In those days, we had no medical insurance and still had old bills we were paying on monthly. My husband worked so hard. Now, there would be even more expenses. I felt like such a burden.

Things moved quickly after that fateful day. The doctor amputated my right leg about six inches below the knee. My stump healed beautifully since the infections were gone. He was able to work with healthy tissue.

Back then, the usual waiting period for the first fitting was eight weeks. I was ready in six. Being young and fairly healthy helped a whole lot. After a five-day hospital stay I came home on crutches. I was glad it was over. I wasn't suffering any more pain than I had been before, on a day-to-day basis. Knowing this pain would eventually go away filled me with new hope.

My husband worked as a body man for a salvage yard. He managed to purchase a burned automobile and completely restore it over the six weeks

I was waiting for my first fitting. The price he received for that automobile covered the exact amount needed for the hospital bill plus the new limb. It was remarkable.

To this day, I believe receiving that precise dollar amount came directly from "divine intervention." Otherwise, how did the dollars work out to the penny? Coincidence? I don't think so.

The rest is history. In retrospect, after being an amputee for forty-six years, I can tell you that it is not the worst thing that could ever have happened to me. I walk very well for age seventy-four. I have no more complaints than most folks my age have about their discomforts. In fact, I probably have a lot fewer because I am quite active.

Breaking it down into a percentage, my missing part is only about ten or fifteen percent of the "entire me." That's not a whole lot. Before, it was painful, disfigured, and threatened to undermine the health of my entire body. It was a miracle that it could be removed and my health restored. What more could anyone ask?

I'll admit there have been times when I have been disgruntled over fitting problems. At those times, I have been frustrated and cranky, but on the whole, those times have been few and far between. The technology of today's prosthetics is absolutely amazing. Most people never notice I am wearing an artificial limb (nor do I).

The secret—adjusting to the change and having a willing attitude about your new way of getting around.

If you are satisfied with watching life pass you by while you sit, then you will never get where you are going. If you really want to be a part of life, you certainly can be. The best part about being busy is that you forget about the prosthesis. At least, that's how it has worked for me.

People have always complimented me about "my wonderful attitude." I guess the thought of losing part of your body has a deeper emotional impact upon people than internal ailments. Probably because it is so visual.

So, why would I have anything but a good attitude? After all, I have two legs, two arms, and a healthy body to live with every day.

I have a strong belief that God has been carrying me forward since the day the doctor "pronounced my doom," or what I thought was the end of world for me. It was only fear of the unknown that caused such anguish.

I couldn't have been more wrong. There are so many things I can do, and have done.

Obedience training three large dogs, seventy-five pounds plus, presented a challenge, but the wonder was, I "trophied" with all three.

I am no longer as fast a swimmer as I was before the amputation (missing one of my flippers) but I can swim like a fish.

Can I dance? You bet. Not particularly the slow dances like a waltz or tango that require long strides and perfect balance. I can dance them, but not gracefully. I can certainly jitterbug, polka, cha-cha, or do any of the dances that have quick, short, steps.

I played recreational volleyball two different periods, in past years, and was a terrific "spiker" at the net.

My home has always been clean and organized as we raised our family. Even now, I cook healthy, tasty meals every day, and feasts for the holidays. My life has been filled with activity. I am humbled and grateful for any, and all, of my accomplishments.

I cannot relate to "handicapped," "crippled," or even "physically challenged." To me, better words would be "slightly limited," but aren't we all in some way?

Bragging was not my intent. I only spelled out some of my "can do's" as an example of what is possible.

I acknowledge all the rich blessings that have been bestowed upon me over my lifetime. I have been able to keep walking forward to reach whatever destination I chose.

Only through my faith in God, in myself, and with prosthetic technology could I have kept walking this long course.

Life is good.

—Joyce E. Sudbeck

生命中仅有的残缺是消极的生活态度。

——斯科特·汉密尔顿

　　我坐在医生对面，问医生："诊断结果如何？医生。"这是一个经常被问及的问题。他说："必须对腿部膝盖以下的部分进行截肢。"

　　听到这个结果，一阵恶心之感涌上来，我差点儿昏厥过去。回望过去，没有什么能像医生的那番话一样，让我如此震惊。等到平静下来，我又问了医生一些问题，结果很明显，必须截肢。尽管是否进行截肢手术是可以选择的，但当时那不是选择，二十八岁的我别无选择。

　　医生解释说，如果我继续等，可能会有坏疽的危险，到那时，截肢位置将根据分界限（健康组织和坏疽组织之间形成的一道浮肿红线）而定。我知道坏疽这种病，我曾因此失去过两根脚趾。如果由医生决定截肢位置，那么拥有一条健康的腿的机会会更大一些。

　　在回家的路上，我一边痛哭，一边想着截肢将给我生活的方方面面带来的影响。情景令人沮丧，我心中充满恐惧。

四年来，我一直忍受着病痛的折磨。因为植骨手术，引发了一系列并发症；又因残余感染，整个脚已经坏疽。这是艰难的四年，但我从未想过会以这样的方式结束，我不想戴假肢。但是，没有人能使我的脚和腿康复，损伤已经太过严重。

医生已明确地说，需要尽快进行手术。我害怕让老公知道这件事。四年来，无数次的手术、住院以及治疗，我们已经无力支付。而且在那个时候，我们没有医疗保险，还要每月偿还旧账。老公已经很努力地工作了，如今，又要承担更多的医疗费用，我感觉自己像个沉重的负担。

自性命攸关的那天起，事情进展得很快。医生在我右腿膝盖往下六英寸处进行了截肢。紧接着，感染消失之后，断肢恢复得很好很快，能像健康组织一样正常工作。

第一恢复阶段一般需要八个星期，因为我还年轻并且体质较好，所以到第六个星期就已经康复。我在医院住了五天，就出院了，自己拄着拐杖走回了家。我特别高兴，一切终于结束了。我不用再像以前一样，要一直备受病痛的折磨。因为这些病痛终会消失，我的内心充满希望。

我丈夫在一家报废机器拆卸场当保安。在那里，他买了一辆烧坏了的汽车，花了六个星期的时间修理它，那时正是我恢复的第一个阶段。汽车最后的出售价格正好可以抵销医院费用和买新假肢的费用。多么令人惊奇的巧合！

直到今天，我相信这样的巧合肯定是缘于"上帝的帮助"。否则，为什么这么巧？纯属巧合吗？我不这么认为。

后来发生的事情也都成为过去。回想起来，我失去右腿有四十六年了，但是对于我来说，截肢不是最糟糕的事情，我七十四岁了，依然可以稳健地走路。和同龄人相比，我对于这些不便，没有很多的抱怨。其实，我之所以抱怨得少，是因为我自己比较积极。

若从比例的角度看，我失去的部分只是"整体"的百分之十或百分之十五，那不是生命的全部。之前，残肢带来的痛楚和身体的残缺，威胁到我整个身体的健康，通过截肢手术使身体康复已是一大奇迹，还能再要求些什么呢？

我承认，在假肢是否合身这个问题上，好多次我都非常不满意。在那些时候，我自己心情沮丧，情绪也不稳定，但这种时候并不多。今天的假肢制造技术绝对令人惊叹，很多人都没有注意到我戴着假肢（我自己也看不出）。

我能够如此面对现实的秘诀——适应改变，以积极的态度接受现在的状态。

如果你满足于坐看生命与你擦肩而过，那么，你永远不会到达你想去的地方。如果你真的想融入生活，你就可以。忙碌的意义是可以让你暂时忘记假肢的存在，至少，对于我来说这样很有效。

别人总是称赞我有"良好心态"。我想，与身体上的疾病相比，失去身体的一个部分在感情上可能给人的冲击更加强烈。也许是因为这个更明显些。

所以，我为什么不以良好的心态去面对这一切呢？毕竟，我还有双腿双手和健康的身体。

我始终坚信，自医生给我"宣判末日"起——我自己也认为那是我的世界末日，上帝就一直伴我前行。因为对未知的恐惧，才会有这样的痛苦，我不能再犯这样的错误。有很多事情值得我去做，有的也已经做到。训练三只重达七十五英磅的巨型犬，是一项艰难的挑战，但神奇的是，我竟然成功做到了。

我不能像截肢以前那样游泳（因为失去了一个脚蹼），但我仍可以像鱼一样游泳。

　　我可以跳舞吗？你肯定觉得我不能跳华尔兹或探戈，因为它们需要迈大步和完美的平衡感。不过，我可以，但不是很优美。我还会跳吉特巴舞、波尔卡和恰恰，或者其他任何一种快速短步舞蹈。我还曾经两度打排球，过去，我在球场上还是个了不起的扣球手。

　　我们家总是那么干净整洁。即使是现在，我每天做健康可口的饭菜，而节假日里就做丰盛的美味佳肴。总是有各种各样的活动需要我去参加。我感激生活中点点滴滴的成就。

　　我从来不认为自己有"身体缺陷"，或称自己是"跛子"甚至"残障"。我觉得更好的说法是"轻度受限制的"，而事实上，我们不都在某种程度上受到限制吗？

　　我不想自夸。我只是想举出些我"能做的事情"来，说明什么是可能。

　　感激上苍，这一生中，赐予我如此多的祝福。我会继续前行，想着我心中的梦想和目标。

　　我相信带着对上帝的信仰、对自己的信心和假肢技术的信任，自己可以继续前行，走过这漫长的人生路。

　　生活很美好。

——乔伊斯·E.萨贝克

Faith to Share
分享信仰

Every evening I turn my worries over to God. He's going to be up all night anyway.

—Mary C. Crowley

"I hate the way chemotherapy makes me so sick. I wish I could go the rest of the summer without these treatments." My husband Glen picked up my hand as we sat in our side-by-side recliners in front of the television screen, neither of us caring what was on it. Having made a living by operating heavy equipment for thirty years, even the palms of his hands had always been rough. I noticed how soft they were becoming. "I don't even know why I bought that boat. It won't do anybody any good tied up at dock all summer. I wish the kids would go ahead and use it, but you know they won't."

"The kids will use the boat all right—with us." I squeezed his hand. "I believe you'll get an extension on your break from chemo. We'll be camping and fishing soon. And we'll take our family vacation again this year, too. You just wait and see."

"Oh, I'll be back on chemo for the rest of the summer. I've been off it since April. I hate this stuff, but I guess if it prolongs my life, I'll have to take it. Being with you and the kids means a heck of a lot more to me than putting up with a little nausea and needle sticks, so I'll take the chemo again." He spoke in a low but determined tone. "But you do know, don't you, that there will come a time when I will have to say 'no more'?"

I swallowed to keep the lump in my throat from choking me. "I know, and it is your decision. We have agreed not to influence you. When that time comes, you will know, and we'll understand." I tried to lighten my voice. "But for now, we will enjoy your vacation from chemo and nausea. We'll enjoy the next three months."

"I don't have a clue what you're talking about. The doctor said I can't be off that rubbish more than a few months, or the mass will double in size. Don't you remember he said that?"

"I know what the doctor said, and I know how much being able to spend these summer months relaxing with the family means to you. But, you see, I have it on a higher authority that you won't be taking treatments for three more months. We'll have this summer together, so plan the vacation. Rachel wants to go to Myrtle Beach, I think."

My husband of forty-two years looked at me as if I were mad. He had been suffering from lung cancer for two and a half years. It had spread into his lymph nodes and the adrenal gland, but chemotherapy was keeping the lungs stabilized and preventing the mass from spreading to other vital organs. When Glen wasn't suffering from the side effects of the chemo, such as violent nausea and extreme exhaustion, he appeared quite healthy. His breathing had become almost normal. The doctors who did his study were amazed.

Although the chemotherapy did a good job fighting the cancer, after so many treatments, his body demanded a rest period. His blood vessels and his nervous system couldn't handle any more poison being pumped into his body. The damaged nerves in his feet caused so much pain he could hardly walk, and his veins wouldn't hold the needles. So, the doctors decided to give his body a break from the torture of chemotherapy. He had been resting and gaining strength all spring, but the threat that stopping the treatment would allow the masses to grow in leaps and bounds hung over us. Now it was time to see the doctors and get the results of the latest scans.

"What in the world are you talking about, woman? How could you know something like that? Why would I be off for another three months?"

"Because that's what I asked for—three months," I answered.

"Oh, I know. You're talking about religion again." He let go of my hand and fumbled with the remote control. Deciding there was nothing on TV to hold his attention, he switched off the set. "Hon, I wish I had your faith, but the truth is, I don't, and you better be prepared to accept what the doctor has to tell us."

I wasn't ready to accept such a summation. "I asked God to give us just three months to enjoy this summer. He said 'yes.' That's all there is to it."

My husband turned toward me, giving me his full attention, his eyes probing my face. "You know I'm not much of a churchgoer, but you are so confident you almost make me believe." He touched my fingers to his lips.

I searched my heart, asking God to give me the right answer, before I replied. "Okay, Glen. Please, just try it this way. If you don't have enough faith of your own, try leaning on mine for a little while. I promise you there will be no more chemotherapy for three months." I'm not sure if my faith or my stubbornness kept my voice from trembling as I made that promise.

Our daughters, Rachel and Beth, met us at the Kentuckiana Cancer

Institute the next morning. They never missed any new scan reports. You wouldn't believe a twentynine-year-old and a twenty-seven-year-old could be such Daddy's girls. Beth sat on his knee, while Rachel stood, arms around his neck, waiting for the doctor to come into the room.

"Don't you girls go worrying, now." Glen's jovial mood turned sober. "We're gonna get a three-month reprieve." My eyes widened in surprise. Had I heard him correctly? Then he added, "Mama says so." I thought he was joking until I perceived the somberness in his voice. He did believe.

The door opened and the doctor, smiling as always, bounced in. "Well, Glen, we got good news. I don't know how, and I sure can't explain it, but the cancer cells haven't doubled in size; actually, they've shrunk. I don't think we'll need any treatments just now." And then he said the magic words: "Come back in three months."

As he shook the doctor's hand, Glen said, "My family's been praying."

"Well, you tell them to keep it up," the doctor said before he exited the room. "You know you really shouldn't be here. You should have left us two years ago. Yeah, you tell the family to keep on praying."

Sunday morning, Glen was dressed and waiting for me to get out of bed. "Well, come on, woman, get up and get ready. We don't want to be late for church today."

With a smile in my heart and a lilt in my voice, I hummed "Amazing Grace" all the way to church.

—Jean Kinsey

Chapter 2 Health Challenges
第二部分 健康挑战

每晚，我向上帝倾诉担忧。不管怎样，他一直都在那里倾听着。

————玛丽·C. 克罗雷

"我讨厌化疗，那种恶心的感觉很难受。我不想再接受这些治疗，只想平静地度过这个夏天。"丈夫格伦握着我的手，我们并肩坐在电视机前的躺椅上，都没在意电视上播放着什么。三十多年来，丈夫一直靠操作重型机械谋生，因此手掌一直很粗糙，我注意到它们开始变得柔软。"我不知道为什么我会买那艘船。整个夏天都拴在码头上，没派上什么用场。我希望孩子们能用得上它，但是你知道她们用不上。"

"孩子们很快就会用上的——和我们一起。"我握紧他的手说，"我觉得化疗间隔时间会延长，这样的话，我们很快可以去露营钓鱼。今年我们又可以一家人一起去度假，你就等着看吧。"

"整个夏天，我都要到医院去化疗，我四月就已经取消了度假计划。我虽讨厌化疗，但如果可以延长生命，我愿意接受。与忍受病痛和针管相比，对我来说，与你和孩子们在一起更重要，所以我会继续接受治疗。"他用低沉而坚定的口吻说，"但是你应该明白，总会有那么一天我不得不说'不必治疗了'？"

我深深地吞咽了一下，不让喉咙哽咽。"我明白，那是你的决定，我们同意不去影响你的决定。到那时，你会知道，我们也会理解。"我极力使自己听起来很轻松，"但是现在，我们可以尽情享受假期，没有化疗，也没有恶心。接下来的三个月，我们会很快乐。"

"我不明白你在说些什么。医生说过，治疗间隔不能超过几个月，否则，肿块会成倍增大。你不记得了吗？"

"我记得。我也明白，这个夏天能够与家人一起放松对你的意义。你知道，我已经从更权威人士那里确知，你可以三个多月不用接受治疗。因此这个夏天我们可以一起度假，所以计划一下假期吧。我觉得雷切尔想去默特尔比奇。"

四十二岁的他盯着我看，好像我疯了一样。他患肺癌已有两年半了，癌变已经扩散到淋巴结和肾上腺，化疗帮助稳定肺部的情况，防止进一步扩散到其他重要器官。不用忍受化疗的副作用的时候，格伦看起来很健康，呼吸几乎正常。负责治疗他的医生都很惊讶。

虽然化疗确实有效地抵抗了癌症，但经过这么多次的治疗，他的身体需要休息。他的血管和神经系统已经不能承受任何药物。因为脚部神经受损，他痛到不能走路，血管也脆弱得不能再承受任何针头。所以，医生决定让他的身体休息一段时间，停止了化疗。整个春天，他都在调理恢复，积蓄力量。但因为停止了治疗，肿块可能会迅速长大，这种威胁一直困扰着我们。现在，该去找医生进行最近结果检查。

"你到底在说些什么，老太太？你怎么会知道我可以再休息三个月？为什么？"

"因为那是我要求的——三个月。"我回答道。

"哦，我知道了。你又在说你的信仰。"他松开我的手，摆弄着遥控器，看到电视上没有什么节目可以吸引他的注意力，他关掉了电视，"亲爱的，我希望我能和你一样，有这样的信念，但我没有，你最好做好听医生分析结果的准备。"

我没有听从："我祈求上帝给我们三个月的时间，让我们一起享受这个夏天。他说'可以'，就是这样。"

丈夫转过头来，全神贯注地打量着我的脸："你知道我并不经常做礼拜，但你如此自信，几乎让我不得不相信。"他把我的手放到嘴边。

我在心里一直祈祷，希望上帝给我答复。"格伦，试一试。如果你没有足够的信心，就试着从我这里获得支持。我向你保证，三个月内你将不用再做化疗。"我做出那个承诺时，不知是不是坚定的信仰和执着的坚持没让我的声音颤抖。

我们的女儿，雷切尔和贝丝，第二天来到肯塔奎那癌症研究院。她们从没漏掉过一次检查报告。你简直不敢相信，一个已经二十九岁，另外一个二十七岁，竟然还像是爸爸的乖宝宝。贝丝坐在爸爸腿上，雷切尔揽着爸爸的脖子，等医生过来。

"孩子们，你们不要担心，"心情大好的格伦变得认真严肃起来，"我们要停止三个月的化疗。"我把眼睛瞪得很大，感到十分惊讶。我听清楚他说的了吗？随后他又说道："妈妈这样说的。"我以为他在开玩笑，直到感觉到他声音里透着的深沉。他相信了。

医生走过来，像往常一样带着笑容："嗯，格伦，我们接到好消息。我不知道怎么回事，我也不知如何解释，但癌细胞没有变大，相反它们在变小。我想现在我们不需要做任何治疗。"然后他接着说了很有魔力的一句话："三个月后再回来。"格伦一边握着医生的手，一边说："我的家人一直在祈祷。"

"告诉他们继续祈祷，"医生离开前说，"你明白你本不应该在这里，两年前，你就该离开了。告诉你的家人，继续祈祷吧。"

星期日早上，格伦穿戴好，等着我起床："快点儿，老太太，快起床准备。今天做礼拜，我不想迟到。"

我的心情很好，在去教堂的路上，我一直高兴地哼着"上帝的恩宠"。

———琼·金西

I Am Woman
我是女性

When you treat a disease, first treat the mind.

—Chen Jen

In 1997, I learned what it meant to be a woman. Not how other people define womanhood, mind you—I was well past puberty, had already been married and experienced childbirth twice. I learned how to define myself in other ways, as I faced the loss of what I thought made me female.

Six months after the birth of my daughter, I went for my annual exam. I'd been exercising and feeling great and had no worries. The doctor completed her exams and I returned home. A week later, the doctor called and told me that she needed to perform a cervical biopsy, based on my test results. Scared and a bit squeamish, I appeared dutifully for the colposcopy. A week later, I was told that the cells were not cancerous, and that lowering my stress would likely improve my cervical health. I was informed that I would be returning to her office twice per year to have exams instead of annually due to the increased risk.

Two months later I met with the doctor again, this time because I was pregnant with my second child. Despite a few hiccups with the pregnancy, things went relatively well, and I gave birth to a healthy son eight months later.

Six weeks after the birth, I headed to the doctor's office for a postpartum exam. While I thought that all was well, the doctor was concerned about some "suspicious" skin discoloration near the suture sites. While it seemed reasonable to me that the area might be freaking out given what I'd been through, the doctor was not so pleased. I was told that I would be returning to her office for a biopsy the following week. After the last biopsy, I wasn't looking forward to any other procedure being performed in the area, but agreed to do so anyway.

A long week later, the doctor did a punch biopsy. I left the office sore, and began the long wait for the results. A few days later, we learned that there was no cancerous explanation for the radical change in coloration—it was, as I'd suspected, just a part of my reaction to childbirth.

I felt like I had a new lease on life! Two close calls, but all clear now! I enjoyed my children, my family and my work, and settled into the working mother routine. I tried to focus on what was positive and to distract myself from the stressors that seemed to be creeping in day by day. I made marketing calls, attended networking events, and when my son was six months old, I entered training as a Medical Intuitive. I was going to be all that I could be, no matter what else was happening in my life.

As much as I loved the training and felt like I'd finally discovered myself, I watched the distance grow daily in my marriage. I had entered a new world, filled with Light and healers—a place where he didn't fit. He travelled more often, and the silence between us grew. When we interacted, it was about the house or the children, but little else. I distracted myself from the reality I lived in, until one morning I found a lump in my left breast.

I contacted my doctor, who gave the lump a cursory exam and ushered me into Radiology. The tech performed an ultrasound, and I watched as the amorphous beast appeared on the screen. While I was used to the tiny fibrocysts I'd had all my life, this mass was much larger than anything I'd ever felt, and its presence on the screen shocked me. Appearing a little pale, the technician left the room and returned with the radiologist, something I'd never experienced despite the fact that I'd had numerous ultrasounds during my pregnancies. The radiologist turned to face the screen and grimaced. She then turned her gaze to me and told me that the mass had to be biopsied and likely removed, and that I would need to meet with a breast surgeon immediately. She left the office and returned with a sheet of paper as I pulled my clothing back in place. I was to head over to the surgeon's office while she called to schedule an emergency appointment.

I drove across town, finding it difficult to breathe. A half hour later, I was sitting in yet another doctor's exam room, being told that no biopsy would be performed due to the inherent risk of a potentially-cancer-filled mass leaking its mutant cells into my chest cavity. And, as the surgeon scheduled a radical lumpectomy for my left breast, the tears came like a torrent. I was thirty-one years old and in the previous twenty-four months, I'd had two children, and had faced cancer scares in all of the organs that I thought made me inherently female. Somewhere, here, there was a message for me.

I spent the weekend not with my husband, or even my children, but with a group of healers of all kinds. I had my palm read, got a massage, had some acupuncture, then spent hours in past life regression. In all of the lives in which I died as a result of bodily injury or illness, the healers diligently worked to resolve and release the energy trapped there. Then, on Sunday, anxious but more at peace, my tribe and I went to see G.I. Jane. After two hours, I came out physically and emotionally exhausted. Over dinner, I told my women friends that if Demi Moore could shave her head and be a badass, then I could certainly surrender my breasts in order to survive.

Monday morning found me on a gurney, staring up at the man who was about to remove most of my left breast. We made an agreement that if the path slide were positive for cancer, he'd remove both of my breasts and schedule reconstruction as soon as possible. I slipped into the nothingness of anesthesia, chanting my prayers, as I was wheeled into the operating room.

I awoke to the most incredible blue eyes staring at me, smiling.

"Ah, good, you're awake!" greeted the doctor.

I still felt so fuzzy, but wanted to know what they had found. I tried to reach up to my chest, but I couldn't seem to move my arms.

"That'll wear off soon," the surgeon soothed. "But, you don't need to check —they're both still there," he said, smiling again.

Then, as my tears of joy consumed me, he reached out to touch my arm. He leaned in close to me, with his lips just to my ear and whispered, "I don't know what you did, but I've never seen cancer vanish! You think someday you can teach me that trick?" He stood up, gave me a wink, and strode away.

My whole life, I thought that being a woman was about having a uterus, a vagina, breasts, and long hair. But, in 1997, I learned that being a woman was about acknowledging the awesome Light within, filling every crevice with peace, joy and love, and knowing that no body part would ever again define me.

—Sage de Beixedon Breslin, Ph.D.

要治病，先改变思想。

——陈仁

　　直到 1997 年，我才真正认识到作为一个女人的意义。我所认识到的和别人定义的女性不同，我已经历青春期，也已结婚并且有两个孩子。当我失去之所以成为女性的子宫时，我学会了用其他方式定义自己。

　　在女儿出生六个月后，我去医院做体检。因为我一直都坚持运动，感觉身体状态很好，所以没担心什么。医生给我做完检查，我就回家了。一个星期之后，医生打电话告诉我，根据检查结果，我需要做子宫颈活体检查。我有些害怕，就听从她的建议，做了阴道镜检查。一个星期过后，医生告诉我细胞没有发生癌变，但是要注意减轻压力，这样有助于子宫颈健康。医生说因为患病的风险增加，我需要每年到她的诊室进行两次检查，而不是一年一次。

　　两个月后，我又见到这位医生，这次是因为我怀了第二个孩子。怀孕期间，除了有些打嗝儿，其他一切都好。八个月后，一个健康的儿子出生了。

生产后的第六个星期，我去医院进行产后检查。自己觉得一切都好，医生却对缝线处的皮肤色斑有些疑虑。我想生产后，这些异常情况也是合情合理的，医生却没有像我这么乐观。医生说下星期再来她诊室做活体检查。自从上次活体检查之后，我不愿再进行这项检查，但还是同意过来检查。

漫长的一个星期过后，医生给我做了钻取活组织检查。检查完伴着疼痛就离开了医院，之后开始了漫长的等待结果的过程。几天后，我们得知结果：皮肤颜色强烈变化并不是癌变征兆——正如我猜想的，只是生产后的正常反应。

我感觉如获新生。两次性命攸关的时刻，都侥幸脱险！我爱自己的孩子、家庭以及工作，也适应了职业母亲的生活。我努力把注意力放在积极的事情上，虽然压力一天天增加，但努力地分散着注意力。我做营销工作，参加各类社交活动，儿子六个月大的时候，我参加医学实习生的培训。不管以后会发生什么，我要尽力做我能做的。

我喜欢参加这样的培训，感觉终于找到了自我价值，但同时也感觉到婚姻中我和丈夫两个人之间的距离在拉大。我已经进入一个全新的世界，那里有希望，有医生——一个他格格不入的地方。他经常外出旅行，我们之间变得越来越沉默，交流的时候，除了房子和孩子，几乎没有其他事情。我把注意力从现实生活中转移开来，直到一天早上，我感觉到左侧乳房有个肿块。

随后，我联系了我的私家医生，他为我简单地检查了一下，又带我到放射科。放射疗法运用的是超声波技术，我看到显示屏幕上的乳房，没有固定形状。我体内一直有这种小型囊变性纤维瘤，已经习以为常。与其他能感觉得到的囊肿相比，这个肿块要大得多，它显示在屏幕上的样子吓到了我。那些医生的脸色有些苍白，他们离开诊室，后来又与放射科医生一起回来。我从未经历过这样的情况，即使是在怀孕期间，那时做过无数次超声波检查。放射科医生转过脸对着屏幕，表情凝重，然后，她转过头盯着我。她说需要对肿块进行活体检查，肿块好像已经转移，我需要立刻做胸部手术。她离开诊室，拿了一张单子回来，我也穿好了衣服。她打电话给我安排急诊，我立刻赶往外科手术室。

我开车穿越小镇，感觉呼吸有些困难。半小时后，我已经坐在另外一位医生的检查室。医生说我不可以进行活体检查，因为潜在的癌变肿块的变异细胞可能已经扩散到胸腔。外科医生给我安排乳房肿瘤切除手术的时候，我的眼泪奔涌而出，如倾盆大雨。我只有三十一岁，前两年，才孕育了两个孩子。我也曾面临女性器官癌症的威胁，在某些地方曾有暗示。

这个周末，我没有陪丈夫和孩子，而是和几位医生在一起。我做了按摩、针疗，然后回想着过去。我想，若死于身体疾病，这些医生也曾努力拯救。到了星期日，我们一伙人又一起去看望简。两小时后我们离开，已经身心俱疲。吃饭的时候，我跟我的女性朋友说，如果黛米·摩尔剃光头发当坏蛋，那我就放弃我的乳房，来求得生存的机会。

到了星期一早上，我发现自己躺在病床上，盯着医生，他将给我做左侧乳房切除手术。我们达成一致，如果情况不利，将切除两个乳房，并尽快安排修复治疗。被推进手术室时，我进入麻醉状态，内心却一直祈祷着。

醒来后，一双蓝色的眼睛微笑着看着我，带着一副难以置信的表情。

"太好了，你醒了！"医生说道。

我很困惑，想知道他们发现了什么。我试着摸找自己的胸部，但胳膊好像动弹不得。

"药力过会儿才能消失，"医生安慰道，"你不必检查了——它们还在那里。"他说，又微笑起来。我难以控制快乐的泪水，任凭它流下来。他抓住我的胳膊，靠近我耳边，轻轻地说："我不知道你做了什么，但从没有见过这样的情况，癌症自己会消失！将来有一天，你一定要教教我你是如何做到的！"

他站起身，朝我眨了眨眼，大步走开。

我一直认为，女人就是要有子宫、阴道、乳房还有长发。但是，就在 1997 年，我真正了解了女性，女性就是要有好的心态，充满平和、爱和喜悦，并且知道没有哪个身体部位可以定义自己。

——塞奇·贝克斯顿·布雷斯林博士

My Purpose
我的目标

He who has a why to live can bear almost any how.
—Friedrich Nietzsche

"Syringo-my-what?" My eyes widened and my heart skipped two beats as my neurosurgeon gave me the diagnosis.

"Syringomyelia—a very rare disease. You have a syrinx, or a cyst, inside your spinal cord. It's growing toward your brain. Should do surgery soon as possible."

What was going on? I hadn't been sick— just some numbness, tingling and a few sensations resembling electrical shocks. Scary but not painful.

"I don't understand. What are you saying?" I wasn't sure I wanted to hear the answer.

The doctor patted my shoulder and spoke softly. "If that thing continues to travel upward, you have only a few weeks to live."

"What's the prognosis if I have the surgery?"

He sat on a stool and swiveled it to face me. Gentle concern filled his eyes. "I am a Christian and I pray before every surgery, but sometimes God has his own plans for my patients. This is a dangerous operation; I will not lie to you." He waited a moment for me to absorb what he said. "You may never walk again or you may die. You could be quadriplegic, or you could be well. I have to puncture the spinal cord, insert drainage tubes, and decompress the hindbrain. I promise to do all I can."

"But, Doctor, I can't die. I have two small children. They need me."

"Then we better get started. Do you want me to set a date?"

"Have—have you done this surgery before?" Again, I feared his answer.

I was more frightened when he answered, "Yes, one, and the results were good."

Telling my husband was almost as hard as hearing the words coming from my doctor's mouth. "Honey, we need to get a second opinion," he said. But this doctor told me he never went into surgery without praying first. I wanted him!

Several weeks later, I walked out of the hospital. I wore a neck brace and dragged my foot, but with the help of a walker and God, I walked!

Until this time, I had considered myself a good Christian person, who went to church—when it was convenient, who loved my church family—when I thought about them, who taught my children to say their nightly prayers—when we weren't too busy or too sleepy. Sometimes skipping them until the next night, or the next. The word "miracle" seldom crossed my mind.

Thank God, my church wasn't as lax as I. My pastor, who couldn't sit upright because he'd recently undergone a spinal fusion, rolled himself into the backseat of his automobile while his wife drove him to see me every day for the many weeks I was hospitalized. After returning home, several weeks later I was able to attend church. My loving church family had prepared a special seat so I could sit without hurting my neck. I no longer had my top seven vertebrae.

My life, as I knew it, came to a halt. I learned to expect the unexpected and to accept the unacceptable. My condition forced me to learn new skills and gracefully put the old ones behind me. I learned to appreciate the few true friends who stuck around through it all. I learned what a financial drain a prolonged illness can have on a working-class family.

But most important, I learned what love can overcome. My husband and I had planned to travel as school schedules allowed. He surprised me earlier than I'd anticipated. One day he came home driving a big brown, used motor home.

Shocked, I looked at those big steps leading from the ground to the entrance. "Did you forget I can't do steps? Can you take it back? I think our plans may have to be put on hold or maybe canceled."

"Yes, I can take it back. I haven't closed the deal yet. But did you forget I have arms? I can carry you up the steps." He pointed to a vacant spot in front of the window. "A comfortable recliner or even a lift chair will fit just fine there." We kept the motor home.

I had been an avid bowler for years, bowling in two leagues a week. By the time the winter season began, I had improved somewhat, yet I was still weak, wore my neck brace and used a cane. My teammates asked me if I would come and watch just to cheer them on. But when I got there, they said, "Of course, if you think you can do it, we still need a bowler. We decided not to replace you just yet."

"I can't. Besides, I'd kill all chances of you having a winning team." We'd won the league two years in a row.

"We want you, if you'll try."

"Well, maybe," I answered. Since I couldn't hold onto my heavier ball, I chose one of the children's balls, put on my bowling shoes, held onto the ball return and laid the ball on the lane. It stayed on and I picked off three or four pins. The building full of people began to applaud. I returned to my spot on the team, hobbling on a cane, neck brace and all. It didn't take long for my 165 average to drop into the low eighties, but I was bowling! I even won a trophy. My team ordered me a special one, engraved "Most Courageous Bowler." It's still my most cherished trophy. We received a team trophy also—we earned last place!

Perhaps I would have never stopped to evaluate my friends, my family and my Christianity if I had not been stricken with syringomyelia. I even learned that I had a hidden talent. I began to write articles for the American Syringomyelia Alliance Project newsletter. "FACES" profiled SM sufferers from around the country, helping individuals to feel less alone. I started a local support group and joined a group of peer supporters, answering calls from frightened SM sufferers from all over the world. I feel blessed that God has taken a misfortune and turned it into a blessing, making me a better person.

But, alas, time has taken its toll. The cyst has elongated the length of my spine. There are no more surgeries for me. Someday, unless God intervenes, and I believe He can and might, I may lose the remaining use of my arms, legs or both. But the beautiful truth of this is that I know as long as the Lord has work for me to do, He will make a way.

My cloud has a silver lining that refuses to dissipate as long as I know I have a reason to exist. Some say it is a miracle that I still have even limited mobility in all my limbs after twenty-five years of living with this malady. But I say, God has worked His miracle on me, not by miraculously giving me a new body, but by giving me peace within myself.

—Jean Kinsey

一个人一旦有了生活的目标，就能够承受得住任何事情。

——弗里德里希·尼采

　　"脊髓空……什么？"当神经外科医生告诉我这个诊断结果时，我睁大眼睛，心怦怦直跳。"脊髓空洞症是一种非常罕见的病。你的脊髓有空洞或者说是囊肿，正朝着大脑方向生长。应当尽快做手术。"怎么回事？我并没有生什么病，只是会有麻木感、刺痛感和一点儿类似于触电的感觉。感觉有些可怕但并不痛。

　　"我不明白你在说些什么？"我不确定是否想要得到答案。医生拍拍我的肩，轻声说："如果脊髓空洞继续向上发展，你也就只有几个星期可活。""如果我做手术的话，预计还能活多久？"我问道。他转过椅子，面向我，眼神里满是温柔的关怀，"我是个基督徒，在每次手术前都会祈祷，但有的时候上帝有他的安排。这个手术很危险，我不想说谎。"他停下来，给我时间理解，"你也许再也不能走路，也许会死掉。你可能会四肢瘫痪，也可能痊愈。我需要刺穿你的脊髓，插入引流管以减轻后脑的压力。我保证，我一定会尽我所能。"

"但是，医生，我不能死，我还有两个小孩子，他们需要我。"

"那么我们最好尽快准备手术。你要让我安排时间吗？"

"那你以前做过……做过这种手术吗？"我又一次害怕得到他的答案。

当他回答说"是的，做过一次，结果是好的"，我更加害怕。

要把这件事情告诉我的丈夫很困难，就像当我听医生说出这些话的时候一样。"亲爱的，我们需要咨询一下其他人的意见。"他说。但是这位医生说，他手术前一向都会祈祷，所以我相信他。

几个星期后，我走出医院，戴着颈托，拄着拐杖。上帝保佑，我能走路了！直到这个时候，我已经把自己当成一名虔诚的基督徒。平时在方便的时候，我会去教堂做礼拜。我知道自己深爱着我的教会家庭，它教会孩子们在不是很忙或者不是很困的时候每晚做祷告。有时候，我会不去教堂祈祷，一直拖延到第二天晚上或再往后。我从来没有想过"奇迹"这个词。

感谢上苍，我的教会不会像我一样松懈。我的教父刚刚做了脊柱融合手术，所以不能直起身坐着，就蜷卧在汽车后座里。在我住院的那几个星期，由他妻子每天载着他来医院看我。回到家几个星期之后，我就能做礼拜了。贴心的教会家庭已经为我准备了一个专门的座位，所以我可以坐下来，还不会弄疼脖子。我已经失去了七块顶部脊椎骨。

我的生活，如我所预料，忽然停滞不前。我学会了期待意外的发生，接受无法预料的事情。我的情况迫使自己学习新的技巧，而且以优雅的姿态忘记过去。我学会了感激始终陪伴在身边的朋友，那些真正的朋友。我明白了持久病痛会给一个工薪家庭带来多大的经济消耗。

但更重要的是，我懂得了爱可以战胜一切。在学校的工作安排允许时，我和丈夫计划一起去旅行。他曾给过我一个惊喜，比我预料的要早。

一天，他开着一辆大大的褐色二手露营车回到家。我惊讶地看着几层大台阶从地面通向入口，"你忘了我不能爬台阶吗？我想我们的计划可能得延期或者取消了。""记得，我可以把它送回去，我还没完成交易。但是，你难道忘记了我还有胳膊吗？我可以抱你上台阶啊。"他指着窗户前的一块空地。"一个舒服的躺椅，或者一个升降椅刚好可以安放在那里。"我们把它留了下来。

好多年前我就是个狂热的投球手，每个星期都会在两个社团里玩儿投球。初冬时候，身体已好转，但仍然很虚弱，仍然需要戴着颈托，拄着拐杖。我曾经的队友们问我要不要去看比赛，只是为他们加油呐喊。但等我到那儿的时候，他们说："当然了，如果你觉得可以，我们还需要一个投球手，我们决定暂时不换掉你。"

"我不行。如果参赛，我可能会毁掉你们获得胜利的机会。"我们已经连续两年赢得联赛冠军。

"我们需要你，如果你想试一试的话。"

"嗯，好吧。"我回答。因为抓不稳重球，我选了一个孩子们的球，穿上我的保龄球鞋，紧紧抓住球转身把球放在了滑道上，它停了下来，我打倒了三四个球瓶。室内满座的观众开始为我鼓掌。我拄着拐杖，戴着颈托，拿着其他的东西，蹒跚着回到了我在球队里的位置。没多久我打的一百六十五平均值就落到了八十名之后，但是我竟然可以打保龄球了！我甚至还赢得了奖品。因为我们队专门为我定制了一份特别的奖品，上面刻着"最勇敢投球手"。直到现在它仍是我最珍惜的奖品。我们还赢得了团队奖，虽然我们是最后一名！

如果不是患上了脊髓空洞症，也许我就不会停下来思考什么是真正的朋友、家人和基督教。也因此，我发现自己还有一项能力——我开始为美国脊髓空洞症联盟项目写文章。通过"脸谱"网站，简单介绍了全国各地患有脊髓空洞症的患者，让那些患病的个体不再感到孤单。我还成立了一个当地的互助团体，召集了一队支持者，他们帮助回复那些来自世界各地的电话，就是那些恐慌的脊髓空洞症患者的电话。我现在觉得很幸福，虽然上帝带给我不幸，但又把它变成祝福，让我成为更有用的人。

唉，但时间不饶人，囊肿已经有脊椎那么长了，我已经不能再做手术了。除非有一天上帝帮助我，我相信他能够并且可能会。也许我会丧失胳膊的功能，也许是腿的，又或许是二者的。但是，美好的事实是，只要上帝有事让我去做，他就会让我做下去。

我阴云密布的生活中有了一线希望。只要我有生存的理由，希望就不会消失。有些人说，我患这种病虽已有二十五年，但四肢仍然有一定的活动力，真是个奇迹。但我得说，上帝已经让奇迹在我身上发生。他没有不可思议地给我新的身体，而是给我平静的内心。

——琼·金西

心灵鸡汤：
每一次跌倒，
都是最好的成长

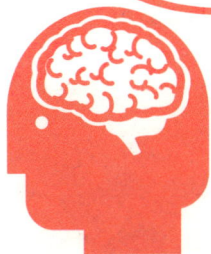

第三部分　每一天都是特别的

Chapter 3
Every Day Is Special

Each day comes bearing its own gifts. Untie the ribbons.

—Ruth Ann Schabacker

....

每一天都带着自己的礼物而来。请解开它的丝带。

——露丝·安·夏巴克

Every Day a Friday
每天都是星期五

Monday is a lame way to spend 1/7 of your life.
—Author Unknown

I love Fridays, and I'm not alone. Most people associate the last day of the workweek with feelings of relief, relaxation, and anticipation of good times to come in the weekend ahead. You know there has to be something special about a day when the feeling of celebration that accompanies its arrival is even commemorated in the name of a restaurant chain!

And so I, too, celebrate Fridays. After dropping my son off at school I head to Starbucks, to pick up a coffee treat of one type or another. Then instead of driving straight home I generally take a long route through the most scenic roads I can find, which usually includes my favorite corner of the local state park. On and on throughout the day I find myself smiling and happy for no other reason than that the day's name starts with an "F" rather than a "M," "T," or "W."

When I pick my son up again hours into the afternoon we high-five physically and vocally, our chorus of "FRIDAY!" resonating at least as loudly as our hand slap. Then we point out to each other the signs of beginning celebration in the college town we drive through. We see footballs being passed on fraternity lawns, hamburgers being thrown on grills, people parked on front porch swings, and parties everywhere swinging into action. Sometimes it seems as if the whole world is celebrating Friday!

The other day I emerged from a doctor's office happy over a positive prognosis in a health situation I was concerned about. My good mood was amplified by the signs of spring that were bursting all around me—flowers blossoming, birds singing, bright sunshine warm upon my back. I was suddenly ready to celebrate, and java-scented thoughts wafted through my brain. I whispered the word "Cappuccino!" and headed for the specialty coffee bar that was conveniently located just around the corner.

My mind rebelled. "What are you doing? It's Tuesday! Coffee treats are reserved for Fridays!" And suddenly I realized how ridiculous that line of thinking was! Why should Fridays be any more special than any other day of the week? Why waste six days while waiting to rejoice on the seventh? Minutes later I was walking back to my car with a big grin on my face and a raspberry mocha in my hand.

A small victory, to be sure, but it's also an accurate example of how many of us live our lives. We're waiting for conditions to be right before we allow ourselves to enjoy our time here on earth. Maybe when we finally graduate from college and get a job it will be time to celebrate, or perhaps when our toddlers are old enough to be in school all day. We'll rejoice when the car is paid off, or enjoy life when we're finally able to retire. And in that waiting we waste so much of the life that God has given us and the happiness that can be found in our todays. What if we moved a little of that "Friday feeling" into our rainy-day Mondays, our gloomy Tuesdays and our mid-week Wednesdays? Surely our lives would be much happier as a result.

It's interesting to note that T.G.I. Friday's isn't open for business on just the last day of the workweek! No, they celebrate all week long and into the weekend.

So should we.

—Elaine L. Bridge

星期一是耗费你七分之一生命的颠簸小路。

——逸名

我喜欢星期五，当然不只是我如此。许多人都把一个星期的最后一天与惬意放松和即将到来的周末美好时光联系起来。你知道这样的一天确实比较特别，为了庆祝它的到来，甚至还用连锁餐饮店的名字来纪念。

因此，我也要庆祝星期五。在把儿子送到学校后，我就直奔星巴克，点上一杯咖啡。我不会直接开车回家，而会选择一条路程较长风景优美的道路，在那儿能看到当地国家公园我最喜欢的一角。随着时间的流逝，我发现自己会因为这一天的名字是以字母"F"而不是以"M""T"或"W"开头而开心不已。

当几小时过去，到我下午去接儿子的时候，我们会击掌，异口同声地喊道："星期五！"嗓音比击掌声还要大。沿路行驶，我们会一一指出大学城里其他开始庆祝星期五的标志性活动。我们看到兄弟会草坪上传递着的足球、被放在烤架上的汉堡、秋千前休息的人群，和随处可见的行动起来的欢庆派对。有时感觉似乎整个世界都在庆祝星期五！

　　几天前，我从医生那儿得知自己所关心的身体状况为良好，开心不已。我愉快的心情伴着四周春天的迹象而荡漾着——繁花似锦，鸟儿鸣唱，明媚的阳光温暖地照在我的背上。忽然间我好想庆祝一下，咖啡的香气从脑海中飘过。我低声说道："卡布奇诺！"随后我直奔坐落在街角的那家十分便利的精品咖啡店。

　　我的理智开始抗议了："你在做什么？今天是星期二！咖啡应该留到星期五啊！"我突然感觉到这种思路的滑稽可笑！为什么星期五要比一个星期中的其他日子更加特别？为什么要浪费六天的时间而等到第七天才庆祝？几分钟后，我手拿一杯覆盆子摩卡，乐呵呵地回到了车里。

　　诚然，这只是一个小小的胜利，但它确实是我们当中许多人真实生活的写照。我们总是在等待正确的时机，才允许自己享受快乐：我们大学毕业后，找到一份工作时；当我们蹒跚学步的孩子已到了适合入学的年龄；我们在还完汽车贷款时；在最终能退休时。在这种等待中我们已经浪费了太多上帝赐予我们的生活和现在可以找到的幸福。如果我们能够把"星期五的感觉"分一点儿给多雨的星期一、阴郁的星期二和中间的星期三，会怎样呢？无疑，我们的生活会因此更加幸福。

　　有趣的是，我注意到"星期五餐厅"（美式休闲连锁餐厅）只有在工作日的最后一天不营业！哦不，他们要将庆祝持续整个星期，一直到周末。

　　我们也应该这样。

——伊莱恩·L.布里奇

The Gift of Brain Cancer
脑癌的礼赠

The excursion is the same when you go looking for your
sorrow as when you go looking for your joy.

—Eudora Welty

In August 2002, I received the greatest gift of
my life when I was told that I had terminal brain
cancer and would be dead in four to six months.
I had been married exactly five months when this
happened. My career was going well, my family and
friends loved me. I was as happy as I had ever been.
So why was this such a great gift? Why?

Because I had to face my death.

It was the middle of the night in January 2003.
I was wandering outside in the cold, alone and
bitter. The clinical trial I had entered was fraught
with uncertainty and danger. I could only participate
because I was terminal, my survival quite unlikely. I
was confused, constantly nauseous, and hardly able
to walk, even with a cane.

I was infuriated by my circumstances: I hated the cancer, myself, the doctors, and God. I found myself shouting, screaming, crying, raging against the injustice. For the first time in fifty-four years I had finally found happiness in my life, and now this horrific disease was ripping from me not only the joy of life, but also any semblance of stability, comfort or peace. Was I destined for continuous detestable rotting away every day in my pathetic limp to a cold grave?

Then suddenly, amidst all the virulence, came the inspirational voice of a very dear old friend, employer, and mentor, W. Clement Stone, one of the first people to write about Positive Mental Attitude, or PMA. In my mind I could hear him say, as he had thousands of times, "Every Adversity carries within it the seed of equivalent or greater benefit to those who have a Positive Mental Attitude!"

What?

Are you serious?

Greater Benefit?

What on earth was the greater benefit of dying of brain cancer, old man? (I was unaware that Mr. Stone had passed away just five months earlier at the age of 100.)

His words kept running through the part of my brain that was still functioning. Not some adversity, he had said, but every adversity, EVERY adversity, carries within it that seed of equivalent or greater benefit! You have to be kidding!

Fortunately, the many years of his being my mentor, teacher and hero had left its mark—the words "I reasoned" were ablaze like sun above my head. He used "I reasoned" frequently—very often in describing critical situations he faced in life. Once, a loaded gun was held to his head by a desperate, depressed, and hopeless person who told him that he had lost everything—he was going to kill Mr. Stone, and then turn the gun on himself. While most of us would panic in such a spot, Mr. Stone said calmly, "I reasoned," and then proceeded to think of a logical plan to save not only himself but the other person as well. He later set the person up in business, where the man was successful and prosperous the rest of his life.

"So," I said to myself, giving in to his message, "Let's reason." Immediately, I was at peace and felt rational—for the first time in months.

So... what were the possibilities for me? After all, life at that point had not provided me with very good options.

I certainly didn't have the option of "live happily ever after"—or did I?

The fact is one of two things was going to happen: I was either going to die very shortly, or, much less likely, live a long time.

So what if I died soon?

Well, "I reasoned," if I were bitter and angry, then I would have spent the last few months of my life in sorrow and isolation, making a living hell for my loved ones, and would be remembered, if at all, as a bitter old man who let brain cancer defeat him. I would receive their temporary show of sympathy, but in the end they would only have contempt for me and how I left them.

On the other hand, what if I were positive and hopeful? It wouldn't change the date of my death one bit!

But, it would mean that I would spend the last months of my life breathing deeply and clearly, contented, blissful, and in love with my family and everyone I met. I would die a happy man, and be remembered as that brave soul who faced a terrible death with courage, fortitude and aplomb. I would be cherished by those who knew me.

On the other hand, what if I made it? What if I lived?

Then I had no reason to be bitter and tormented! Why waste months of my life wailing about an end that wasn't even near?

So there it was—I had every reason to be positive about my condition, and absolutely no reason to be negative.

It was at that point, that very moment in time, for the first time in my life, that I stopped dying and started living.

I started telling everyone I met and knew that having brain cancer was the greatest thing that had ever happened to me, and today I believe that with all my heart.

A little over a year ago, I learned that the brain cancer had returned. Treatment today is more researched and predictable, prognosis is better; however, the outcome is never certain. After a year of radiation and chemotherapy the tumor board doctors have decided to continue my chemotherapy indefinitely and have scheduled me for monthly MRIs, with absolutely no promises.

How has this disturbing news affected me? It has made me even more positive!

From that special moment—that cold, dark night in January 2003, I have not wasted one second of my life fretting about dying. All the moments of all of my days are spent living.

Brain cancer the first time made me a better man. The second time is making me a good man. Brain cancer is the greatest thing that has ever happened to me.

So what about you? You will have good things and bad in life. Sometimes life will give you great fortune, other times it will rip you like a brick across the face.

What happens to you will happen, and you only have two ways to respond— you can be positive and happy, or negative and miserable. That's it. The good news is that the choice is always up to you! You choose how happy you will be every day of your life, every way that life happens, no matter when, no matter what, no matter who.

Make the decision today to live, not die. To be positive, not negative. Don't endure a tragedy such as mine to figure it out. Live every day, live every minute, live every second of your life.

—Tom Schumm

寻找痛苦的旅程和寻找快乐的旅程是一样的。

———优朵拉·卫尔蒂

　　2002 年 8 月，当我被告知得了脑癌仅剩下四到六个月的生命时，我收到了人生中最好的礼物。那时我结婚仅仅五个月，事业逐渐有了起色，家人和朋友都很爱我。我像从前一样开心地生活。但是为什么会是这样的礼物？为什么？

　　因为我不得不面对死亡。

　　那是 2003 年 1 月的一个深夜，我独自一人在寒冷的街上徘徊，孤独而心酸。临床试验充满了不确定因素和危险性，而我只能进行，因为我已经快走到生命的尽头，生还已几乎无望。我有些神志不清，时常恶心，即使拄着拐杖，也几乎无法行走。

　　我为自己的境况恼羞成怒：我怨恨癌症、怨恨自己、怨恨医生、怨恨上帝。面对这样的不公，我吼叫、咆哮、哭喊、恼怒。五十四年来，我终于第一次感受到了人生的快乐，然而这种可怕的疾病不仅剥夺了我生活的幸福，还有安宁与平静。难道我注定要继续堕落下去，悲哀地蹒跚着走向冰冷的坟墓吗？

　　然而突然间，在所有的悲悯之中，传来了一位挚友鼓舞人心的话语。他是我的老板，也是我的良师益友——W. 克莱门特·斯通，最早进行积极心态写作的人之一。在我的脑海中，似乎数以千次地听到他说："对于心态积极的人来讲，每一次挫折都能带来同等或者更多的收获！"

　　什么？

　　你是认真的吗？

　　更多的收获？

　　老伙计，在这世上到底什么是死于脑癌更大的收获呢？（我当时并不知道斯通先生在离自己百岁生日只差五个月的时候便与世长辞了。）

　　他的话萦绕在我仍旧运转的那部分大脑中。他曾说，不是某些挫折，而是所有，每一次挫折都会带来同等或者更多的收获！你一定是开玩笑吧！

　　幸运的是，他在作为我的导师和偶像的那些日子里给我留下了深刻的印记——"我推断"这几个词就像炫目的阳光一样在我的头脑中闪耀着，他经常说"我推断"——尤其在他描述他所面临的人生关键期时。一次，一个因极度绝望而铤而走险的家伙拿枪指着他的脑袋，告诉斯通先生他失去了一切，要杀死斯通先生，最后却掉转枪口，妄图饮弹自尽。当我们在场的多数人都惶恐不安时，斯通先生镇静地说"我推断"，然后他想出了逻辑严密的计划，不仅保全了当事人，还保护了其他人。随后他在事业上提拔了此人，让他的余生飞黄腾达。

　　"那么，"我自言自语道，听从了他的话，"让我们推断一下吧。"立刻，我恢复了平静与理智——这是数月来的第一次。

　　那么……什么对我才是可能的呢？毕竟生命在那时没有给我提供太好的选择。

　　我确实不知道"从此幸福生活"的选择是什么——难道我知道？

事实总会二选其一，要么我会很快地死去，要么我会比较长寿。

如果我很快就死了该怎么办？

好吧，"我推断"如果我苦恼气愤，我会在哀伤和孤单中度过我生命的最后几个月，会使爱我的人像生活在可怕的地狱一样，会给人们留下一个被脑癌击垮的令人悲痛心酸的老头儿的糟糕印象。

另一方面，如果我能够积极乐观呢？我的命运也不会发生什么改变！

但是，这意味着我可以快乐满足地深深呼吸，在家人和所遇到的每个人的关爱中度过余生。我会快乐地辞世，会以勇敢坚毅、泰然自若面对死亡的形象，被那些认识我的人所缅怀和祭奠。

另一方面，如果我成功了呢？如果我活下来了呢？

那么我就没有理由再痛苦心酸、饱受折磨了！我为什么要浪费掉生命中几个月的时间去悲叹那个尚未到来的终点？

那么我就有足够的理由对自己的状况保持积极的心态，完全没有消极的理由。

在那一刻，我的生命第一次停止走向死亡，开始重新生活。

我开始告诉认识的每一个人得了癌症是我遇到的最棒的一件事，现在我完全相信。

又过了一年多，我得知我的脑癌又复发了。现在的治疗更具可研究性和可预测性，预后更佳。然而，结果永远难以确定。在经过了一年的放疗和化疗之后，我的肿瘤医生决定无限期延长我的化疗时间并为我安排了每月的核磁共振成像检查，当然这也不能绝对保障。

这些令人不安的消息对我有什么影响吗？它们让我变得更加积极！

从那个特殊的时刻——2003年1月那个寒冷而阴暗的夜晚开始，我不再为烦恼死亡而去耗费生命的一分一秒。我把生命的所有时光都用来生活。

第一次，脑癌让我成了更好的人。第二次，它正在让我成为好人。脑癌是我遇到的最棒的事。

那么你呢？你的生命中既会经历好事，也会经历坏事。有时生活会给你带来好运，有时也会向你脸上扔砖头。

要发生的事终究会发生，而你只有两种应对方式——可以积极乐观，也可以消极悲观。就是这样。好在选择的权利始终在你的手中，无论任何时候，无论发生任何事，无论你是谁，你都可以选择在生命的每一天里你将有多快乐。

今天就决定继续活着，而不是死去；要积极，而不是消极。不要像我一样在承受如此沉痛的折磨后才弄明白这件事情。为每一天而活，为每一分而活，为每一秒而活。

——汤姆·舒姆

Eleven Minutes
十一分钟

Act as if what you do makes a difference. It does.
—William James

Wednesday starts ordinarily enough. I turn off my alarm and drift back into the warm softness of my bed, listening to the soft breathing of my husband and my daughter's rhythmic sucking on her fingers as they sleep.

As I start to go back to sleep, I force my eyes to open and sit up. There is a reason I want to wake up at the ridiculous hour of 5：30 AM! I quickly put on my running gear and head out to the car.

It is still dark as I drive to the track and I wonder if I'll ever get used to getting up before the crack of dawn. Orion is still very bright in the sky, even as the horizon lightens.

I don't recognize the people running or walking together around the unlit track. I see a woman walking by herself. Is that Marisa? She said

Chapter 3 Every Day Is Special
第三部分　每一天都是特别的

yesterday she might not be up to coming today. I stretch my hamstrings waiting to get a closer look.

Nope, not her. Just a stranger wearing a navy windbreaker.

Walking onto the track, my leg feels pretty good today. I am up for some good running spurts today as soon as I warm up. I walk past the bleachers and off to my right on Cherry Avenue, I see Leanne and her running friends jog swiftly past. One day I'll be able to keep up with them.

A runner passes me on the left. He looks like Leanne's husband Todd. Does he come to the track while she runs, too? No, that wouldn't make sense. I bet Todd is home with…

WHAM!

The runner collapses. Hard. His head hits the track with a sickening thud, like a bowling ball dropped on concrete.

"Oh!" exclaims the woman in the navy windbreaker, jumping back. She is a few feet away from him.

"Is he all right?" I call out. I'm about thirty yards away, and walk quickly to get to them.

The man on the track makes no sound. No screams of pain.

"Does anyone have a phone? Call 911!" says Navy Windbreaker.

I pull out my phone and dial 911. He's breathing harshly. Ring. His eyes are open, but staring, his tongue sticking out. Ring. His legs are bent at an odd angle. Ring. I walk around him looking for a leg injury.

"Hello, what is your emergency?"

"A man just collapsed at the Willow Glen High School track on Cherry Avenue. Please send an ambulance."

"Okay, one moment."

The rest of the folks at the track are starting to gather, murmuring quietly. No one touches him.

"Can you tell me what hurts? Are you okay?" I ask loudly. I don't understand why he isn't talking. It still hasn't hit me that his injuries aren't visible. He looks fairly healthy and is probably in his mid-forties.

The dispatcher on the phone says, "Hello, what is your emergency?" I realize that the long pause was the call being transferred to the local San Jose 911 dispatcher.

"A man just collapsed at the Willow Glen High School track on Cherry Avenue. Please send an ambulance," I repeat.

"Okay, one moment."

We are all quiet, watching. Waiting for something. His breathing is slowly getting quieter and quieter. Less air now. Even less air. Now just a soft wheezing.

Oh… My… God!! He is dying right in front me! We all are frozen for a moment as we realize this.

"He's not breathing!" I yell into the phone. "Does anyone know CPR?" I shout. It has been years since I was trained. I'm squeamish about giving mouth-to-mouth, but I remember how to do chest compressions so I move in to get started.

I straighten his legs first and then kneel down next to his chest. I don't adjust his head or check his pulse or listen for a heartbeat. I hold the phone against my face with my left shoulder and immediately start chest compressions.

"One and two and three and four and," I count off and then pause.

"He's not breathing. Can someone give him mouth-to-mouth?" I call out to no one in particular.

"One and two and three and four and," I press down at each count on his chest, pumping his heart.

I touch his face, cup his cheek and look in his eyes. His skin is smooth and clammy. His eyes are open and unseeing. It looks like his tongue might be blocking his airway.

Barbara, a fit and active grandma with thick, bobbed gray hair, kneels down to adjust his head. Her hands are shaking.

"Squeeze his nose," someone suggests behind me.

"Put his head back," another person calls out.

"One and two and three and four and…" I count and compress.

Barbara tries to move his tongue with her finger. He bites her in an unconscious response. "Ow!" she exclaims.

"One and two and three and four and…"

Barbara valiantly pinches his nose before giving him a breath. His chest rises and the air rushes out again.

The 911 dispatcher starts giving instructions for CPR.

Another big breath from Barbara. "Stay with us!" she yells at the man. "It is not your time yet!" Movie scenes flash in my head where a disembodied spirit is floating above us, watching us working on him. I wonder if that is happening now.

The dispatcher is telling me how to hold and place my hands, etc. I am frustrated hearing detailed instructions about things I'm already doing while trying to coordinate the compressions and check for his breathing.

"But I've been trained," I interrupt the dispatcher irritably.

"Ma'am I just want to make sure you don't do it wrong!" I get it. I shut up and let her talk.

"Now, you need to do six hundred compressions."

"Six hundred?" I'm confused.

"Yes, six hundred. Don't stop. Count as you go. I want to hear you count."

"One… two… three…" I'm counting out loud.

Barbara gives him another big breath, and it looks like he is starting to breathe on his own.

"We're not ready to have you go yet!" she continues to yell at him.

"Nine... TEN... one... two... three..."

I get into a rhythm and almost drop the phone. My neck is starting to hurt holding it against my shoulder. I ask someone to hold the phone for me and put it on speakerphone.

"Nine... THIRTY... one ...two ..."

Barbara has stopped giving mouth-to-mouth as he is taking big shuddering breaths on his own. His tongue is still slack in his mouth and the exhale is a loud and welcome sound.

"He is breathing on his own now," I tell the dispatcher.

"Eight... nine... ONE HUNDRED... one... two..."

"Wow," a man says behind me. "He has had a massive heart attack. Just massive."

It finally occurs to me that his injuries must all be internal. I cannot stop what I am doing. I am pumping his heart for him! For the first time I think to check his pulse in his neck. I don't feel anything. Maybe I'm feeling in the wrong spot? I keep my counting and compressions.

"TWO HUNDRED... one... two..."

It seems like forever since I first called 911. Where are the paramedics? There is only so much we can do.

"Eight... nine... TWO EIGHTY... one... two..."

"Do you need a break?" someone asks behind me. "Are you doing okay there?"

I don't look up. "No thanks, I'm okay."

My lower back is starting to feel a little tight, but I am afraid to stop long enough to let someone take over. I don't want to stop. I cannot stop. I am in the zone of counting and compressions. Counting and compressions. Counting and compressions.

"Eight… nine… THREE FIFTY… one… two…"

My anxiety settles a bit while I concentrate on counting, but then suddenly realize too much time has passed already! The sun has come up and it is no longer dark.

"Where is the ambulance?" I snap at the dispatcher, irritated.

"They are on their way," she assures us. "Keep going. You are doing a good job."

"Nine… FOUR TWENTY… one… two…"

I can feel the growing anxiety of the crowd.

"They should be here by now!" someone says in frustration.

"Eight… nine…" I lose track counting and guess "… FOUR EIGHTY."

We hear the sirens. They are on the high school's main street behind us.

"They are on the wrong road!" someone exclaims, panicking.

"No, they know where they are going," the dispatcher calmly explains. "Keep going. You are doing a good job."

The sirens come closer and we see a fire truck stop on the street. Firemen in blue uniforms get out calmly and get their gear. They start walking to the track.

"Why aren't they running? They need to go faster!" Someone to my left is upset.

"Eight… nine… FIVE HUNDRED AND TEN… one… two…"

The crowd backs up a bit for the firemen and one puts his bag down and starts putting on his latex gloves, unpacking his gear. Very calm. He assesses the two of us.

"Okay, you can stop now," he tells me. His eyes look sad. "I'll take over."

I stand up and back away as he starts up the chest compressions again. Someone hands me my phone back.

"They are here now," I tell the dispatcher.

"Okay, I see they are on site. You did a good job." And with that, the dispatcher hangs up.

An ambulance arrives and more EMTs join the firemen. They put an air bag on him, and then have to clear the airway and put in an oxygen tube. CPR continues, and they each take turns. The chest compressions the EMT does are really hard… his limp legs move on each push and I am worried that my compressions didn't do the job. Were mine too soft? Maybe they didn't work.

The EMTs don't find a pulse. They work efficiently and quietly together, cutting open his shirt to apply the pads of the AED. The entire team stands up and backs away as someone says, "CLEAR!" and they defibrillate him. His arms and legs jerk as his torso tenses with the jolt.

Still no pulse. More chest compressions. No pulse.

They defibrillate him again. "CLEAR!" His body contorts stiffly and then relaxes.

There is a solemn silence as we all wait to hear the heart monitor.

"Beep… beep… beep."

Everyone lets out a collective sigh of relief as we hear the soft sound of his heart beating on its own.

"They got his pulse back!" someone shouts.

Others around me clap and cheer. They all seem relieved and surprised. Somehow, I don't feel that surprise. It had never even occurred to me that he wasn't going to be okay. Am I in shock?

A fireman finds a house key in the runner's shorts. There is no other ID. No wallet. No cell phone. No way to notify his family about where he is. He must live close by. I'm horrified at the thought of someone waiting for him to return home from his run and not knowing what has happened.

The ambulance is driving off and a few firemen remain to clean up the trash on the track from the emergency supplies. One is the fireman with the sad eyes.

Sad Eyes walks over to me and says, "Wow. We usually don't see that."

"Yeah," adds another fireman. "Usually we don't get them back."

I'm stunned.

"What? Why? People just stand around and watch?"

"No, it's not usually witnessed. They were in another room and find someone on the floor. Maybe it has been too long since it happened or they don't know how long it has been or they don't know CPR."

"How long was it after he fell that you started CPR?" asks Sad Eyes.

I have to think. "Umm. Less than a minute?"

"Well that was it then. One minute is really good. The sooner CPR starts, the better the chances are for recovery." He continues to fill out his report on his clipboard.

Now I understand the sadness I first saw in his eyes. Arriving at the scene, I don't think he expected a good outcome. His rescue experience and knowledge had taught him that, in cases like this, the story was not going to have a happy ending.

Navy Windbreaker is standing next to me and has started to react to what happened. I reach out to give her a hug; she is still really shaken up.

"What's your name?" she asks me, wiping her tears.

"I'm Heather. What's yours?"

"Suzanne. Oh, I could have never done that. Heather, I will never forget you. You did a great job. I just keep thinking that could have been my husband…." she trials off, still emotional.

Navy Windbreaker is now Suzanne.

I check the time on my phone. 6：15 AM. I'm surprised it all happened in less than thirty minutes! It felt so much longer. I don't need to be home until 6：30 AM. Should I run now? I haven't even walked once around the track. I look around and see others starting to run around the track and think it looks odd. To just go on with life… I'm not ready for that yet. I want to go home. I say goodbye to the group and start to walk to my car.

"Ma'am!" someone calls out behind me. I turn around and it is Sad Eyes the fireman again.

"Hey, I just want to say again that you did a great job. I'm going to go to the hospital to pick up my guys who rode with him in the ambulance. If I find out more information about his status, do you want me to call you?"

"Well sure. That would be great. I am really interested to find out how he does. And whether his family finds him." I give him my name and cell phone number and he writes them on his clipboard.

"What's your name?" I ask him.

"Dave." Sad Eyes is now Dave.

"You guys did a great job too, Dave. It is an honor to meet you," I say with a smile.

I get in the car with this feeling that maybe I shouldn't go home. That I should help more, but I don't know what else to do. I wave absently to the policemen on the street and drive home on autopilot. I pass the first intersection and my eyes start to tear up when I realize the gravity of it all. That man could have died this morning! I hope he will make it through okay. I wish I could go tell his family, to not let them worry when he doesn't come home this morning. I think of all the things I could have done sooner. I worry I didn't do enough to help.

The house is quiet when I get home but for the water running in the shower. I am definitely shaken now and consider having a glass of wine to settle my nerves. Since it is 6：20 AM and I need to drive the kids to school, I figure wine is not really a good option right now. Tempting, though.

There is a voicemail from Marisa letting me know that she isn't coming today. I realize how close I came to not being there to help! If I had checked my voicemail or if I had gone back to sleep... I would have stayed home. If I hadn't been there today, then someone else surely would have stepped up, but I can't be sure they would have been there in time or had a cell phone with them.

I am again reminded that everything happens for a reason. I was there today for a reason. To help save a life. To learn my own inner strength and grace under pressure. To be reminded again that there is a higher source I can trust to give me opportunities to live my purpose. I walk back to my bedroom, in a bit of a daze.

"There is a reason I woke up today. " I tell my husband.

"Hold on, Babe. I can't hear you. I'm almost out," he calls out from the shower.

I wait in the doorway of the steamy bathroom, absorbing the warmth of the room. I take off my sweatshirt and start to put my phone on the dresser. I pause to check my last call, curious how long I was on the phone with 911.

Eleven minutes.

Eleven minutes for my life to briefly intersect with his. Enough time for me to be his heartbeat until help arrived. Enough time to save his life. Enough time to change mine.

—Heather Gallegos

要表现得好像你的工作与众不同。的确如此。

——威廉·詹姆斯

　　星期三一如平常地开始了。我关掉了闹钟，缩回到温暖的被窝，倾听着睡梦中的丈夫温柔的呼吸声和女儿有节奏地吮吸着手指的声音。

　　当要再次睡着的时候，我强迫自己睁开眼睛，坐了起来。我想自己会在清晨五点起床一定是有原因的！我迅速换上了跑步的装备，冲出门直奔汽车。

　　当我驶入跑道的时候，天仍然是一片漆黑，我怀疑自己能否习惯在破晓前起床。虽然地平线逐渐变亮，但猎户星座在天空中仍旧十分显眼。

　　我没有认出在旁边没有灯光的跑道上跑步或者说是行走的那个人，只是看到独自一个女人。那是玛丽莎吗？她昨天说今天可能不会出现的。我抻了抻腿，准备近距离看清楚。

　　不，不是她。那只是个穿着深蓝色防风夹克衫的陌生人。

　　走在跑道上，我感到今天腿脚特别轻快。我尽快做好热身，准备开始冲刺跑。我跑过了露天看台，还有右侧的樱桃大街，看到了琳恩和她的一起跑步的朋友飞快地跑了过去。将来有一天，我会和他们一样快。

一个跑步的人从我左侧经过，他看起来像琳恩的丈夫托德。他也同她一起来跑步吗？不，这讲不通。我猜托德在家里……

哐！

那个跑步的人忽然倒下了，他的头砰的一声碰到了跑道，就像一只保龄球掉落在混凝土地面上。

"哦！"那个穿深蓝色防风夹克衫的女人大叫起来，跳了回去。她离他只有几英尺远。

"他还好吗？"我大声叫喊道。我离他们大约三十码远，迅速地跑到他们那儿。

那个倒在跑道上的人没有发出任何声音，没有痛苦的叫喊声。

"有人带电话了吗？快打911！"那个穿深蓝色防风夹克衫的女人说道。

我拿出手机，拨打了911。他喘着粗气……"嘟嘟"……他的眼睛睁着，但目不转睛，舌头伸了出来……"嘟嘟"……他的腿奇怪地弯曲着。电话里传来"嘟嘟"声。我在他身旁绕来绕去查看他的腿伤。

"您好！请问您遇到了什么紧急情况？"

"有一个人在樱桃大街威洛格伦高中的跑道上晕倒了，请快派救护车来。"

"好的，请稍等。"

跑道上其他的人开始聚集过来，大家窃窃私语，没有人去触碰他。

"你能告诉我哪里痛吗？你还好吗？"我大声问道。我不知道他为什么不说话，我也不清楚为什么找不到明显的受伤处。他看起来很健康，四十几岁的样子。

电话中调度员说道："您好！请问您有什么紧急情况？"我意识到刚才长时间的间歇是为了将电话转接到圣何塞当地的911调度员。

"有一个人在樱桃大街威洛格伦高中的跑道上晕倒了，请快派救护车来。"我重复道。

"好的，请稍等。"

我们都在那里安静地看着，等待着。他的呼吸越来越微弱，气息很弱，更弱了，现在只剩下了一丝喘息。

哦，我的天哪！！他就在我面前奄奄一息了！当我们意识到的那一刻，我们都僵直在那里。

"他没有呼吸了！"我在电话里喊道。"有人懂心肺复苏法吗？"我大喊道。我在很多年前曾接受过这类培训。我对进行人工呼吸感到有些不安，但是还记得如何进行胸部按压，所以我马上行动起来。

我首先拉直他的腿，然后跪在他身旁，没有去调整他的头、检查他的脉搏或听他的心跳，而是用左肩和脸夹住电话，马上开始胸部按压。

"一、二、三、四……"我数着数，然后停下来。

"他没有呼吸了！谁可以帮他做人工呼吸？"我向周围的人群大声喊道。

"一、二、三、四……"我一次次按压他的胸部，维持他心脏的跳动。

我摸了摸他的脸，捧着他的脸颊，看了看他的眼睛。他的皮肤光滑而湿润，眼睛睁着，眼神却很茫然。他的舌头似乎堵住了气管。

芭芭拉是一位很不错的积极热心的老太太，她有着浓密花白的头发，她跪下来用颤抖的双手扶正他的头。

"捏住他的鼻子。"有人在我身后建议道。

芭芭拉试图用手指移开他的舌头，他无意识地咬到了她。"哦！"她大叫道。

"一、二、三、四……"

芭芭拉勇敢地在每一次给他呼气前捏一下他的鼻子。他的肺部鼓了起来，气流再一次呼了出来。

Chapter 3 Every Day Is Special
第三部分　每一天都是特别的

911 调度员开始指导我们施行心肺复苏法。

芭芭拉深呼了一口气："我们开始吧！"她对那个人吼道："这还不是你倒下的时候！"电影中的画面在我的脑海中闪过，脱离躯壳的灵魂飘浮在我们上面，看着我们在拯救他。我猜想这就是现在所发生的。

调度员告诉我怎样摆放双手等，听到那些我已经在做的细节指导，我有些沮丧，我要努力协调按压，检查他的呼吸。

"但是这些我已经接受过培训了。"我急躁地打断了调度员的话。

"女士，我只是想确认你没有做错！"我明白了。我不再说话了，就让她继续说下去。

"现在，你需要按压六百次。"

"六百次？"我很困惑。

"是的，六百次。不要停。边数边做。我希望能听到你数数的声音。"

"一……二……三……"我大声数着。

芭芭拉又给他呼了一大口气，看起来他似乎可以自己呼吸了。

"我们还没准备好让你走呢！"她继续对他叫喊着。

"九……十……一……二……三……"

我渐渐形成了节奏，几乎要扔掉电话了。我的脖子连同肩膀开始疼痛，我让人帮我拿着电话，我的嘴对准话筒。

"九……三十……一……二……"

芭芭拉停止了人工呼吸，因为他自己开始颤抖着大口呼吸了。他的舌头依旧松软无力，呼气的声响很大。

"他现在能够自己呼吸了。"我告诉调度员。

"八……九……一百……一……二……"

"哇，"我身后的一个人说道，"他是突发严重的心脏病了。很严重。"

我终于明白了他的伤是内在的，我不可以停下来，我继续帮助他做心脏勃起！突然，我想到要检查他颈部的脉搏，但是我没有感觉到。或许我找错了位置？我继续数数、按压。

"二百……一……二……"

从我拨打 911 开始，时间似乎就开始变得非常漫长。医护人员在哪里？我们所能做的就只有这些。

"八……九……二十八……一……二……"

"你需要休息一下吗？"我身后的人问道，"你还好吗？"

我没有抬头看："不用了，谢谢，我能行。"

我的下背部开始有点儿紧，但是我担心换别人接替会耽搁太长时间。我不想停下来，不能停下来。我忙着数数、按压……数数、按压……数数、按压……

"八……九……三十五……一……二……"

当我集中精力数数时，紧张的情绪稍有了缓和，但是突然间，我意识到已经过去了很长时间！太阳已经出来了，天也放亮了。

"救护车在哪里？"我恼怒地向调度员呵斥道。

"他们在路上了，"她安慰着我们，"继续，你做得很好！"

"九……四十二……一……二……"

我能感受到人群中紧张的情绪在蔓延。

"他们现在应该到了的！"有人沮丧地说道。

"八……九……"我数乱了，猜想着，"……四十八。"

我们听到了警笛声。他们已经在我们身后学校的主道上了。

"他们走错路了！"有人惊慌地大喊道。

"不，他们知道在哪里。"调度员冷静地解释着，"继续，你做得很好。"

警笛声越来越近，我们看到了一辆消防车停到路边。穿着蓝色制服的消防员镇静地走出来，准备他们的装备。他们向跑道走来。

"他们为什么不跑呢？他们需要更快些！"我左边的一个人有些不安。

"八……九……五百……十……一……二……"

人群为消防员让路，向后移动了一些，一名消防员放下背包，开始戴他的乳胶手套，取出装备，非常冷静。他打量着我们俩。

"好的，你们现在可以停下来了。"他告诉我，他的眼神看起来很忧伤，"我来替你们。"

我站在那里往后退了退，他便开始了胸部按压。有人把我的手机递了过来。

"他们现在到了。"我告诉调度员。

"好的，我看到他们在现场了。你做得很好！"说完后，她挂断了电话。

一辆救护车到了，更多的内科急救专家加入到了救援当中。他们为他戴上了气囊，又为他清理呼吸道，插上氧气罐，他们轮换着对他进行心肺复苏按压。内科急救专家进行的胸部按压十分用力……每一次按压，他无力的双腿都会向前移动，我很担心我进行的按压没有起到作用。难道我用力太小了？它们可能没有起作用。

内科急救专家也没有感觉到脉搏。他们高效而安静地工作着，剪开他的衣衫，为他放置自动体外除颤器。所有的援救队员都站了起来，退后，有人喊道："注意安全！"他们就为他进行除颤。他的四肢抽搐着，身体也紧绷着摇晃起来。

仍旧没有脉搏。他们给他做了更多次的胸部按压。仍旧没有。

他们又一次为他除颤。"注意安全！"他的身体僵直扭曲，然后放松下来。当大家都在倾听着心脏检测器时，周围一片肃静。

"嘟嘟……嘟嘟……嘟嘟。"

当听到他的心脏在自己跳动的时候，大家都松了一口气。

"他们让他恢复脉搏了！"有人叫喊道。

我周围的人鼓掌欢呼着。他们看起来既放松又惊讶。

无论如何，我都无法感到惊讶。虽然我从未想过他会没事。我是受了惊吓吗？

一名消防员在这名跑步者的短裤中找到一把房子的钥匙，没有其他的身份证明，没有钱包，也没有手机。他们没有办法通知他的家人他在这里，他一定是住在附近。我想到有人正在等他回家，还不知道发生了什么，不禁有些心惊胆战。

那辆救护车开走了，几名消防员仍在清理跑道上急救留下的废弃物。其中有一个就是那名眼神忧伤的消防员。

他走过来对我说："哇。我们通常不会看到这一幕。"

"对，"另一名消防员补充道，"通常情况下，我们救不了他们。"

我不知所措。

"什么？为什么？人们就只站在那儿围观吗？"

"不是的，人们通常不会发现。他们可能在另一个房间里，发现某个人倒在地上。或许已经发生太长时间了，或许他们不知道发生了多长时间，或许他们不懂得做心肺复苏。"

"从他倒下到你开始做心肺复苏有多长时间？"眼神忧伤的那个人问道。

我想了想："嗯，不到一分钟？"

"嗯，那就是了，一分钟非常好。越早开始做心肺复苏，恢复的概率越大。"他继续在笔记板上填写报告。

现在，我明白了第一次在他眼中看到的忧伤。我想到达现场时，他并没有期待一个好结果。他的营救经验和知识告诉他，像这样的情况，事情往往不会有令人愉快的结果。

穿深蓝色防风夹克衫的女人站在我的旁边，看来已经对所发生的事情反应过来了。我伸开双手，给了她一个拥抱，她仍旧有些惊慌。

"你叫什么名字？"她边问我，边擦拭着眼泪。

"我叫希瑟。你呢？"

"苏珊娜。噢，我从没有做过这样的事。希瑟，我永远都不会忘记你。你做得很棒。我只是一直在想如果我的丈夫……"她试图克制情绪，但是仍然十分激动。

穿深蓝色防风夹克衫的女人现在成了苏珊娜。

我查看了一下手机，时间是早上六点一刻。我十分惊讶这一切都发生在不到三十分钟的时间里！感觉却是那么漫长。我到六点半才需要回家去。我现在应该跑步吗？我连一圈都没有跑完呢。我环顾四周，看到其他的人开始绕着跑道跑起来了，感觉这有些奇怪。继续正常的生活……我还没有准备好呢，我想要回家。跟大家告别后，我向汽车走去。

"女士！"背后有人叫住我。我转过头去，发现还是那名眼神哀伤的消防员。

"嘿，我只想再说一次，你做得很棒。我现在要去医院接那些跟着救护车把他送到医院去的伙计，如果我找到更多关于他身份的信息，你想让我打电话给你吗？""当然，那太好了，我很想知道他怎么样了，还有他的家人是否找到了他。"我把姓名和手机号码告诉了他，他记在了写字板上。

"你叫什么名字？"我问他。

"戴夫。"眼神忧伤的人现在成了戴夫。

"你们做得也很棒，戴夫。很荣幸认识你。"我笑着说道。

我上了车，心里却觉得或许我不该回家去，我应该多帮帮忙，但是我不知道还能做什么。我对路上的警察视而不见，利用自动导航系统驾车回家。在经过第一个十字路口时，我突然意识到了这件事的重要性，不禁潸然泪下。那个人有可能今天早上就死了！我希望他能够安然无恙，我希望能去告诉他的家人，不要因为他今天早上没有回家而担心。我想所有这些事可能我都能尽早完成，我担心我做得还不够。

当我回到家中，除了浴室里"哗哗"的流水声，屋里一片安静。刚才我完全被震撼住了，想要喝点儿红酒来定定神。因为那时是早上六点二十，我需要送孩子们去上学，所以我想红酒不是合适的选择。但是它确实对我充满诱惑。

语音信箱里收到了一条玛丽莎发来的信息，告诉我她今天不来了。我意识到本来今天我很有可能不会在那里帮忙！如果我查看了语音信箱或继续回去睡觉……我可能会待在家里。如果我今天不在那里，那么一定会有其他人站出来，但是我不确定他们是否会及时出现在那里，或者是否带了手机。

我再一次想起了万事皆有因果。我今天出现在那里也是有原因的，为了帮助拯救一个生命，去体会压力之下我内心的力量与慈悲，去再一次提醒自己我有更大的源泉去获得活出自己目标的机会。我回到卧室，有点儿头晕目眩。

"我今天早上那么早醒来是有原因的。"我告诉我的丈夫。

"等一下，宝贝儿，我听不清你说的话。我马上就出去了。"他从浴室里向外喊道。

我在雾气蒙蒙的门口等候着，感受着屋里的温暖。我脱掉了运动衫，正要把手机放到梳妆台上，我停下来查看了下手机，想知道和911通了多长时间的电话。

十一分钟。

我的生命里只有短暂的十一分钟与他有交集。这已足够让我在救援到达前成为他的心跳，足够拯救他的生命，足够改变我的生命。

——希瑟·加利西亚斯

It's in the Little Things
小事见真情

Enjoy the little things, for one day you may look back and realize they were the big things.

—Robert Brault, www.robertbrault.com

It was one of those days when there was way too much to do. I had fallen behind in most of my household chores. I hadn't been to the grocery store in nearly forever and we were out of pretty much everything. The laundry was piled up well above the tops of the hampers and the house was stretching even my reasonably loose standards of cleanliness. And besides all that, I had two article deadlines and needed to spend some serious time at my computer.

All of that, and my four children were on a break from school. They were thrilled to be home and asked me repeatedly how we would spend their day off.

They were going to be disappointed with my plans for the day. There was absolutely nothing fun about them. Nothing special, nothing school break-worthy at all.

The kids woke up that morning, expecting their usual bowls of cold cereal. But we were out of milk, and my kids hate dry cereal. There were no eggs and no bread, which left few breakfast options. I searched through the freezer, hoping for a box of frozen waffles. No such luck. I rooted around in the fridge, finally finding a tube of buttermilk biscuits. I sprinkled them with cinnamon and sugar, baked them, and gave them to the kids.

"I'm sorry that I can't offer you anything better this morning, but I haven't had time to go shopping," I said. The kids didn't bother responding. They were too busy shoving my makeshift cinnamon rolls into their mouths.

After breakfast, I started a load of laundry and sat down at the computer. My youngest daughter, Julia, walked toward me, wearing her I'm-about-to-whine face. "But, Mommy, I thought we were going to do something fun today," she said. "Since it's our day off from school."

"I know it's your day off, but it's not Mommy's day off," I explained. "I have work to do."

"Can you play a game with me?" she begged. "Like Candy Land? Or beauty shop?"

I sighed. I really didn't have time to play. I desperately needed to get some work done. But then I had an idea. "Can we play beauty shop while I work?"

So I got my article done, and my toenails painted at the same time.

My oldest, Austin, volunteered to fix lunch so I could keep working. The younger kids were thrilled with his selections. Not exactly the choices the food pyramid people advise, but the kids had fun and I met my writing deadlines.

Shortly after lunch, we made the trek to the grocery store. Austin pushed the cart, while the younger kids collected coupons from the little dispensers scattered throughout the store. I got what I needed—with a few additions from my entourage, of course.

Back at home, the kids decided to play "grocery store" with the coupons they had collected during our trip. They lined up the canned goods on the kitchen counters and the snacks on the island and pretended to re-buy our groceries.

For the remainder of the afternoon, I cleaned house, folded laundry, and started dinner. The kids continued with their game until my husband, Eric, walked through the door.

He spotted me and grinned. "So how was the kids' big day off today?"

I began to explain that we hadn't done anything special because I'd been too busy with chores. But the kids interrupted me.

"Daddy, did you see Mommy's toenails? She let me sit under her computer desk and paint them while she typed!" Julia said. "It was so much fun!"

"And, Dad, we had the best breakfast today," said Austin. "Have you ever made those special biscuits for Dad? They were awesome!"

Eric gave me a questioning look and all I could do was shrug. My two middle kids, Jordan and Lea, piped up to tell their dad about the coupon game and Austin's special lunch. "We had such a great day today, Dad! It was a blast!"

I looked at my children's faces. They were lit up with excitement. Excitement about makeshift cinnamon rolls, a most unhealthy lunch, coupons from the grocery store, and painted toenails.

"You guys really had a good day? You're not disappointed that we didn't do something fun?" I asked.

Austin shrugged and said, "Life is only as fun as you make it, Mom."

I nodded, realizing how right he was. Happiness is far more about our attitude than our circumstances.

I hugged my kids and thanked them for reminding me to look for happiness in the little things.

Julia smiled and said, "And the little things that make you the happiest are us, right, Mommy?"

Wow, my kids sure are smart.

—Diane Stark

要欣赏生活中的小事情，因为当某天蓦然回首的时候，你可能会认识到那些其实都是有意义的大事情。

——罗伯特·布拉特，www.robertbrault.com

又是一个有太多的事情要忙的日子。我的家务活儿已经落下很多了。已经不记得多久没有去过杂货店了，所有的东西差不多都用光了。要洗的衣服堆得高出了篮子好多，屋子里即使用我那非常宽松的清洁标准来衡量也是乱七八糟的。除此之外，我还有两篇文章截稿日期已近，急需我认真地花些功夫在电脑前面待着。

除了这些事之外，我的四个孩子也放假回来了。他们兴高采烈地回到家里，不停地问我怎么度过这个假期。

他们会为我这一天的计划感到失望的，绝对没有什么他们感兴趣的事，没有什么特别的事值得在学校放假的这一天去做。

那天早上，他们醒来，期待着平时的麦片粥。但是我们已经没有牛奶了，而我的孩子们讨厌吃干麦片。我们没有鸡蛋，也没有面包，没有任何其他可以选择的早餐。我找遍了冷藏柜，希望找到一盒冷冻华夫饼，但结果令人非常失望。

翻遍了冰箱，最终找到了一盒酸奶脆饼干。我撒上了肉桂和糖，烘焙了一下，给孩子们吃。

"我很抱歉，今天早上没法给你们准备更好的东西了，因为我没有时间去购物。"我说道。孩子们没有搭理我，他们忙着把我临时将就做的肉桂卷往嘴里塞。

早餐过后，我开始洗衣服，然后坐到了电脑前。我的小女儿朱莉娅走到我跟前，一脸不悦的样子。"但是，妈妈，我还以为我们今天会干些有趣的事。"她说道，"因为这是我们放假的日子。"

"我知道你放假，但是妈妈不放假啊。"我解释道，"我还得工作。"

"你可以跟我做游戏吗？"她恳求道，"糖果乐园？或者美容院？"

我叹了一口气。我真的没有时间玩儿，我迫切地需要完成工作，但是我有了一个主意。"我可以一边和你玩儿'美容院'一边工作吗？"

所以，我写完了文章，同时被涂好了脚指甲油。

我的大儿子，奥斯汀，主动帮忙准备午饭，这样我就可以继续工作，两个年幼的孩子对他准备的食物高兴极了。食谱并没有完全参照人们建议的食物金字塔进行搭配，但是孩子们很开心，我也按时完成了写作计划。

午饭过后不久，我们便长途跋涉去了杂货店。奥斯汀推着车子，年纪小的孩子们从商店里遍布的自动出票机中收集着优惠券。我需要做的当然就是为我的小随从们再补充点儿东西。

回到家里，孩子们决定用他们一路上收集的优惠券玩儿"杂货店"的游戏。他们在橱柜上摆放好罐装的食物，在架子上摆放好零食，假装再次出售我们的杂货。

在下午剩余的时间里，我打扫了房间，整理了衣物，并开始做晚餐。孩子们继续做游戏，直到我的丈夫埃里克走进门来。

他看到了我，咧着嘴笑了："孩子们放假的大日子过得怎么样啊？"

我开始解释我们没做什么特别的事情，因为我只忙着做家务了。但是孩子们却打断了我的话。

"爸爸，看到妈妈的脚指甲了吗？她让我坐到电脑桌下面，在她打字的时候帮她涂的！"朱莉娅说道，"太好玩儿啦！"

"爸爸，我们今天吃了最好吃的早餐。"奥斯汀说道，"你给爸爸做过这种特别的饼干吗？它们太棒了！"

埃里克用疑惑的眼神看着我，我只好耸耸肩膀。排行中间的两个孩子，乔丹和李，开始向他们的爸爸炫耀优惠券的游戏和奥斯汀做的特别的午餐，"今天过得太棒了，爸爸！太令人兴奋啦！"

我看着孩子们的脸上都洋溢着兴奋的表情——为临时将就的肉桂卷兴奋，为不健康的午餐兴奋，为从杂货店带回来的优惠券兴奋，还为涂抹的脚指甲兴奋。

奥斯汀耸耸肩膀说："妈妈，只要你制造快乐，生活就会充满欢乐。"

我点点头，意识到他的话是多么正确。快乐更多的是关于我们的态度，而不是环境。

我拥抱着孩子们，感谢他们提醒我从小事中寻找快乐。

朱莉娅微笑着说："让你最开心的小事就是我们，对吧，妈妈？"

哦！我的孩子们确实很聪明。

——黛安娜·斯塔克

In Full Bloom
鲜花盛开

Some people are always grumbling because roses have thorns; I am thankful that thorns have roses.

—Alphonse Karr

She was outside, looking at the flowers. "I don't think I mentioned this earlier, but one of my hobbies is taking photos of flowers," she said, contemplating the few blooms left in my yard. "Let me get my camera."

"Knock yourself out," I shrugged, wondering why anyone would bother. I had not planted much this year, cutting back on nearly everything since losing my job. But if she wanted to take pictures...

It had been a difficult year. Just when I thought I was done with the bitterness, it would all come rushing back. The last thing on my mind was flowers.

She aimed her lens at a rose. I hadn't seen her in nearly twenty years, since college in New York. The world had changed, yet we seemed the same.

We could still party like old times, as long as we were home by eleven, wore comfortable shoes, and took a couple of aspirin and an antacid. And since we couldn't see our crows' feet without our reading glasses, essentially we were the same. Close enough, I reasoned.

I fiddled with the television remote. My laptop was on the coffee table next to a magazine I was reading. That was me, doing a dozen things at once, packing everything I could into a moment. I was busy with graduate school, an arduous job search, and being the stereotypical valiant, strong, single mother of two boys.

She steadied herself near the last rose of the season, quiet and still, taking photo after photo. Eventually even the dog got bored with her endeavor and walked away.

Suddenly a song from Mary Poppins filled the air. I was pretty sure it was coming from outside my head. This day was getting progressively stranger.

"That's my cell phone," she remarked. "I set the alarm on it to remind me to take my medicine. 'Spoonful of Sugar'—get it?"

"An alarm for meds?" I laughed. "Are we that old?" I still refused to write grocery lists, insisting on carrying the list around in my head. I'd forgotten many things that way, but so what? It was the principle of the thing. I would get old when I was good and ready.

Anger kept me young, I figured. Those days were bittersweet, my fury harsh but healthy.

"Strange looking pills," I remarked as she pulled them from her purse.

"They're for my liver," she took a drink of water. "Actually, it's not MY liver. I'm just borrowing it." One corner of her mouth curled upward.

Every few hours, Anne took anti-rejection medication to keep her body from attacking her donated organ. Eight years earlier, she had been diagnosed with a rare liver disorder, one so rare that her doctor missed it completely.

Somehow, though, she knew something was wrong. But she didn't know exactly what.

"It was a fluke, really," she said. "What are the chances of meeting a liver specialist at a party? And he was cute!"

She had a slew of flukes in her life. After her liver transplant, she came down with thyroid cancer, discovered by chance during a checkup by a doctor touching the base of her throat. "I told him he was examining the wrong end of me," she giggled. She could giggle at the damndest things.

One day she felt dizzy. With her track record, her doctor sent her for an MRI, which revealed a small tumor in her brain. "It's no bigger than your fingernail, and it hasn't grown at all, so that's a good sign. After all, size is everything!" That was Anne —ever hopeful, giggling and fluky. Even a brain tumor was not beyond joking about. I envied her attitude, but certainly not her situation.

She'd be leaving soon. I was just fine alone. It was great to have her here, share old times, but I was comfortable on my own. I didn't need anybody.

With a hug, she was off. I grabbed a beer from the fridge.

Later that day, an e-mail popped up from her, taking forever and a day to load, especially to an impatient, moody grump like me. Sheesh, I huffed, I have things to do.

It was filled with her flower photos—still, clear, and beautiful. She had taken a few blooms and made them glow, made them perfect, made them timeless. Just a few raggedy flowers.

Damn, I thought. She had gotten past the anger, past the pity. She was on the other side, capturing giggles and picking flowers, making an incredible, everlasting bouquet while I grumbled and whined. That, too, wasn't fair.

I wanted to be able to do that. Here I was trying to cram all sorts of events into my life so it would count for something, as she blithely took one moment at a time, polished it until it shined, and shared it with everyone. She made it look easy. Compared to many things in her life, I guess it was.

Quietly she was able to stop the world from turning, keep it still for a moment, insisting that it take the time to look at a single, lowly daisy. Even more extraordinary, the world would do it.

"Wow," I wrote back. "These are incredible." Lame, I know, but for once I was beyond words.

"Annie," she replied, knowing what I was thinking. "We don't know what tomorrow will be. We don't know if we'll even have a tomorrow. So I choose to focus on today. That's why I take pictures. That's why I came to visit you. That's why I'm here."

I shifted my gaze to outside. I got it now. I was stubborn and thickheaded but finally I got it. And I had thought I was the strong one.

She'll be back to visit again—I'm sure of it. Until then, I have her flowers, in full bloom. Actually, I always had them, but it was Anne who got me to really see them.

—Annie Mannix

有些人时常埋怨玫瑰有刺，我却庆幸刺里有玫瑰。
——阿方斯·卡尔

　　她站在外面，看着鲜花，"我觉得好像之前没有提起过，但给鲜花拍照确实是我的爱好之一。"她对着我院子里的那几朵鲜花深思熟虑了一下，接着说："我去拿相机。"

　　"随便点儿，不用客气。"我耸了耸肩，思考着为什么有人会这么执着。我今年没有种多少东西，自从失业以来，我把能缩减的东西几乎都缩减了。但是如果她想拍照片的话……

　　这真是难熬的一年。正当我以为一切苦难都要结束了的时候，它又突然回来了。我脑海里的最后一件事情就是鲜花。

　　她把镜头对准一朵玫瑰。从在纽约上学到现在，我已经将近二十年没有见过她了，整个世界都改变了，然而我们依旧是老样子。我们还可以像过去一样聚会，只要十一点前到家，穿着舒适的鞋子，吃两片阿司匹林或抗酸剂。虽然我们已经到了不戴老花镜就看不到乌鸦的爪子的年纪，依旧是这样。我想，我们就是如此亲密。

我摆弄着电视遥控器，笔记本电脑放在咖啡桌上，旁边是我在读的杂志。这就是我，同一时间做着各种事情，把所有事情都压缩到同一段时间里。我忙着研究生院的事情，面临着严峻的就业问题，还是一名典型的带着两个男孩儿的勇敢坚强的单身母亲。

她让自己安静地待到这个季节里最后一枝玫瑰凋零前，一张接一张地拍着照片。最后，连小狗也厌烦了她的工作，弃她而去了。

忽然，空气中飘荡起玛丽·波宾斯的歌曲。我很确定它是从我的灵魂之外的地方传来的。这一天渐渐地变得奇妙起来。

"这是我的手机。"她说道，"我在上面设了铃声来提醒我吃药。'满满一匙的糖'——知道吗？"

"设闹钟提醒吃药？"我大笑道，"我们有那么老吗？"我现在仍旧拒绝写杂货清单，坚持把清单记在自己脑子里。用这种方式，我会忘记很多东西，但是那又能怎么样？这就是做事的原则。等一切就绪的时候，我就已经变老了。

我猜想，是愤怒让我年轻。日子苦乐参半，我的愤怒虽然尖刻但健康。

"看起来很奇怪的药片。"当她从钱包里拿出它们的时候我说道。

"这是治疗肝脏的。"她喝了一些水，"事实上，不是我的肝脏。是我借来的。"她的嘴角轻轻上扬。

每隔几小时，安妮就要吃抗排异的药物来避免她的身体攻击别人捐献的器官。八年前，她被诊断患有肝病，但由于这种病太罕见，以至于被她的医生完全忽视了。然而，不知怎么回事，她感觉有点儿不对劲儿，但是不知道到底哪儿出了问题。

"真是侥幸，"她说，"怎么会在聚会上遇到一名肝病专家呢？他太可爱了！"

她的人生中经历了许多劫后余生。在接受了肝脏移植手术后，她得了甲状腺癌，这是在医生为她做检查时，偶然触摸到她喉咙底部时发现的。"我告诉他，他一开始就检查错了。"她咯咯地笑着说。她可以在最糟糕的事情面前咯咯地笑出来。

一天，她感到头晕。根据她之前的病史，医生把她送去做核磁共振检查，最终在她的大脑里发现了一小块肿瘤。"它还没有你的手指甲大，而且也没有长大，这是个好的征兆。毕竟，大小就是一切！"这就是安妮——永远充满希望，咯咯傻笑，侥幸脱险，甚至连脑瘤也在她开玩笑之列。我羡慕她的态度，当然不是她的处境。

她不久就要离开了。我独自一人也还不错，与她一起回想过去很棒，但是独自一人让我舒适惬意。我并不需要任何人。

她给了我一个拥抱，便离开了。我从冰箱里拿了一罐啤酒。

那天晚些时候，一封她发来的电子邮件突然出现了，我这个极其没有耐心、喜怒无常、坏脾气的人花了好长时间去下载。天哪，我怒气冲冲，这下子有事情可做了。

里面都是她拍的鲜花的照片——恬静、清新、美丽。她让鲜花绚丽夺目、完美无瑕、永恒不朽。它们本来只是几朵不起眼的鲜花。

天哪，我想，她已经超越了愤怒和忧伤。在我满腹牢骚、诉苦抱怨的时候，她却在捕捉欢笑、采摘花朵，精心制作着难以置信的永恒的花束。这太不公平了。

我也想能够这样。我试图把所有的东西都塞进我的生活里让它更有价值，而她却每次都愉快地抓住一个细节，打磨它，直到让它发光，并与大家一起分享。她让这看起来如此简单，和她人生中的许多事相比，我想确实是如此。

宁静之中，她能够让整个世界停止运转，让它在那一刻静止，坚持让它在那一刻来欣赏那一枝简单而卑微的雏菊，即使是更加不同寻常的事情，世界也会去做的。

"哇！"我回信写道，"这些真是不可思议。"我知道这样说很蹩脚，但是第一次我无法用语言表达自己的感受。

"安妮，"她回复，知道我正在想些什么，"我们不知道明天会怎样，我们甚至不知道会不会有明天，所以我选择关注今天。这就是我拍摄照片、来看望你、来到这里的原因。"

我把视线转向了窗外。现在我明白了，我虽固执愚钝，但最终还是明白了。我原本以为我是一个坚强的人。

她还会再回来的——我确信。到那时，我还会让她的鲜花盛放。事实上，我一直拥有它们，是安妮让我真正地看到它们。

——安妮·曼尼克斯

A Timely Lesson
及时的一课

We can only be said to be alive in those moments when our hearts are conscious of our treasures.

—Thornton Wilder

"The kid was only eighteen. He dropped on the basketball court. SADS. It's what a lot of those young athletes die of."

"Yeah, what's SADS?"

"Sudden Arrhythmia Death Syndrome."

As I listened to the actor's words on *NCIS*, I popped up on the couch, dumping the *New York Times* crossword onto the floor. Extricating myself from the heavy paws of our Lab-mix, Yoshi, I moved to the computer and typed in "SADS."

I wove through research about this syndrome, which is characterized by a cardiac electrical glitch. It was probably what had snuffed out our teenaged son's life seventeen years earlier. Maybe if Josh had been born later, he could have been saved. SADS no longer had to result in sudden death, but it was genetic, so close relatives should be examined.

Jeff and I have always been grateful that our third child, Maliq, born eighteen years after our first, has had solid ground under his feet. Life has tossed this kid very few lemons.

Young life was different for our middle child, Miles. Losing his big brother when he was only eight cast a shadow across his childhood. Miles had held hands with mortality too early. Now at twenty-seven, he was a father himself.

I called him to talk about getting checked for SADS.

"Mom, I had an EKG a few months ago because I had those bruised ribs. They didn't find a problem. Are you worried? Should I be? For Mikah?"

Miles hadn't planned on children. He brought his dad and me the ultrasound picture as a way to tell us that he was going to be a father. He was happy. And terrified.

"Mom, all that can go wrong..."

"Yeah, but all that can go right. Look at you; look at Maliq."

There's a lot Jeff and I, as parents, don't get worked up about since Josh died; fender-benders, money problems, adolescent piercings, and pretty much anything that isn't a death threat stays in perspective.

***

Now we were having Maliq checked for SADS. The doctor and nurse swept into the small exam room that was packed full of our family. The doc took one look at Maliq, who even when seated, dwarfed him, and began firing questions: History of eye problems, scoliosis, heart murmurs? I knew where he was going because I had already been there during one of my many Internet searches. Marfan's Syndrome.

"Listen Doctor, I understand I'm not a cardiologist, but I've researched

Marfan's thoroughly. Maliq doesn't fit the criteria." I knew even as the sentences flew anxiously out of my mouth that this doctor wasn't taking me seriously.

"How tall are you, anyway?" Just fifteen, Maliq already measured in at 6'3". The cardiologist put stethoscope to chest. His face changed. He listened for a long time, then had his nurse listen.

Damn, I knew that expression. I had seen it enough times with Josh. I looked over at Jeff. His face seemed to lose muscle, sagged as he too recognized the shift.

The doc listened again. "There's definitely a murmur."

Maliq's face, lean and sculpted, was open and mostly unconcerned.

"I think this young man has Marfan's Syndrome."

Maliq looked at us, then at the doc. "What's that?"

"It's a syndrome that includes serious heart problems. Young man, as of right now, you are on complete athletic restriction."

Maliq's eyes registered shock as tears rolled down his face. Maliq's world was spinning. The door was slamming shut on the life he had constructed, on the future he had assumed. Maliq had been a soccer goalkeeper since he was four.

Miles moved to his brother's side, put his arm around Maliq, moved his head in close and whispered in his ear. Time paused as I watched my sons together. Their relationship deepened in that moment, narrowing the span of years between them.

I jumped in to compensate for the doc's obviously underdeveloped bedside manner, my voice stern enough to cause my husband to grimace, and Miles to smile.

"What other tests are needed to confirm or rule out the diagnosis, and when can we get them done?"

The cardiologist looked startled by my tone and set of my jaw. Years of navigating the medical system had helped me be just a little scary, when need be.

"We can do the EKG here. He needs to go over to the hospital for the echocardiogram."

Maliq had rearranged his face, stopped his tears.

They squeezed the machine into the room. Jeff and I sighed in relief when no long QT, which is a marker related to SADS, and no other abnormality showed in the EKG's squiggly lines.

My schedule was such that I would take Maliq over to the U for the echo. As we walked to the car, I reached up to hug Maliq. He was a good hugger—never gave passive squeezes—but this time he held on a lot harder and longer than usual.

"How're you doing, Darling? Do you have questions?"

Tears showed again. "Is he saying I might have the same thing that killed Josh?

"Yes, but Josh died a long time ago. Things have changed. What Josh had can now be treated."

"Mom, I have never loved soccer as much as I do this very minute. If I have this heart thing, is there surgery so I can play again?"

"Yeah, I think there is."

"Okay, then if I have it, I want the surgery soon, so it won't mess up my season."

And for the first time that day, I started to cry, because here it was, that thing you can always count on embedded in adversity. Within minutes, Maliq's priorities had crystallized. He knew, without a doubt, what he was willing to do to keep the life he had previously taken for granted.

"Mom, is this going to be okay?"

I answered from the logical part of my brain. "It's going to be fine, and here's the good news; this morning, soccer got taken away, and when you get it back you'll appreciate it like you never have before."

"Mom, do you really believe that, or are you just being positive?"

This child knew me well. "I do believe it, and I'm also being positive."

Finally at 9:45 that night, the cardiologist called. "The echo came back clean."

I let out the breath that I hadn't realized I'd been holding. "Great. That means Maliq doesn't have Marfan's or SADS?"

"You still need to meet with the geneticist, put all the pieces together."

The appointment with the geneticist ended up being scientifically interesting but thankfully, clinically insignificant. She found no Marfan's, and ruled out SADS.

Maliq started running sub-six-minute-miles. His soccer team made it to the state tournament and in a shoot-out where Maliq was up against arguably the best goalkeeper in the state, he blocked the most kicks and his team won.

Later, fork paused over the last of about ten meals he had eaten that day, he said, "Mom, I took it for granted before. I figured there was always time to get serious about soccer. Now, I know, I can't take anything for granted; we don't really ever know what kind of time we have."

I was so grateful that a lesson I learned through tragedy, this son was able to learn through a near miss.

—Lindsay A. Nielsen

据说我们只能活在那些心能感受到我们的价值的时刻。

"那孩子只有十八岁，他倒在了篮球场上。是 SADS。有许多年轻的运动员就是这样死的。"

"是的，什么是 SADS?"

"成人猝死综合征。"

当我听着电视剧《海军罪案调查处》里演员的台词时，我突然从沙发上弹了起来，把上面有纵横字谜游戏的《纽约时报》扔到地板上，我把自己从我的混血狗耀西的爪子中挣脱出来，走到电脑前，输入"SADS"。

我浏览了和这一病症有关的调查研究，这种病的特征是心力衰竭。这或许就是十七年前扼杀我只有十几岁的儿子生命的元凶，或许如果乔希出生得晚一点儿，他就可以得救。SADS 不再一定会导致猝死，但它确实是有遗传基因的，因此近亲应该接受检查。

杰夫和我一直很感激我们的第三个孩子马利克在第一个孩子出生十八年后降生，那时他的脚下已经有了坚实的基础，生活没有让他体味太多心酸。

我的第二个孩子迈尔斯的童年却是不同的，八岁时失去自己的兄长，给他的童年留下了阴影，迈尔斯过早就与死亡打过交道。他现在二十七岁，自己也即将做父亲了。

我给他打电话，讨论关于 SADS 检查的事情。

"妈妈，我几个月前因为肋骨挫伤做了心电图检查，他们没有发现问题。你很担心吗？我也应该为麦卡担心吗？"

迈尔斯本来并没有打算要孩子。他给我和他父亲带来了超声波照片，告诉我们他即将成为父亲了，他很开心也很惊慌。

"妈妈，一切都可能会出错……"

"是的，但是一切都可能是正常的。看看你，看看马利克。"

作为父母，有许多人跟杰夫和我一样，在孩子离世后内心焦虑不安，汽车的小擦撞，花钱的问题，青春期时在身上穿孔，任何除了死亡威胁之外的问题都存在着。

* * *

现在我们正在让马利克接受 SADS 检查。医生和护士们拥进了被我的家人塞得满满的小小的检查室。医生看了一眼因为坐着而变得更加矮小的马利克，便开始像机关枪似的发问："有眼疾、脊柱弯曲、心脏杂音病史吗？"我知道他会问到哪里，因为我在上网搜索时已经找到相关的信息，是马凡氏综合征。

"医生，请听我说。我知道我不是心脏病专家，但是我已经彻底研究过马凡氏综合征了。马利克不符合这种病的症状。"我知道即使我迫不及待地说出这些话，医生也不会太当真的。

"那么，你有多高？"马利克虽然只有十五岁，但已经有六英尺三英寸高了。心脏病专家把听诊器放到他的胸前，他的脸色变了。他听了好长一段时间，然后又让护士听。

天哪，我记得这种表情，在陪乔希检查时，我看到过许多次。我望向杰夫，当他也意识到这种变化时，他的面部肌肉变得松弛无力，垂陷下去。

医生又听了一次，"确实有心脏杂音。"

马利克的脸瘦削而突兀，张着嘴，一点儿也不担心。

"我想这个年轻人得了马凡氏综合征。"

马利克看看我们，又看看医生："那是什么？"

"是一种带有严重心脏问题的综合征。年轻人，从现在起，你不能参加任何体育运动了。"

马利克的眼睛里透出惊愕，眼泪从他的脸上滚落下来。马利克的世界在旋转着，医生把他所构建的生活、他设想的未来都砰的一声打碎了，马利克从四岁就开始当足球守门员了。

迈尔斯走到他弟弟的旁边，用胳膊抱住了他，把头靠近，在他的耳旁轻声低语。当我看到儿子们抱在一起时，时间仿佛静止了。在那一刻，他们的关系更加亲密了，年龄的差距也似乎缩小了。

我马上开始想为刚才医生对病人那种明显不合时宜的态度做些弥补。我的语气太过严厉，以至于我的丈夫扮了个鬼脸，迈尔斯也笑了起来。

"我们还需要为这个诊断做哪些测试？什么时候我们可以做完？"

心脏病专家为我的语气和唠叨吃了一惊。多年游走在医疗机构让我在需要的时候会变得有些可怕。

"我们这里可以做心电图。他需要到医院去做超声心动图。"

马利克重新调整了自己的表情，停止了哭泣。

他们把仪器拖进了房间。当看到没有出现与 SADS 相关的长 QT（心电图上的 QT 间期代表了心室从除极到复极的时间）标志，也没有显示心脏异常的曲线时，我们都舒了一口气。

我计划带马利克去做超声心动图，当我们朝车子走过去的时候，我走上前去拥抱了马利克。他是个很会拥抱的人——从不跟人被动地紧拥——但是这一次他比平时拥抱得更用力，时间也更长。

"宝贝儿，你还好吧？有什么问题吗？"

马利克的眼泪又一次流了下来："他是说我得了和乔希一样的病吗？"

"是的，但是乔希已经去世很久了，情况已经改变了，乔希得的病现在已经可以医治了。"

"妈妈，我从没有像现在这样热爱足球。如果我有这样的心脏问题，有可以让我重新踢球的手术吗？"

"是的，我想有的。"

"好的，如果有的话，我想尽快做手术，那样就不会打乱我的赛季安排了。"

那一天，我第一次流下眼泪，因为它是当你陷入逆境之中时唯一可以做的事情。几分钟内，马利克的权利就被否决了。毫无疑问，他知道他之前把要活下去这件事看作理所应当的事情了。

"妈妈，会没事吧？"

我从逻辑思维的角度回答了他的问题："会好的，这是件好事。假设今天上午你的足球丢了，当你把它找回来时，你就会像从未拥有过一样珍惜它。"

"妈妈，你真的相信吗？还是你太乐观了？"

这个孩子太了解我了。"我相信，而且我也很乐观。"

那天晚上九点四十五分，心脏病专家打来了电话，"心脏杂音消失了。"

我长舒了一口气，刚才都没有意识到自己屏住了呼吸，"太好了。这就是说马利克没有得马凡氏综合征吗？"

"你还需要去见见遗传病专家，把这些情况整合一下。"

与遗传病专家的会面以得知她对此现象的科学研究非常感兴趣而结束，庆幸的是，临床上并不显著，她既没有发现马凡氏综合征，也排除了 SADS。

马利克开始了六分钟之内要完成一英里的跑步练习。他所在的球队成功晋级国家联赛。在一次点球大战中，面对公认的最佳守门员的激烈竞争，马利克扑出了最多的进球，他的球队也最终取得了胜利。

那天晚些时候，他吃了大约十顿饭饭量的食物。放下餐叉后，他说道："妈妈，我以前把它看作理所当然的，我总觉得有时间可以认真对待足球。现在我知道，我不能把任何事当成理所当然的，我们确实不知道自己还有多少时间。"

我很感激能从悲剧中学到一课，我的儿子能够在万幸中有所收获。

——林赛·A.尼尔森

Childhood Delights
童年的欢乐

So our human life but dies down to its root, and still puts forth its green blade to eternity.

—Henry David Thoreau

My mother was diagnosed with Alzheimer's long after I accepted the gradual changes I saw in her. I had grown used to partially listening to her repetitious stories and filling in the missing words of her sentences.

I imagine I might have continued to deny my inklings had she not been admitted to the hospital for a short hospital stay. During the night, apparently she had become disoriented and the nurses found her roaming the hallways. A neurology consultation had taken place and the doctor told me that my mother was approaching the middle stages of Alzheimer's.

The doctor was kind and compassionate as we sat in a hospital conference room. He explained that for people with dementia, once a memory was lost it could not be relearned as in the case of a stroke. I thought I understood that concept, but over the coming months, I often had to fight the urge to say, "I already told you that."

My mother lived with our family since her retirement. We enjoyed a deep friendship and she led a very independent life filled with activities. Almost overnight our family life dramatically changed with the pronouncement of that one word: Alzheimer's.

Those happy, active days dropped away from my consciousness as I suddenly felt trapped by the challenges that I imagined lay ahead for all of us. Somewhere in the process of hearing and accepting this diagnosis, my focus shifted from being with Mom to taking care of Mom.

Each day led to a new discovery as I learned what Mom knew and what she could no longer remember. For example, my heart sank the day I realized she could no longer read written directions. She stood in front of the microwave holding her frozen dinner, not knowing what to do. That was also the day that I knew she would need someone to stay with her while I was at work. It was the only way I could ensure that she would eat during the day.

I thought about the best way to take care of Mom all the time. I was vigilant in my discreet observations of her. Looking back, I wonder if despite my well-meaning intentions, I arrogantly took it upon myself to decide what I thought was best. Possibly in the process I curbed some of her independence and neglected to consider her capability to express her feelings and opinions in the moment.

Driving the car was a major decision and dilemma as I wondered whether she could drive to the grocery store and find her way home. When was it time to remove her car keys from her purse? Fortunately it turned out to be a mutual agreement when she called me crying from the mall, "I can't find where I parked the car. Help me!" Thankfully she remembered the phone number, probably because she had dialed it hundreds of times over the years.

That one decision struck a major blow for each of us. It signaled a huge loss of independence for Mom and huge dependence on me. I also began wondering how I could convince her to wear a medical alert bracelet with her name and address without destroying her dignity.

Each day more memories were lost but slowly I discovered that every cloud does have a silver lining. Because my mother did not have memories of the past, I grew to know her in new and different ways that were free from the baggage that most of us carry throughout our lifetimes. Resentments with a sister-in-law no longer mattered and she would talk to her on the phone again. She could go to the hair salon on a Tuesday instead of a Saturday because each of her days really did begin with a clean slate.

Slowly I let go of the firm notion of taking care of Mom and being with Mom. We began to share a companionship. Often we would engage in an activity and it was as if she was experiencing it for the very first time. I would see delight on her face blowing out candles on her birthday cake, coloring with crayons, or picking flowers in the park.

It was surprising to see some amazing changes of imprinted patterns that evolved. She forgot that her back bothered her and I no longer had to drive around a parking lot to find the closest parking space to the store. She even began taking walks up and down our street.

One day we went to a buffet and I will admit I was a bit shocked and embarrassed when she stuck her hands in the salad bin and stacked her plate with a wide variety of foods. She didn't remember what she liked or disliked and I watched with fascination as she tried and enjoyed some of those foods.

As time passed, I noticed Mom was able to take care of herself in some new ways. She dressed herself but she didn't care if her clothes matched. This was the same person who bought me matching box-pleated skirts, cardigan sweaters, and knee socks as a child. I noticed with amusement and sadness that she took over the control of the television remote. Her taste in movies changed from her cherished classics to the Western channel.

She was unaware of the growing to-do list added to my schedule. She was free from paying bills, making dinner, driving herself to doctor appointments, laundry and numerous other details that make up a person's day.

Mostly she was happy just to be with me. She would follow me from room to room and was always ready to jump into the car for errands or an outing. Slowly I began to recognize her individuality as she displayed her likes and dislikes and a full range of unpredictable emotions. She was Mom, not just a human being with a disease.

One of my most treasured memories occurred when I took her to an outdoor band concert. They were playing music from the Big Band Era. By that time she was barely able to carry on a conversation, yet once the music started she sang the words to almost every song! For more than forty-five minutes, I was filled with awe and gratitude that somewhere deep inside her there was still a bridge to the outside world. I can still recall the joy and contentment on her face.

Alzheimer's helped me to learn to appreciate Mom and not just take care of her. As her memory fell away, I discovered in her an almost childlike innocence. She taught me to view the world from a different perspective and to notice how precious each moment can be. It is with a sense of irony that the less she remembered, the more present we both became in our lives.

—Jean Ferratier

我们人类的生命即使绝灭，只要绝灭不了根，那根上仍能萌生绿叶，直至永恒。

——亨利·戴维·索罗

我观察到了母亲的变化并慢慢接受了这一事实，之后过了很久，她最终被诊断出患有阿尔茨海默病。我已经开始习惯了只听一部分她那些唠唠叨叨的故事，并把她话语中漏掉的词语补充上去。

我想如果不是她短期住院了的话，我可能会继续否认我的猜测。那天晚上，她显然是迷失了方向，护士发现她在走廊里游荡。经过神经学临床会诊，医生告诉我，我的母亲已经接近阿尔茨海默病的中期。

我们坐在医院的会议室里，医生和蔼而富于同情心。他解释说患有痴呆症的人，如果在中风的情况下，一旦丧失记忆，就无法再重新拾起。我想我明白了它的意思，但是在之后的几个月里，我常常不得不抑制住说这句话的冲动："我已经告诉过你这些了。"

母亲自从退休后一直和我的家人住在一起。我们非常享受这种深厚的感情。她过着一种非常独立的生活，参加各种活动。而几乎一夜之间，我的家庭生活因为阿尔茨海默病这个词的宣布而面目全非。

那些开心快乐的日子从我的知觉中消失了，忽然感到我正面临着曾经设想过的挑战。在听说和接受诊治结果的过程中，我的注意力从跟随母亲转变为照顾母亲。

当我去注意母亲还知道哪些和已经不记得哪些的时候，每天都会有新的发现。例如，那天当我发现她已经看不懂书面指示时，我的心情非常沮丧。她站在微波炉前面，手里举着冷冻食品，却不知道该做什么。也就是那一天，我知道我需要在工作时找个人陪她，这是唯一可以确保她在白天能够吃上饭的办法。

我总是想着尽最大的可能照顾好她，小心谨慎地观察着她。回想起来，我想知道是否自己太过自负地想当然地选择了我认为最好的方式，即使这是出于好意。可能在这个过程中，我限制了她的自由，忽视了她在那一瞬间表达自己感受和看法的能力。

开车是一个重大的决定和难题，因为我怀疑她是否能够开到杂货店并找到回家的路，她知道什么时候该把车钥匙从钱包里取出来吗？幸运的是，后来我们还是达成了共识。她从购物中心打电话来喊道："我忘记把车停到哪里了。快来帮帮我！"谢天谢地，她还记得电话号码，或许是因为她这些年已经拨打了成百上千次。

有一个变化使我们每个人都受到了巨大的打击——母亲几乎完全失去了独立性，必须在很大程度上依赖我。我开始考虑如何在不伤害她的自尊心的情况下，说服她佩戴带有姓名和住址的医用警觉识别腕带。

每一天，她都会丢失更多的记忆。但是我很快发现黑暗之中总有一线光明。由于母亲失去了过去的记忆，在抛出了那些我们大多数人在人生中始终背负的包袱后，我开始用全新的不同的方式认识她。她原本对一个已经不再联系的姑嫂充满怨恨，但现在却能够跟她在电话里再次交谈。

她可以星期二去发廊，而不是星期六，因为她的每一天都是从头开始。

对于照顾母亲和跟随母亲的想法，我渐渐释怀了。我们开始享受这种伙伴关系。我们常常投入一项活动中，就好像是她第一次体验一样。我能看到当她吹灭生日蛋糕上的蜡烛，用蜡笔上色和在公园里采摘鲜花时脸上流露出的喜悦。

令人惊讶的是，一些根深蒂固的模式也发生了令人惊奇的变化。她忘记了一直烦扰她的背部疼痛，不再为找到离商店最近的停车位而转遍整个停车场，她甚至开始在街道上散步。

有一天，我们去吃自助餐。我必须承认，当她把手伸进盛放沙拉的盒子里，并在她的盘子里塞满各种各样的食物时，我有一点儿震惊和尴尬。她已经不记得自己喜欢或不喜欢吃的东西，我好奇地看着她尝试并享受着那些食物。

随着时间的推移，我发现母亲能够用一些新的方式照顾好自己。她自己穿好衣服，但并不介意它们是否搭调，她曾是小时候给我买搭配好的箱形褶裙子、开衫毛衣和及膝袜的那个人。我既开心又有些伤感地注意到她接过遥控器时的变化，对电影的品位从她珍爱的经典之作变成了西部频道。

她并没有意识到我的计划表里增加的任务清单。她可以不用付账，不用做饭，不用自己开车去复诊，不用洗衣服，不用做许许多多其他人每天要做的杂务事。

大多时候，只要和我在一起，她就会很开心。她会跟着我从一个房间到另一个房间，随时都准备跳进车里外出办事或郊游。在她表现出自己的喜好和各种各样不可预测的情绪之中，我意识到了她的个性。她是我的母亲，而不单单是一个患病的人。

我最珍贵的记忆之一是有一次带她去一个户外乐队演奏会。他们正在演奏大乐队时代的音乐。那时，她已经很少能进行对话了。然而当音乐一响起来，她几乎唱出了所有歌曲的歌词！在那长达四十五分钟还要多的时间里，我心里充满了敬畏，感激她的内心深处仍保留着通向外界的桥梁。我仍然能回想起她脸上流露出的快乐与满足。

　　阿尔茨海默病帮助我学会了去欣赏母亲，而不仅仅是照顾她。当她的记忆消失后，我在她的身上找到了孩子般的纯真。她教会我从不同的角度去看待世界，让我意识到每个时刻的宝贵。有些讽刺意味的是，她记得的越少，我们就越多地生活在当下。

——琼·费偌蒂尔

People First
以人为本

I always prefer to believe the best of everybody, it saves so much trouble.

—Rudyard Kipling

When I attended Open House at my son's school, I scanned the bulletin board outside his first-grade classroom. I spied Cody's handiwork in a colorful sea of papers tacked to the board. My expectant smile froze.

In one circle he was supposed to write or draw what he didn't like.

"MEN," he scrawled in capital letters.

Uh-oh, I thought as fear iced me. How could Cody not like men? He loved his daddy! Did some man do unspeakable things to my child?!

"Cody," I said casually. "Can you tell me about your work here?"

"Yeah," he replied, then carefully recited each word slowly. "I... don't... like... mean."

Such is the world of phonics, writing words the way they sound.

That exercise served to reinforce how our kids perceived the world, divided into two classes: good and bad.

It didn't matter to them what the person looked like. You were either good or you were bad. Take our neighbor next door, for instance. She was a good person, giving the kids treats when they deserved it. Now the bully on the bus who hit Cody in the stomach…

"He's mean, Mom!" cried Cody. "He's a bad boy!"

"He's not a bad boy," I replied, drying his tears. "What he DID was bad. There's a difference."

That's what the parenting magazines tell us to say. And it makes sense, this mass campaign of programming us to think in terms of "people coming first."

People with or without disabilities.

People with or without a steady income.

With or without a home.

With or without goodness.

People first.

But I doubted Cody understood my logic.

Until one warm Saturday morning.

Cody and I arrived at a pizza parlor where a birthday party was being held for his classmate, Kristi.

"Cody!" Kristi shouted, walking toward him in a cloud of pink ruffles, her thick, blond hair combed into one long braid down her back. She was radiant as she hugged him.

"Why, Kristi," I said, "you look beautiful!"

"Thank you," she responded, twirling around. "Let's go play some games, Cody!"

Cody, unfazed by being the only boy in the handful of attendees, bounced gleefully from one game to another, feeding tokens to hungry machines.

When several pizzas were delivered to the balloon-bedecked tables, Kristi made a point of asking Cody to sit next to her. When Cody asked for pink lemonade, she informed the waitress, with a trace of authority in her voice, "I'll have what he's having."

When it came time for opening presents, she announced, "I want to open Cody's present first!"

He handed her a small package, a pink Ooglie toy that made funny and irreverent noises when one pulled its tail.

"It's for your book bag," Cody said shyly.

"Oh, I love it!" she gushed, hugging Cody. "Thank you!"

While everyone was eating cake, Kristi leaned over to me and said, "Mrs. Oliver, Cody is always so nice to me every single day at school. He's the only one who's never, ever mean to me."

I blinked back tears. Not just because a little girl was sweet enough to acknowledge Cody's sensitivity to his mother. But for knowing how cruel kids could be, especially to skinny-challenged girls like Kristi.

My heart ached from the sudden surge of pride that coursed through it.

All I could think of was, by golly, he got it.

Cody got it.

People first.

—Jennifer Oliver

Chapter 3 Every Day Is Special
第三部分 每一天都是特别的

我总是宁愿相信每一个人最好的一面，这样就可以避免许多麻烦。

——鲁德亚德·基普林

在参加儿子学校的家长开放日的时候，我浏览了他所在的一年级教室外的布告板，我发现了科迪用彩色纸张做的手工艺品被钉在了上面。但是，我满怀期待的笑容凝固了。

在一个圆圈里，他被要求写出或画出自己不喜欢的东西。

"人。"他用大写字母潦草地写道。

哦不，我想到了可怕的冷冰冰的自己。科迪怎么会不喜欢人呢？他喜欢他的爸爸！有什么人对我的儿子做了不可告人的事吗？！

"科迪，"我若无其事地说，"你能告诉我关于你这个作业的事情吗？"

"可以，"他回答道，然后开始认真地慢慢讲出每一个词语，"我……不……喜欢……坏人。"

这就是自然拼读法，就是根据读音来拼写单词。

这种练习可以强化孩子们对世界的观察方式，分成两类：好的和坏的。

对他们来说人的样子并不重要。你或者是好

人，或者是坏人。拿我们隔壁的邻居为例吧。她是个好人，给了孩子们应有的一切。而当小霸王在公交车上打到科迪的腹部时……

"他太坏了，妈妈！"科迪大声喊叫着，"他是个坏孩子！"

"他不是个坏孩子。"我回答，擦干了他的眼泪，"只是他做的事情不对，这是有区别的。"

这是亲子杂志上告诉我们要说的话。这种为我们确定"以人为本"的思维方式的大众宣传是有道理的。

四肢健全或肢体有障碍的人。

有稳定收入或没有稳定收入的人。

有家或无家可归的人。

信仰上帝或不信仰上帝的人。

以人为本。

但是我怀疑科迪是否理解我讲的道理。

直到一个温暖的星期六上午。

科迪和我去了一家比萨屋，他的同学克里斯蒂的生日聚会正在那里举行。

"科迪！"克里斯蒂叫喊着，向他走过来。她在粉红色荷叶边儿的簇拥之下，浓密的金发在背后梳成了一根长长的辫子。当她拥抱科迪的时候，容光焕发。

"哦，克里斯蒂，"我说，"你看起来太漂亮了！"

"谢谢您，"她回应道，转着圈圈，"我们一起做游戏吧，科迪！"

科迪虽然是为数不多的出席者中唯一的男孩儿，但他没有丝毫畏惧，兴高采烈地从一个游戏换到另一个游戏，并把代币券塞进游戏机里。

当几份比萨送到用气球精心装饰过的桌子上时，克里斯蒂点名让科迪坐在她的身旁。当科迪点了粉红柠檬水的时候，她用命令的口吻告诉

Chapter 3 Every Day Is Special
第三部分　每一天都是特别的

服务员："我要喝和他一样的。"

当到了拆礼物的时候，她宣布："我要先打开科迪的礼物！"

科迪递给她一个小包裹，里面是一个粉红色欧格力玩具，一拉它的尾巴，它会发出滑稽有趣的声音。

"这是为你的书包准备的。"科迪害羞地说。

"哦，我喜欢它！"她激动地拥抱了科迪，"谢谢你！"

当所有人都在吃蛋糕的时候，克里斯蒂俯下身来对我说："奥利弗太太，科迪在学校每一天都对我很友好。他是唯一一个从未、也永远不会对我刻薄的人。"

我眨了眨眼睛，把眼泪忍住了。不只是因为一个讨人喜欢的小女孩儿把科迪的善解人意告诉他的妈妈，还有知道了孩子们可以多残酷，尤其是对像克里斯蒂这样瘦小的女孩儿。

当一阵自豪感闪过时，我的内心感到了痛楚。

我所能想到的是，天哪，他明白了。

科迪明白了。

以人为本。

——珍妮弗·奥利弗

心灵鸡汤：
每一次跌倒，
都是最好的成长

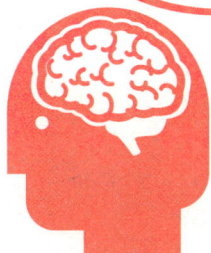

第四部分　榜样

Chapter 4
Role Models

A good example has twice the value of good advice.

—Author Unknown

好榜样比好建议更有价值。

——逸名

A True Thanksgiving
一个真实的感恩节

I would maintain that thanks are the highest form of thought; and that gratitude is happiness doubled by wonder.

—G.K. Chestertond

A few years ago, right before Thanksgiving, I was dumped without warning by the man I thought I would marry. The next day, I was laid off from my administrative assistant job. The day after that I turned forty.

I'd lived in New York City for ten years trying to make it as an actress. While I'd had some luck on stage, nothing had paid enough for me to make a living at it. I was single, broke and approaching middle age in a profession that worships youth and beauty.

The last thing I wanted was to go home to Florida for Thanksgiving and catch up with my younger, married and successful cousins. At least we would all meet at Brooks, my favorite restaurant back home and a family holiday tradition for twenty years.

The day before I flew to Florida, I got a terrible cold. I was lying in bed feeling very sorry for myself when the phone rang. It was my mother.

"Darling," she said. "I have wonderful news!"

This made me cringe. Her last report of wonderful news was she had married a man she met online two weeks before. Now, recently divorced for the fourth time and living in a new apartment complex for "active elders," I feared the worst.

"What is it?" I sniffled.

"Well..." she replied, pausing for dramatic effect, "you know how every year we have dinner at Brooks. This year, I've decided to make dinner for the family myself. Well, with your help, of course. Let's see, we should have... twenty-five people, not including us. Won't that be so much fun?"

Could I have pretended she had the wrong number? Yes, if I hadn't been so stoned on cold medicine and thinking clearly. Instead I mumbled "Yeah... great... can't wait" and hung up, pulling the covers over my head before passing out.

The next day, I arrived at the Ft. Lauderdale airport looking and feeling absolutely miserable.

I picked up my luggage from baggage claim and walked outside to look for my mother. A platinum blonde pulled up to the curb beside me and honked the horn. "Do you like it?" my mother exclaimed. She leaned out of the car window to toss her formerly salt-and-pepper curls, now flat-ironed and reaching her shoulders.

"Who are you and why did you steal my mother's car?" I replied.

She laughed like a girl of sixteen. "Silly! This is to celebrate my wonderful new life!"

"Oh. Wonderful," I said.

I should have been happy for her, but at that point my mom looked and sounded ten years younger than me.

The next day was madness. I shopped and cooked more by noon than I had in years. At midnight, I was bent over the sink, elbow-deep in a still-frozen turkey, trying to pull out the gizzards with both hands.

Even though the activity helped take my mind off my troubles, I still felt sad about my life and worried about what I would do when I got back to New York.

Thanksgiving Day, we woke up at 6：00 AM to finish cooking. I never thought we would pull it off, but somehow, we managed to prepare everything, clean the house, fit four card tables next to the dining room table in a one-bedroom apartment, polish the silverware, find matching plates and even create four miniature pumpkin centerpieces.

We put out our casseroles and hot dishes on the buffet, checked the turkey, and just had time to change clothes before the first guests arrived. Soon the house was overrun with family. No one asked about my boyfriend or if I had gotten any acting work lately. They all just oohed and ahhed over the table. They couldn't believe we did it all ourselves.

Before we ate, we said grace and went around the table to say what we were thankful for. I've always loved doing this each year but now, even though I was proud of helping my mom and glad to see everyone, I didn't really feel like contributing.

Mother's turn came before mine. She said, "I am thankful for my health, my family and my friends. I am especially thankful to my daughter Alyssa who taught me the meaning of gratitude on a Thanksgiving thirty-nine years ago."

I looked up from my plate. What did she mean by that?

She continued. "Alyssa's father Ed had just gotten out of the Army. I was a new wife and mother of a one-year-old. We left Ft. Polk in Louisiana for Pittsburgh because that's where Ed found work. Well, the Army lost all our furniture in the move and we had no money to buy more. We also couldn't afford to go home for Thanksgiving.

"I went out and bought one baby food jar of strained turkey and one of strained carrots for Alyssa and two turkey sandwiches for us. We sat on the floor in our empty apartment and cried over our misfortune. Then we heard Alyssa laughing."

My mother looked over at me with tears in her eyes. "You were so happy. You were singing and having such a good time playing with your food in that cold empty apartment. I pray that you will always find happiness in every living moment, my darling daughter."

I was stunned. I had asked myself how a woman of sixty-five who lived alone on a fixed income decided to become a hot blonde and make Thanksgiving dinner for almost thirty people.

Now I had my answer. She was just following the example I had set so long ago and had forgotten.

When I returned to New York, I had a new sense of purpose and thankfulness for life.

I also went blond.

—Alyssa Simon

我认为感谢是思想的最高形式，感恩所获得的幸福会因为惊奇而加倍。

——G.K. 切斯特顿

几年前，在感恩节前，毫无征兆地，我被原本打算结婚的对象甩了。第二天，我失去了行政人事助理的工作。那天后，我四十岁了。

我在纽约住了十年，试着在那个舞台上表演。虽然在舞台上有点儿运气，但是那却不能让我维持生计。我单身，没钱，人到了中年，从事的还是一个年青貌美的人吃香的职业。

我最不想做的事是回到佛罗里达的家里过感恩节，碰到我那些年轻、已婚又成功的表妹。感恩节那天，我们会在布鲁克斯碰面，那是我最喜欢的当地的饭店，而在那里过感恩节也是我们二十年来的家庭传统。

在去佛罗里达的前一天，我得了重感冒。我躺在床上，感觉很糟，这时手机响了，是我妈妈。

"亲爱的，我有好消息要告诉你！"

这让我畏惧。她上次告诉我的好消息是她和一个在网上认识两个星期的人结婚了。最近，她结束了第四段婚姻，搬到一个叫"活跃的老年人"

的公寓大楼里。我担心还有更坏的情况。

"怎么了？"我哼哼着鼻子问。

"那个……"她回道，为了达到戏剧效果，还故意停顿了一下，"你知道我们每年在布鲁克斯过感恩节。今年，我打算准备家庭晚宴。当然，需要你的帮助。让我看看，我们应该约……除了我们二十五个人。这该多有趣啊！"

我能假装她打错了电话吗？可以。如果当时我没有因为感冒药昏沉沉的，还保持思维清晰的话。然而，我却含糊地说："嗯，好，迫不及待了。"然后挂断了电话，在失去知觉睡着之前，我拿掉了头上敷的东西。

第二天，我到了劳德代尔堡机场，看上去很糟，感觉很糟。

我从行李认领处取到自己的行李箱，走出来等我妈妈。一个金发女郎把车停在我身边，将喇叭按得嘟嘟响。"你喜欢这样吗？"我妈妈大叫，身体探出车窗。她原来黑白相间的鬈发被拉直了，披在肩上。"你是谁啊，怎么偷了我妈的车？"我答道。

她笑得像个十六岁的少女："你傻啊，这是为了庆祝我的美好新生活啊！"

"哦，真美好。"我说。

我本应该为她开心，不过那时我妈妈看起来好像比我年轻十岁。

第二天简直让人抓狂。我要购物、准备晚餐，做的事情比我过去几年都多。半夜的时候，我弯着腰，在深到肘部的水槽旁处理冰冻的火鸡，两只手试着把鸡胃拿出来。

尽管这些事让我暂时忘了烦心事，我仍然觉得活得很悲哀，担心我回到纽约后该怎么办。

感恩节那天我早晨六点就醒了，继续准备食物。我从来没想到我们能顺利完成，但不知不觉间，我们准备好了所有的东西，打扫了她那一室一厅的寓所，在餐桌旁边准备好了四张牌桌，擦干净了银质的餐具，找到相匹配的盘子，甚至做了四个小型的南瓜装饰品摆在餐桌中央。

我们拿出砂锅，把热菜放在自助餐桌上，查看火鸡的情况，只剩一点儿时间在第一批客人来之前换了衣服。很快家人都来了，房间变得拥挤起来。没人问我关于男朋友的事，或者问我找没找到新工作，他们只是边吃边聊天。他们都不相信这些都是我们准备的。

在开饭之前，我们做了饭前祷告，围坐在饭桌前表达我们的感恩。我以前每年都喜欢祷告，然而现在，虽然我为帮妈妈准备的一切感到自豪，很高兴见到所有的人，但是我并没有感觉自己做了贡献。

妈妈的感恩祷告在我之前。她说："我感谢主让我健康，让我的家人和朋友在我身边。我特别要感谢我的女儿阿莉莎，她在三十九年前的感恩节教会了我感恩的意义。"

我的目光从眼前的盘子上移开，抬起头来想她这么说是什么意思。

她接着说："阿莉莎的爸爸艾德那时候刚退伍。我和他刚结婚不久，阿莉莎只有一岁。我们离开了路易斯安那州的波尔克堡，前往匹斯堡，因为艾德在那里找到了工作。军队在给我们搬家的时候弄丢了所有的家具，我们没有钱买新家具，也没有钱回家过感恩节。

"我出去买了一个小号的挤坏了的火鸡罐头，买了一个挤得变形了的胡萝卜给了阿莉莎，我们自己买了两个火鸡三明治。我们坐在空荡荡的公寓的楼梯上，感伤我们的不幸。而那时我听到阿莉莎在笑。"

妈妈眼中含泪地看着我："你当时很开心。你唱着歌，在那个冷清而空荡荡的公寓里玩儿着食物。我祈祷你能在活着的每一天感到幸福，我亲爱的女儿。"

我很吃惊。我曾问过自己，一个六十五岁的单身女人，靠着固定工资，怎么变成一个火辣的金发女郎，为将近三十个人准备感恩节晚餐。

现在我有答案了。她只是按照我以前所做的去做，而我却忘记了那些。

回到纽约后，我对生活有了新的感受，对生活充满感恩。

我也变成了金发。

——阿莉莎·西蒙

Unbreakable Faith
坚定不移的信仰

Every tomorrow has two handles. We can take hold of it by the handle of anxiety, or by the handle of faith.

—Author Unknown

Like most moms of her generation, our Italian mother has mantras for every life event. For medical ailments—whether a broken bone or toothache, her advice is to "take two aspirin and grease it with Vicks." When something she predicted didn't exactly happen the way she believed it would, Mom's reply is, "I may not always be right, but I'm never wrong."

One of the most inspiring attributes of our mom is her ability to face adversity and not come out defeated. She always emerges with a renewed spirit and infectious sense of hope. Her outlook on tragic events is typically met with: "Hey, nobody died, nobody has cancer; we'll get through this, too!" But by far, our mother's most widely used mantra is, "For the love of God, count your blessings! It could be worse!" And she should know. Four of my parents' five children, myself included, are afflicted with a rare genetic bone disease called Osteogenesis Imperfecta, known as "brittle bones," as are three of their grandchildren. Having children who have collectively broken more than 300 bones would lead some parents to question their faith, but our mom refused to let others pity her or let us feel sorry for ourselves. "Hey, it's just a broken bone... it'll heal. There are worse things children could have. If this is the worst thing I ever have to deal with in my lifetime, I'll take it."

I, on the other hand, needed a little more convincing. Let me illustrate a typical day in my O.I. history. I woke up one morning, slipped on something innocuous, fell and broke my wrist. After Dad splinted my arm, we went to the ER, and I was sporting a heavy white plaster cast before 10∶00 AM. Most parents would allow their injured child to stay home from school for the rest of the day, but not my mother. She scrubbed floors to pay for all five of us to get a Catholic education and by God's grace, she was going to see to it that we didn't miss a day. Whining was out—and so was reason when it came to dealing with my mom.

"But Mom, I have a broken arm. Can't I stay home?"

"It's just an arm, Jodi. You still have two good legs—now get out of the car and use those good legs to walk into that school."

"But Mom, it's my right arm... I'm right-handed. How am I supposed to write?" Protesting was fruitless because Mom had an answer for everything.

"Hey, that's why God blessed you with two hands—use your other one."

Did I mention I'm now ambidextrous? Not by birth, but by counting the blessing of my two hands. Years later, when I learned that I was carrying twin girls, my joy became short-lived when they were born sixteen weeks early. Weighing in at one pound, three ounces each and just under twelve inches in length, my daughters had a large medical mountain to climb. My mother, by my bedside, holding her rosary in one hand and my own hand in her other, told me with great conviction, "They may be tiny, but they're mighty. Count your blessings." Even after Hayley succumbed to pneumonia and died three weeks after she burst into our lives, my Rock-of-a-Mother was there helping me find a way to go on in spite of my incredible grief.

"I know you want your baby here with you," she said in a gentle, loving voice, "but God must have another plan. Maybe he needs Hayley in heaven to be her sister's guardian angel here on earth. Hayley will watch out for Hanna so Hanna can survive." Mom was right; Hanna did survive. Each day for the past seventeen years, I've looked into my daughter's blue eyes and I've known firsthand that I am indeed blessed.

When Hanna was diagnosed with O.I. and people around me started to feel sorry for us, I replied, "Hey, she's not dying and she doesn't have cancer—she'll survive this. Broken bones heal." Then I started to laugh... I had finally turned into my mother.

In 2003, our mother took ill and had to have surgery. When the doctor relayed the unthinkable diagnosis to my siblings while Mom was in recovery—post-menopausal ovarian cancer—my sister called me and said, "Now what do we tell her? We can't say, 'No one's dead, no one's got cancer!'"

As it turned out, we didn't have to say a word. Mom knew even before she was told, and she soothed us when we should have been comforting her. "Hey, let's count our blessings; the doctor got it all and I'm not dead yet. Let's have some faith." As usual, our wise mother was right. She survived not only this bout with cancer, but five years later, she rebounded from another round of cancer—colorectal. She never needed chemo or radiation because miraculously both cancers were contained and surgically removed; and she has been cancer-free for nearly two years and counting.

"Faith; that's all you need," my mom says firmly as she taps the table.

"Feeling sorry for yourself doesn't help anything or solve the problem… pity just adds to your problems. Spend your time counting your blessings instead. You'll see just how well off you really are. That's my motto."

And now we have the good sense to reply, "Yes, Mom… we know, we know!"

Counting blessings is not just a mantra drilled into our heads by our mom. It's become a way of life for all of us. So much so that when I count my blessings, my wise mother is always near the top of the list.

—Jodi L. Severson

明天有两个把手，我们可以握住叫焦虑的那个，或者握住叫自信的那个。

——逸名

　　我妈妈是意大利人，像很多妈妈级的人一样，她对每件事都有箴言。对于小病——无论是骨折或者牙痛，她都建议我们"吃两片阿司匹林，在表面涂上点儿维克斯薄荷膏"。当事情和她预想的不一样时，妈妈就说："我说的可能并不是永远都对，但我从不犯错。"

　　妈妈最突出的一个特点是她能直面不幸，永远不会被打败。她总是与时俱进，用希望感染别人。她对不幸的看法总是："嘿，没有人死了，没有人得癌症，我们会克服的！"但到目前为止，我母亲最常用的口头语是："看在上帝的分儿上，往好处想！事情不会更糟了！"我父母的五个孩子，包括我在内，还有三个外孙都患上了成骨不全症这一罕见的遗传性骨骼疾病。如果你的孩子加起来骨折了三百次以上，你可能会失去信心，但是我妈妈不接受别人的同情，不允许我们自己感到难过。"嘿，只是骨折罢了，会好的。孩子们可能遇到更糟糕的事情。如果这是我这一生要经历的不幸，我会承受。"

　　我，相反地，更需要一点儿信心。我介绍一下我典型的一天。早晨起床，踩到什么东西上一滑，跌倒了，我的腕关节骨折了。爸爸用夹板固定我的胳膊后，我们去了急诊室，早晨十点，我绑上了重重的白石膏。接下来，一般大部分家长会让受伤的孩子待在家里，不去学校。但是我妈妈不这样。

　　妈妈通过擦洗楼梯，供我们五个孩子接受天主教教育，在上帝的保佑下，她确保我们不会错过每一天。没有抱怨——我妈妈就是这么做的。

　　"但是，妈妈，我胳膊骨折了，不能待在家里吗？"

　　"那只是胳膊，朱迪。你还有两条腿——现在下车吧，用健康的腿走进学校吧。"

　　"但是，妈妈，那是右胳膊……我是用右手的，我怎么写字啊？"

　　抗议无效，因为妈妈总是有她的理由。

　　"嘿，这就是上帝给你两只胳膊的原因——用另一只胳膊吧。"

　　我提到过我现在两只手都很厉害吗？那不是天生的，而是知足于我有两只手。几年后，我怀了对双胞胎女儿，对于我，怀孕的辛苦减少了，因为她们早产了十六个星期。她们每人体重只有一磅三英两，身高只有十二英寸，她们有很长的一段时间要进行药物治疗。妈妈站在我床边，一手握着她的念珠，一手牵着我的手。她满怀信心地告诉我："她们可能很弱小，但是她们很有力。往好处想。"在出生三个星期的海莉患上肺炎离开了人世后，还是我的辣妈帮助我走出了巨大的痛苦。

　　"我知道你想要你的孩子陪着你，"她温柔地说道，"但是上帝肯定另有安排。可能他需要海莉在天堂做她妹妹的守护天使，海莉会守护着汉纳，这样汉纳就可以幸存下来了。"

　　妈妈是对的，汉纳的确活下来了。在过去的十七年里，每天看着女儿蓝色的眼睛，我亲身感受到我是受保佑的。

当汉纳患上了成骨不全症时，周围的人都为我们感到难过。我回答道：“嘿，她又不是要死了，她也没有得癌症，她会活下来的。骨折会被治愈的。”然后我开始笑……最后我成了像妈妈一样的人。

2003年，我妈妈身体不大好，做了手术。医生告诉我的兄弟姐妹一个令人难以置信的诊断结果，在我妈妈身体好转的同时，又患上了绝经后卵巢癌。我姐姐打电话给我说：“现在我们怎么告诉她？我们不能说‘没有人死，也没有人得癌症！’”

事实上，我们什么也没说。妈妈在之前就知道了一切。在需要我们安慰她的时候，她反倒安慰我们：“嘿，让我们往好处想，医生解释明白了，我现在不会死。让我们有信心。”和以前一样，我们聪明的妈妈是对的。她活下来了，不仅是这次得癌症，五年后，她得了另一种癌症，结直肠癌。她不需要进行化疗和放射治疗，因为很神奇，这两次癌症都被遏制住了，通过外科手术切除了患癌的部分。她两年没受到癌症的影响。“你只需要有信心。”她一边敲着桌子，一边掷地有声地说着。

“为自己感到痛苦不能帮助你解决问题……怜悯只能增加你的问题，不如花时间往好处想。你会看见自己好起来。这就是我的座右铭。”

现在，我们可以坚定地回答：“是的，妈妈，我们知道了，我们知道了！”

“往好处想”不只是妈妈灌输给我们的箴言，它变成了我们的生活方式。当我往好处想的时候，聪明的妈妈总是我最先想到的几个人之一。

—朱迪·L.塞弗森

The Power of Illusion
错觉的力量

There is no truth. There is only perception.

—Gustave Flaubert

Many years ago, I was sitting in my dear friend Sara's beautifully wallpapered living room. We were discussing my painstaking effort to successfully hang wallpaper in several rooms at my house.

"I can't get the seams to match," I lamented. "It's not straight at the ceiling and it just isn't nearly as pretty as yours. What am I doing wrong? How did you get yours to look so much better than mine?"

Sara sat quietly listening to all my woes. I noticed a small smile on her lips and wondered if she was, perhaps, laughing a bit at me. She had seen the first room I had finished. Maybe she was chuckling to herself about what a poor job I had done. Finally, I wound down my complaining and gave her a chance to respond.

"Donna," she soothed. "It's all an illusion. The

details don't matter. Look at my seams; they aren't perfect either. There is a tear over in the corner, did you notice that?"

I slowly shook my head as I looked more closely at the previously unnoticed imperfections of her living room walls. She continued, "You walk into my house and see the illusion of a beautiful room. You don't notice all the flaws. You did your wallpaper yourself so you know every spot that isn't exactly right. You want your room to be perfect, so you search for anything that may be wrong. No one else will see the mistakes, just like you didn't see mine." As I left her house that day, I knew that she was right and looked less critically at my rooms upon arriving home.

Life went on and I eventually forgot the discussion that I had with Sara that day. Time passed and one of my daughters decided to have her wedding in my backyard. I had worked for many years to make my yard into a beautiful garden—cultivating, transplanting, pruning, trying new varieties of plants. With the help of my husband and sons, we had dug a pond, planted new shrubs and trees and made the area a refuge from the daily world. It was a haven where birds nested, squirrels scampered, and frogs rested on lily pads. I had dreamed that one day one of my children would choose it for a wedding. That day had come and I enthusiastically began planting pale yellow and lavender flowers to match my daughter's chosen colors.

Things were going wonderfully, and then the rains came. Here we were in drought-ridden Colorado and suddenly we were being deluged with day after day of rain. My grass developed a fungus; the weeds thrived with the extra moisture, but it wouldn't stop raining long enough for me to pull them; mushrooms spread from the front to the backyard. The prediction was for clear, dry weather the day of the wedding, but how was I ever to get the yard ready in time?

A few days before the wedding, I was feeling rather desperate. The sun was supposed to be out for a few hours before another thunderstorm was expected. As I was kneeling in mud trying to pull a few obvious weeds, a tree branch brushed caressingly across my shoulder like the soft touch of a tender hand and in the quiet breeze I heard the hushed whisper of Sara's gentle voice from the past saying: "Donna, it's all an illusion. The details don't matter."

And, again, I knew she was right. I looked around and saw that not only had the weeds flourished in the constant downpours, so had the flowers; they were luxurious. The plants and what grass remained green looked emerald and sparkled in the sunlight. The illusion of my yard was a place of peace and tranquility. Once my daughter walked into view in her elegant snow-white dress, with the glow of love in her eyes, no one would notice the weeds or the brown spots in the grass. This outdoor setting was just a fragrant backdrop for an unforgettable event. That's all people would remember, not the details of unfinished gardening.

The wedding was perfect. Well, not perfect, but a perfect illusion of a fairy tale wedding in a magical place. Sara's words of advice to me from many years ago will never again be forgotten. I will always remember as I move through the remaining events of my life: "It's all an illusion. The details don't matter."

—Donna Milligan Meadows

世上没有真理，只有感知。

——古斯塔夫·福楼拜

很多年前，我曾经坐在好朋友萨拉的客厅里，那个客厅贴着很漂亮的壁纸。我们在讨论，我怎样历尽艰辛地把我家几个房间的壁纸贴好了。

"我没法将接口处贴好，"我遗憾地说，"在天花板的地方没贴直，我贴得没有你家的好看。我哪里做错了？你怎么贴得比我的好看啊？"

萨拉安静地坐着，听着我的慨叹。我看见她嘴角微微翘起来，不知道她是不是有点儿嘲笑我的意味。我贴完第一个房间的时候她去看过。她可能在暗自发笑，我怎么贴得那么糟。最后，我慢慢停止了抱怨，让她有机会给我个回应。

"唐娜，"她安慰我说，"这都是错觉，细节并不重要。看看我的接口处，它们也不完美。那个角有个撕口，你注意到了吗？"

我更仔细地观察了她的客厅，发现了以前没有注意到的不完美的地方，我缓缓地点头承认。她接着说："你走进我家，感觉我的房间漂亮，这只是个错觉。你没有看见那些缺陷。在你贴墙纸的时候，你知道每一个不完美的地方。你想让你的房间完美，所以你找到所有可能不对的地方。别人看不到那些错误，就像你看不到我的。"那天离开她家后，我知道她是对的。回家后，我对自己的房间也不再那么苛刻地观察了。

生活在继续，我慢慢忘了那天和萨拉的对话。

时光流逝，我的一个女儿打算在我家后院办喜宴。我花了好几年时间使后院变得那么美丽——栽培、移植、修剪、试验新的树种。在老公和孩子们的帮助下，我挖了个池塘，新种了些灌木和乔木，使后院成了世外桃源。它就像个天堂，鸟儿在这里筑巢，松鼠在这里蹦蹦跳跳，青蛙在睡莲叶子上栖息。我以前梦想，将来我的某个孩子会在这里办喜宴。这天到来了，我满腔热情地开始种植淡黄的和浅紫色的鲜花，使其和我女儿选的颜色相配。

一切进展得很顺利，但随后下起了大雨。我家在干旱的科罗拉多州，但是突然下起了连阴雨。我的草地长出了真菌，野草因为过多的降水疯长，雨一直下，我没有时间拔掉它们，蘑菇从前面一直长到后院。预报说结婚那天不会下雨，但是我怎么能及时修整好院子呢？

在婚礼前几天，我感到很绝望。在预报的雷雨到来之前，只有短暂的日照时间。我跪在泥地里试着拔出一些扎眼的野草，一条树枝轻擦过我的肩头，就好像一只温柔的手抚摸我一般，微风轻轻地吹过，我听到了萨拉以前和我说过的耳语："唐娜，那都是错觉，细节并不重要。"

我知道她还是对的。我环顾四周，发现不仅是野草因为连续的暴雨生长旺盛，花儿也是，它们长势很好。植物仍是翠绿的，像绿宝石一般，在阳光下闪耀着。我的院子一派祥和与宁静。

当我女儿穿着她那高雅的白色婚纱，眼里充满爱的光辉走进大家的视野，我知道没有人会注意野草或者草地上的褐色叶斑。户外环境只是这次难忘婚礼的背景，人们记住的不是未修整完的花园的细节。

婚礼很完美。当然，不是完美，而是完美的幻想——在充满魔力的地方举办了童话般的婚礼。萨拉几年前的建议，我永远不会忘记。我将在以后的生活中永远记着："这都是错觉，细节并不重要。"

——唐娜·米利甘·梅多斯

Cheer Leader
啦啦队长

If I had to sum up Friendship in one word, it would be Comfort.

—Terri Guillemets

The skies were overcast and the sun wasn't even trying to break through. I stood on the steps of Vancouver General Hospital staring at the cold gray exterior, daunted by the size of the building and all the sadness contained in it. Clutching a bouquet of flowers in one hand and a novel in the other, I tried to get past my dislike for hospitals and focus on the task at hand.

My friend Terri and I were both visiting Vancouver, but for vastly different reasons. I was reconnecting with family and friends, and she was in the hospital for tests.

I slowly walked in, feeling helpless and anxious. I got Terri's room number at the information desk and headed for the elevators. As the doors closed I was conscious, not only of our different purposes in the big city, but of the different paths our lives had taken. I'd been blessed with a pretty normal life. Terri, on the other hand, had a particularly tough life. Sometimes I'd look at her and wonder how she had the stamina to survive. In her early 40s, she had already raised two sons when she took on the care of her two preteen nieces when their mother was murdered. Both girls came with a lot of baggage and the younger seemed to be suffering from fetal alcohol syndrome. Caring for them was a stress-filled full-time job.

Terri also has epilepsy and was having increasing problems with seizures. Everyday activities that most of us take for granted carried the threat of a blackout or a seizure. Naturally she could no longer drive a car and had to take the bus everywhere. During meetings at our church we left the fluorescent lights turned off because their flickering could bring on a seizure. Terri signed up for a computer course at the local college but had to quit because she collapsed twice and had to be rushed to the hospital.

Her doctor decided enough was enough and sent her to Vancouver for extensive tests. She was given a private room and was to be bedridden for an indefinite period of time, electrodes implanted in her skull watching for even the slightest change in brain activity. The doctors wanted to know exactly what stimuli would bring on her seizures. I was hoping my surprise visit might cheer her up a bit.

It was with great trepidation that I followed the nurse into Terri's room. I don't like hospitals, even when I'm a mere visitor, and I always get nervous wondering what I will talk about. Besides, this was a person who was having several seizures a day. Maybe my sudden presence would bring on something catastrophic. Maybe a surprise visit was really stupid.

Terri was laying in bed, in the semi-darkness, eyes closed. "Terri, you have a visitor," the nurse whispered.

As her eyes focused, a big smile greeted me. "Lydia! Wow. I can't believe it. Come and sit down. You don't have to worry about touching me," she said laughing. "You won't get electrocuted or anything!"

As I took a chair she quipped about the dozen wires protruding from her head. "What do you think of my new hairdo? It's pretty wild, ay? I thought it was about time I had a change of hairstyle, but this wasn't really what I had in mind."

I laughed with her but it looked kind of painful to me. "Do they hurt?" I asked.

"No. There's a bit of discomfort now and then, but nothing that bothers me. See that TV screen up there? That's most of the TV I get to watch each day. It shows you my brain activity."

I looked at the TV suspended from the ceiling and watched lines and waves and blips floating along the screen.

"Pretty boring stuff, isn't it? Not what most people would want to watch hour after hour. Let me tell you, I had no idea my brain was so inactive. But it does get exciting when I have a seizure. Then bells ring and the nurse comes running in. If that happens, don't panic and don't leave unless they tell you to. Things will calm down in a minute or two."

I was still staring at the screen. "Are they finding what they're looking for?" I asked.

"Nah. We're all hoping I'm going to have a big one, but it hasn't happened yet. Life is too quiet in here. I keep telling them it's related to stress, and what kind of stress do I have here? No responsibilities, no kids, no husband, no telephone, no noise, no dog driving me nuts. I need action to bring on a big one!"

I spent the next half hour with her. We talked about kids and husbands, church and schools, small town drivers and big city traffic. We talked about the challenges of her life and her hopes for the future.

She was looking pretty happy when I left.

And she'd sure cheered me up.

—Lydia A. Calder

如果要用一个词形容友谊，那就是慰藉。

——特里·吉耶梅

天空灰蒙蒙的，没有放晴。我站在温哥华综合医院的楼梯上，看着外面冰冷灰暗的世界，我被医院这座建筑物的规模吓到了，也害怕医院中的哀伤。

我一手拿着一束鲜花，一手拿着一本小说。我想忘记对医院的厌恶，只关注手上的东西。

我和朋友特里一起到温哥华，但出于不同的原因。我是为了和家人、朋友重聚，她是到医院做检查。

我慢慢走进去，感到无助和焦虑。我在服务台问了特里的房间号，然后向电梯走去。当门关上的时候，我意识到我们来到这个大城市，不仅出于不同的目的，还是由于不同的人生轨迹。我很幸运，可以过着简单平常的生活。而特里，和我不一样，生活得很艰辛。有时我看着她，都对她生存的毅力感到惊讶。在她四十出头的时候，养育了两个孩子，还要照顾两个处在青春期的外甥女，因为她们的妈妈被谋杀了。两个女孩儿带着很多行李来到她家，年幼的那个好像还患了胎儿酒精综合征。照顾他们是件很有压力的事，也需要全天候的付出。

特里患有癫痫，而且发作得越来越严重了。我们习以为常的日常活动，对她来说都有暂时失去意识或癫痫发作的风险。自然地，她不能再开车，到哪里都得坐公交。

在教堂聚会时，我们都关上荧光灯，因为闪烁的灯光可能会引起癫痫发作。特里在当地大学报了一个计算机班，但是她必须放弃，因为她病发了两次，不得不被紧急送往医院。

她的医生觉得不能再这样下去了，把她送到了温哥华进行深入检查。她住在私人病房，很长时间都卧床不起。她的头上插着电极，以便时刻观察她大脑活动的细微变化，医生想知道是什么刺激使她发病。我希望我的突然来访能让她开心一点儿。

我忧心忡忡地跟着护士走进了特里的房间。虽然我很少来医院，但我不喜欢医院。我总是不知道该说些什么，尤其还是和每天都要痉挛几次的人。可能我的突然来访会带来毁灭性的后果，可能突然来访是愚蠢的行为。

特里躺在床上，在灰暗的房间里，闭着眼。"特里，你有访客。"护士低声说。

当她的目光集中在我身上后，她给了我个大大的微笑。"莉迪娅！哇，不敢相信。过来坐，你不用担心触碰我，"她边说边笑，"你不会触电而死的！"

在我找椅子的时候，她取笑自己头上插着的十多根线。

"你觉得我的新发型怎么样？有点儿太狂野了，唉，我想换发型很久了，但是这不是我想要的发型。"

我和她一起笑着，不过我看起来更痛苦。"那很痛吗？"我问道。

"不痛，就是时不时有点儿不舒服，但这些并没有影响我。看见那边的那个电视屏幕了吗？那是我每天要看很多次的屏幕，上面的变化反映了我的大脑活动。"

我看到那个电视屏幕悬挂在半空中，屏幕上显示着一些波动的线、波和信号。

"很无聊，是吧？一般人不想成天看着那个屏幕。我告诉你，我不知道我的大脑那么怠惰。不过当我癫痫发作的时候，大脑就会兴奋起来。然后那些铃会响，护士就跑进来了。如果突然发生那种情况，不要惊慌，除非他们让你走，否则不要走。一两分钟后一切都会恢复正常。"

我仍然盯着屏幕。"他们从屏幕上发现了什么吗？"我问道。

"没有。我们都希望我会有次很严重的发病，但是没有发生。在这里生活太安静了。我告诉他们发病和压力有关，我在这里哪有压力啊！没有责任，没有孩子在身边，没有丈夫，没有电话，没有噪音，没有狗对我狂叫。我需要些活动来让癫痫发作！"

我陪她又聊了半小时。我们谈论着孩子、丈夫、教堂、学校、小镇司机、大城市的公交，我们谈论着她生活的挑战，对未来的期许。我离开时，她看起来很开心。

她也让我感动振奋。

——莉迪娅·A. 考尔德

Throw Away the Key
扔掉钥匙

Locks keep out only the honest.

—Jewish Proverb

My godparents Bel and Max met in England during World War II. They became mess hall friends for nutrition's sake: Max liked only meat and Bel liked only vegetables. They began their relationship by swapping foods from their mess trays. Soon they were sharing other parts of their lives.

When they moved into a rickety old house in Berkeley, California, Max carried Bel across the threshold. Then he said, "Hand me your house key."

She did, and he took both their keys and threw them out into the yard.

"I want to live in a home that's open to whoever needs it," he declared.

And so they did. Their home was never locked. Friends wandered in and out, stopping for dinner, taking a cold chicken leg from the refrigerator or curling up in an easy chair for a quiet read. Supper time was always a mish mash of opinions and people: the Kurdish student and the Israeli dissident, the Dallas lawyer and the manufacturer's rep from Denver, the rabbi without a congregation from Brooklyn and the priest with the small church in Santa Fe.

Still, Bel had grown up in Chicago and knew well the value of locked doors.

The unlocked house both exhilarated and terrified her. Sometimes she would lie awake in bed, expecting what her mother would have called "the worst." Robbery, rape and death raced through her mind. And all because her meshuggeneh husband refused to lock the doors.

One Friday night, well past midnight, Bel heard a door open. She heard footsteps and then stumbling. Her hands turned icy and she clutched the covers. She wanted to scream, but her voice dried up in her throat. Then she wanted to be quiet, so the robber would take what he wanted and leave. Downstairs, the furniture scraped and a drawer opened. She nudged Max, but he didn't wake up. She pushed the covers into her mouth so she wouldn't cry out. Then she heard the squeak of the screen door and the closing of the outer door. She shook Max's shoulder. "Max, someone was just downstairs. I think we've been robbed."

"Are we all right?" Max asked sleepily.

"Yes," Bel said.

"Then let's go back to sleep. We'll assess the damage in the morning."

The next morning, Bel could hardly bear to go downstairs. She took one cautious glance at the living room and saw only its familiar rumpled sofas and stack of papers beside the easy chair. The kitchen drawers were all intact; the refrigerator still stocked with leftovers. The Friday night candlesticks were still on the dining room table, her grandmother's sterling was still in the sideboard. Only one thing was out of place: a fresh loaf of challah bread rested on a doily in the center of the dining room table.

"Max, did you buy that challah?"

Max shook his head.

As they settled at the table and drank their morning coffee, Bel said, "Max, we have to lock the house. Something bad could happen to us."

"Or, something good," Max said, as he bit into a piece of fresh buttered bread.

—Deborah Shouse

枷锁只能锁住诚实。

　　我的教母贝尔和教父马克斯二战期间在英国相遇。因为营养的问题，他们变成了一起吃饭的朋友：马克斯只喜欢吃肉，贝尔只喜欢吃蔬菜。他们的友谊始于交换餐盘中的食物，很快他们也开始交流其他话题。

　　他们搬去了加利福尼亚州伯克利市破旧的老房子，马克斯将贝尔带到门口，然后他说："把钥匙给我。"

　　他拿过她递来的钥匙，和他自己的钥匙一起扔到了院子里。

　　"我想我的家可以向所有有需要的人开放。"他解释说。

　　他们也是这么做的，他们的家从来不锁门。朋友可以随便进出，去那里吃饭，从冰箱拿出冷冻的鸡腿或蜷缩在安乐椅上安静地读书。晚餐时间人来人往，不同的人交流着观点：无论是库尔德学生或以色列异己，无论是达拉斯律师或来自丹佛的制造商代表，无论是来自布鲁克林不参加

Chapter 4 Role Models
第四部分　榜样

圣会的犹太人学生或是圣达菲小教堂里的牧师，都聚集在这里。

然而，贝尔在芝加哥长大，她很清楚锁门的重要性。

不锁门对她来说既刺激，又恐怖。有时候她躺在床上睡不着，想着她妈妈所说的"更坏的情况"，她脑子不时想着抢劫、强奸、死亡这些事。这都是因为她疯狂的丈夫不愿意锁门。

在一个星期五的晚上，午夜的时候，贝尔听到门开了，她听到脚步声和磕磕碰碰的声音。她的手变得冰凉，抓住被子。她想大叫，但声音卡在嗓子里发不出来。那时她保持着安静，希望小偷在得到他想要的东西后就离开。她听到楼下储物柜的抽屉打开了。她轻推了一下马克斯，但是他没醒。她咬着被角，以防自己大叫。然后她听见纱门吱吱地响了，外面的门关上了。她摇着马克斯的肩膀："马克斯，刚才楼下有人。我想家里进小偷了。"

"现在没事了吧？"马克斯困倦地说。

"嗯。"贝尔答道。

"那我们继续睡吧，明早再看看损失。"

第二天早晨，贝尔好容易才鼓起勇气下楼。她小心地扫视着客厅，看到一切没变——皱皱的沙发还在，在安乐椅旁放着一沓纸，厨房的抽屉完好无损，冰箱里还放着剩饭剩菜，昨天晚上的烛台仍然放在餐桌上，她祖母的银具仍然放在餐具柜里。只有一样东西不一样：餐桌中间的桌巾上放着一个新买的白面包。

"马克斯，是你买了那白面包？"

马克斯摇摇头。当他们入座喝着咖啡时，贝尔说："马克斯，我们必须关门，否则会有不好的事发生的。"

马克斯咬了一口那抹着黄油的面包说："或者，会有好事发生。"

——德博拉·萧丝

Breakfast with a Friend
和朋友共进早餐

No life is so hard that you can't make it easier by the way you take it.

—Ellen Glasgow

"Good morning." I answered my business line at work.

"Good morning!" came the male voice on the other end. "What do you want to eat this morning?"

The caring voice on the other end was a pleasant surprise. We shared a common interest and problem that neither of us could share with anyone else we knew. There was peace and safety in the early morning question.

Thinking of foods I loved but could no longer enjoy, I responded, "I wish I could have pancakes with lots of butter and syrup."

Feeling tearful over the loss of the sweet pleasure of eating, my mind settled into my new pattern of sadness. The eighty-two-year-old man on the other end of the line interrupted my pity party. "Go get your carrot juice and we'll have breakfast together on the phone."

Running to the refrigerator, I grabbed the all too familiar light blue plastic cup, now permanently stained orange. "Okay, Bill, I've got it."

"Alright," he said from another state, two hours away. "Let's enjoy those pancakes."

Drinking my carrots and celery, I pictured him drinking his juice on the other end of the phone. It was the brightest moment in my dismal mealtime ritual and I was so grateful he'd called to encourage me.

The conversation only lasted a couple of minutes, ending with his signature, "I've gotta go take care of business." His thoughtfulness made me feel like I had my own angel helping me.

A prostate cancer survivor, Bill was remarkable. In his eighties, he still worked from 6：30 in the morning until after 5：00 PM on his lumberyard six days a week, while managing to single-handedly keep up with the other businesses he owned.

The first time I met him I knew he was special. Within moments of meeting me, he asked not about how I could help him and his business, but about my goals and purpose in life. Discovering that I, too, was on an all-juice diet due to medical reasons spurred him to give me juicing recipes and advice.

After being told his cancer was incurable and he would die soon, Bill researched alternative medicines and began juicing every meal every day. The only meal he did not juice was Thanksgiving dinner. I could not fathom going years without a piece of food touching my lips. Yet his resolve encouraged me and drove me.

After his initial early morning phone call, which took me by surprise, I began to relish hearing his morning greeting. Soon I was asking him what he would like to have for breakfast. His response was usually "Coffee, bacon, ham and gravy."

We were two unlikely candidates to become friends—he reminded me of Colonel Sanders and I was a frail twenty-year-old. But the universal prospect of sickness, death, and recovery spanned the generations and miles.

Within weeks I was no longer dreading the various forms of juice that needed to be consumed, thanks to Bill taking time from his busy schedule to encourage a young girl in need. Years later whenever I would pull out my dusty juicer, I would remember Bill's kindness to this near stranger, and would remind myself that being positive amidst the trials of life can propel a person higher than the most advanced medicine.

Some people speak of taking lemons and turning them into lemonade. Only Bill spoke of carrots and celery as if they were country-fried steak. With Bill's positive attitude, even radishes and cabbage can taste like warm brownies with hot fudge and ice cream.

—Erin Fuentes

生活没有那么艰难，你可以活得轻松些。

——埃伦·格拉斯哥

　　在上班时，电话专线响了，我接起了电话说道："早上好。"

　　"早上好！"电话那头的男士说，"今天早晨你想吃点儿什么？"

　　电话那头关心的声音让我又惊又喜。我们有共同的爱好和共同面对的问题，而这些是我们不会向其他认识的人说起的。在一大早问吃什么这个问题让人感到平和、踏实。

　　想到那些我很喜欢但是不能再吃的食物，我回答道："我想吃薄煎饼，要多加点儿黄油和糖浆。"

　　失去享受食物的乐趣让我很伤心，我又陷入了新的悲伤。电话那头八十二岁的老人打断了我的悲伤："去拿你的胡萝卜汁，我们通过电话一起吃早饭。"

　　我跑向冰箱，拿出那些再熟悉不过的浅蓝色塑料杯，不过现在都被染成了橘黄色，"好的，比尔，我拿到了。"

　　"好的，"他在离我两小时车程的另一个国家，"让我们好好享用那些薄煎饼吧。"

　　喝着胡萝卜汁和芹菜汁，我设想他在电话那头喝着他的果汁。进餐让我沮丧，和他一起吃饭是我最开心的时候，我很感激他能够打电话鼓励我。

　　我们只打了几分钟的电话，在他说"我要去工作了"后，我们就挂了电话，他的体贴让我感到好像有个天使在帮助我。

　　比尔曾经患了前列腺癌，后来治好了。在他八十多岁的时候，他仍然早晨六点半起床，在木材场工作到下午五点，一个星期工作六天。同时独立经营其他业务。

　　我第一次见到他就觉得他很特别。在我们见面的时候，他不问我能帮他和他的事业做些什么，却问我有什么生活目标和打算。当他知道我因为身体问题只能吃流食，他给了我些榨汁食谱和建议。

　　在他知道自己患了不治之症、很快就会死去的时候，比尔采用了非常规治疗，每天每顿饭都开始吃流食，他只在感恩节不吃流食。我很难想象长期不吃食物的感受。但是他的毅力鼓励着我，激励着我。

　　他一开始在早晨给我打电话，让我很惊讶，渐渐地我开始喜欢上他早晨的问候。不久，我问他早晨想吃什么，他的答案经常是"咖啡、熏肉、火腿和肉汁"。

　　我们两个本来不大可能成为朋友——他让我想起了桑德斯上校，而我是个柔弱的二十几岁的人。但是无论年纪大小，无论身在何处，人们对疾病、死亡、康复的概念都是一样的。

　　几个星期后，我不再害怕各种各样的果汁了，这多亏了比尔能在百忙之中鼓励我这个需要帮助的年轻女孩儿。几年后，当我拿出那落满灰尘的榨汁机，我想我仍将记得比尔对我这个陌生人的那份善良关怀，也将提醒我积极地看待人生，态度比最先进的药物更有效。有些人说到柠檬的时候，让人想到了柠檬汁的味道。只有比尔说到胡萝卜和芹菜的时候，让人感到他好像在说乡间的煎牛排。因为比尔的积极乐观，萝卜和白菜尝起来都像带着巧克力酱和冰激凌的布朗尼蛋糕。

——艾琳·福恩特兹

She Altered My Attitude
她改变了我的态度

Attitude is a little thing that makes a big difference.

—Winston Churchill

My ninety-year-old grandmother rested quietly in her hospital bed after a visit from her heart surgeon. He explained that she needed a quadruple bypass and she clung to the only good news he delivered: she had the body of a seventy-year-old.

Grandma's vanity required that she still dye her hair and the brown curls framed her porcelain face, her warm eyes, and her thin-lipped smile as she asked, "What would you do?"

My grandfather had died nearly thirty years earlier and Grandma had independently made decisions ever since. I knew she'd made up her mind before she'd even asked, but she liked me to feel included in her life especially after my mother passed away.

"I'd have the surgery," I said.

She nodded and then softly said, "I don't want to go home and wait to die. Besides, I'll be fine."

She was right. A few days later, a post-op nurse allowed me to visit Grandma in the recovery room after her surgery, a rather unusual privilege in hindsight. I was relieved Grandma had survived the operation but had been strangely confident that she would. Surprisingly, she lay naked and unconscious on the gurney, not yet cleaned up or bandaged. She had yellow iodine smeared all over her upper body between her elongated breasts and I was impressed that her enormous incision was stitched together as perfectly as any seam she'd ever sewn.

The sight of her chest rising and falling was comforting, but if Grandma had been awake she would have been embarrassed for me to see her naked. I held her hand and pondered the point at which my body would look like her medically speaking "seventy-year-old" one and worried that given my stressful job, it would be by the time I was forty instead of ninety.

About a year after my Grandma's successful surgery, my partner Ann and I invited her to our house for barbecued ribs. It was one of her favorite meals. I thought she'd enjoy a diversion from the usual mashed potatoes and gravy fare served daily at her assisted living apartment.

That particular Thursday night, both Ann and I got stuck at work. We got home only minutes before Grandma arrived, which killed any hope of serving her normal early dinner. I bought some time by offering to show her my nearby office while Ann got dinner going.

I helped Grandma carefully lower herself into my sports car and then I drove the short distance to my company's headquarters. She almost gasped as I turned down the tree-lined driveway that framed the roadway to the front of the building. Her face was full of wonder, like it always was, and her bright eyes took in everything around her.

"It's so beautiful," she said. "It looks like a park."

I'd never really thought of the grounds that way. My mind was usually distracted by the latest project delay or staff crisis. I drove to the private driveway at the back of the building and used my security card to enter the underground garage. The automatic door slowly opened and I parked my car in my assigned spot and started her tour.

Grandma was impressed with everything: the pristine underground garage, the sheer number of cubicles that stretched as far as the eye could see, the variety of logo-wear for sale at the company store, and the smell of food wafting from the full-service dining room.

As we stepped into the cafeteria I asked, "Given your diabetes, should we grab something here to hold you over until we get home?"

She looked at the herbed chicken dinner, the salad, soup, and sandwich bars and said, "I don't want to spoil my appetite, but do they serve such extravagant meals every night?"

Again, through her eyes I'd taken the quality and convenience of our cafeteria for granted, but the aromas made me want to head home for our own dinner.

"Just one more stop on the tour, Grandma. I want to show you where I sit."

We walked to my office and we both plopped down in chairs around my small conference table. She stroked the mahogany and said, "This is really nice." Then she pointed across my office to the chair behind my desk and asked, "Who sits there?"

Grandmother had always gotten a glazed look on her face whenever I explained what I did for a living, but it seemed she thought I worked at the conference table while "my boss" sat in the big chair behind the desk. Knowing she had been impressed with even that, I giggled as I said, "Well, Grandma... I do... this entire office is mine. I usually sit there at the computer and use this table for meetings with my staff."

Her eyes flashed with astonishment and she looked around my office with a new appreciation. Her response struck me. She'd attended teacher's college—or normal school as she called it—but when she got pregnant with my father she gave up her career. The opportunities for women had expanded far beyond those available to my grandmother: teacher, nurse, secretary, or homemaker.

She went over and sat down in my desk chair. She spun the chair around and then, one by one, she stared at the photographs of Canyonlands, Zion, and Yosemite National Parks that I'd taken while on vacations.

I pointed to one picture on the wall entitled "Attitude." It had a rainbow stretched above a roaring mountain stream and William James' words embossed at the bottom.

"I bought it with your Christmas money last year."

She looked at the picture, drew in a deep breath and then read the words out loud, "The greatest discovery of any generation is that a human being can alter his life by altering his attitudes."

She said, "I like all your pictures, but I think that one's my favorite."

"Me too, Grandma. Are you ready to go home and eat?"

She nodded. As we left my office she stopped outside the door and looked back. She gestured towards my nameplate and said, "I didn't notice that when we walked in."

She touched the letters of my last name... of her last name... and then she looped her arm through mine, patted my wrist, and said, "You've certainly done very well for yourself. I'm so proud of you."

When we got back to my house, Grandma patiently waited for us to serve dinner. It was almost eight when we finally sat down for our meal. Grandma attempted to eat her plate of ribs, but the pork was tough as bricks. When she finished eating what she could, she wiped her mouth with her napkin and unwittingly summed up her philosophy of life: "That barbecue sauce sure was tasty!"

My employer's headquarters, my office, and even my job never looked as wonderful as they did, that day, through my grandmother's eyes—her glistening grey eyes that always sparkled with possibility and only lingered on the good, especially when she looked at me.

—Kris Flaa

态度看似无关紧要，却意义重大。

————温斯顿·丘吉尔

　　我的祖母九十岁了，心脏手术后，安静地在医院的病床上躺着。医生解释说她要做常人四倍的搭桥，而她只注意到他说的唯一的好消息：她的身体像七十岁一样。

　　因为爱美，祖母染了棕色头发，鬈发顺着她白皙的脸颊垂下，她用温暖的眼神看着我，薄薄的嘴唇挂着微笑，问："你怎么想的？"

　　我的祖父在三十年前就去世了，自此祖母总是自己做决定。我知道在她问我之前就已经做好决定了，但她想让我觉得我是她生活的一部分，尤其是在我母亲去世以后。

　　"我会做手术。"我说。

　　她点点头，温柔地说："我不想回家等死。而且，我会好起来的。"

　　她是对的。手术几天后，护士让我去特殊病房看她，这算是一种特殊关照了。祖母的手术顺利地完成了，让我松了口气。手术前我一直坚信她会没事的。见到她，让我吃惊的是，她赤裸裸地躺在轮床上，没有清洗身体，也没有用绷带包扎。她下垂的乳房之间涂满了黄色的碘酒。她身上有个很大的切口，缝得很好，像她以前的针线活儿一样完美，这让我印象很深。

看见她胸部一起一伏安睡的情景，我感到很安慰。不过如果祖母醒了，发现我看着她赤裸的身体，肯定会尴尬的。我握着她的手，想着我将来哪里会有像她现在生理上看起来"七十岁"的身体。因为我工作压力大，我担心我四十岁的时候可能就像祖母现在的身体，而她九十岁还这么健康。

在祖母手术成功一年后，我和我的室友安邀请她到我们家做客，一起烤肋排，那是我最喜欢的食物之一。我想她应该喜欢换换口味，她每天老是吃公寓提供的土豆泥和肉汁。

那是个星期四晚上，我和安都因为工作不能按时离开，我们刚回家，祖母就到了。这样我们就没有办法为她早点儿准备晚餐了。我带着她去看看在家附近的我的办公室，这时安可以准备晚餐。

我小心地帮祖母坐进我的跑车，开了一小段后到了公司的总部。沿路两边都栽有树木。我将车停到公司大楼的前面，她那时都有点儿喘了。她满脸惊奇，像以前一样，她看着周围的一切，眼睛都亮了。

"真漂亮，"她说，"这里就像花园似的。"

我从来都没有这么想过。我总是考虑最近被拖延的方案或是员工危机，无暇欣赏这景色。我把车开到楼后面的私人车道，用我的安全卡进入地下车库。自动门慢慢打开了，我在分配的停车位停下车，开始带她到处转转。

祖母对所有的事物都感兴趣：旧的地下车库，满眼的小隔间，各种各样的提示语——在公司店里穿着销售的衣服，在提供全方位服务的餐厅里要弥漫着食物的香气。

我们走进自助餐厅，我问："你有糖尿病，我们需要在这儿买点儿什么，让你能支持到回家吗？"

她看着那些香熏鸡肉宴、沙拉、汤、三明治条，说："我不想让自己大开吃戒，他们每天晚上都供应这么丰盛的菜肴吗？"

我认为我们自助餐厅保证质量和提供便利是理所当然的。在她眼里，我看到我们的成绩。但是饭菜的香味让我想快点儿带她回家吃饭了。

"我们再去一个地方，祖母。我想让你看看我办公的地方。"

我们走进我的办公室，一起坐到小型会议桌旁的椅子上。她摸了摸那红木，说："这儿真好。"然后她指着我桌子后面的椅子问："谁坐在那里呢？"

在我谈论我如何谋生的时候，祖母脸上总是闪耀着光芒。她好像认为我在会议桌上工作，"我老板"坐在桌子后面的大椅子上。当我意识到她对这些关注的时候，我咯咯笑道："那个，祖母……这个……这整间办公室都是我的。我经常坐在这里看着电脑，在这张桌子上和员工开会。"

她眼里满是吃惊，她重新欣赏了一遍我的办公室。她的反应让我很感慨。她曾经上过师范大学——或者像她说的叫师范学校——但是她当时怀了我爸爸，放弃了学业。现在女性获得的机会比祖母那时候多多了，她们那时候只能当老师、护士、秘书或主妇。

她看完后，坐在我的办公椅上，转着椅子，然后盯着看我度假时拍的峡谷地、锡安山、约塞米蒂国家公园的照片。

我指着墙上的一张名为"态度"的照片——在咆哮的高山流水之上，横跨着一道彩虹，照片底部是威廉·詹姆斯的名言。

"我用去年你给的圣诞节的零花钱买的这幅画。"

她看着这幅画，深吸了一口气，然后大声读出上面的字："人类最伟大的发现，是发现可以通过改变态度来改变生活。"

她说："我喜欢你所有的照片，不过我想我最喜欢这张。"

"我也是，祖母。咱们回家吃饭吧？"

她点点头。我们走出办公室时，她站在门外，往回看。

她指着我的名牌，说："我刚才进来的时候没注意到。"

她摸着那些我的姓氏里面的字母……那也是她的姓……然后她挽着我的胳膊，拍拍我的手腕，说："你做得很好。我真为你骄傲。"

当我们回到家的时候，祖母耐心地等着我们准备晚饭。快八点了，我们才坐下吃饭。祖母打算吃肋排，但是猪肉硬得像砖头似的。等我们吃完晚饭，她拿着餐巾纸擦着嘴，不经意间总结着她的人生哲学："这烤肉酱真是太好吃了！"

我雇主的总部、我的办公室，甚至我的工作从来都没有像那天祖母眼里的那么美好——她那闪闪发光的灰色眼睛里，总是闪烁着可能性，她总是往好处看，尤其是在她看我的时候。

——克里斯·弗拉

Thank You, Mr. Flagman
谢谢你，旗号员先生

It isn't our position but our disposition which makes us happy.

—Author Unknown

The long line of rush hour traffic snaked its way down the rain-slick street as I glanced nervously at my watch. 5：30! It was the third time this week I'd been late picking up the children, and the babysitter would be unhappy. Well, she'd just have to be unhappy, I told myself. My being late couldn't be helped. Nothing had gone right all day, from the dead battery in the car this morning to the secretary's absence throwing the whole office out of kilter. This traffic jam seemed the perfect ending to a horrible day.

All I wanted was to get home and collapse in a tubful of hot, soapy water and enjoy some peace and quiet. But I knew the kids would be clamoring for supper the minute we walked in the door, and I'd left the house in such a mess this morning that I really needed to do something about it before my husband got home. Then after supper there'd be dishes to wash and tomorrow's lunches to pack and a load of laundry that really shouldn't be put off another day. After that, all I'd feel like doing was falling into bed, just like every other night.

I sighed loudly, though there was no one to hear. Lately my life seemed nothing more than a never-ending cycle of chores, work, and sleep, with nothing to break the monotony but weekends filled with more chores. Surely there was more to living than this. I guess I was simply too busy and too tired to look for it.

And then I saw him.

The lone flagman was standing, barely visible but for his blaze orange vest, in the middle of the street, patiently directing four lanes of traffic as they merged into one. But there was something unusual about this flagman, and as I edged my car forward waiting my turn to pass, I realized what it was.

Standing in the midst of dozens of impatient motorists, soaked to the skin and getting more drenched with every icy mud puddle splashed on him, he was smiling. And at every driver that passed, he not only smiled, he waved. Not many waved back, but some did. A lot of them smiled.

As I sat waiting my turn in my warm, dry car, I began to feel ashamed. If this man, who did nothing all day but watch one car after another go by, could stand in the cold rain hour after monotonous hour and still have a friendly gesture for every single person who passed, what right did I have to complain about my life? I thought again about what lay ahead of me tonight—a snug house, plenty of good food needing only to be prepared and, most of all, a caring husband and children who I loved more than anything in the world.

And tomorrow? Tomorrow I had the opportunity to use my skills and intelligence to perform useful, important work. What kind of life did I have?

Chapter 4 Role Models
第四部分　榜样

An absolutely wonderful one.

It was finally my turn to pass the flagman. As if on cue, we waved at each other.

"Thank you," I mouthed through the window. He smiled and nodded and I drove on, spirits lifted, attitude changed. And in the rearview mirror I could see him, raising his hand in greeting to every car that passed.

—Jennie Ivey

地位并不能带给我们快乐，但性格却可以。

——逸名

　　交通高峰时段，路上挤满了车，拥挤的车流弯弯曲曲地行进在雨中。我焦急地看着表，下午五点半了！这是第三次了，我接孩子又晚了，临时保姆应该不开心了，准确来说，我想她肯定不开心了。但对于迟到，我是无能为力了。那天什么事都不顺利，从早晨开始，我车子的蓄电池没电了，秘书没来，办公室一团乱。交通拥堵真为这糟糕的一天画上了完美的句号。

　　我只想回家，泡在热洗澡水中，享受一下平静与安宁。但我知道我一进家门，孩子们肯定喊着要吃晚饭。我早晨走的时候，家里一团乱，在老公回家前，我还要好好收拾一下。晚饭后，我还要刷碗，准备明天的午饭，然后把拖了好几天已不能再拖的要洗的衣服洗完。之后我就倒在床上睡觉。我每天晚上都是这样过的。

　　我长叹了一口气，但是没人听见。最近，我的生活似乎只是在干家务、工作、睡觉间永无止境地循环，没有什么能改变这千篇一律的生活。

周末还要干更多的家务。当然，生活不只是这些。我想我只是太忙太累了，无法去寻找生活的意义。

那天我看见了他。

一个旗号员孤零零地站在马路中间，要不是他那耀眼的橘黄色背心，人们都注意不到他。他耐心地引导着四排车道上的车并为一排。但是我觉得这个旗号员不大一样。当我往前开着，等待通行的时候，我发现他站在车流中，车里坐着焦躁的司机。他浑身湿透了，车子不断通过，他身上被溅到越来越多的冰冷的泥水，而他却微笑着。当车辆通过时，他不仅微笑，还招手。没有很多人会回应他，向他招手，但有些人会。很多司机都会向他笑笑。

我坐在自己温暖干净的车里等候着，我开始觉得有点儿羞愧。如果他每天只是注视着车辆依次通过，站在冰冷的雨中做着单调的工作，但仍然能对过往的每个人做出友好的手势，那么我有什么资格抱怨人生呢？我又想了想，晚上，有个舒适的家在等着我，很多好吃的食物等着我做，最重要的是，有我在这世上最挚爱的丈夫和孩子。那明天呢？明天我有机会通过自己的技能和才智，完成有用而重要的工作。我以前过着什么样的生活？绝对是美好的生活啊。

终于排到了我。我们同时向对方挥了挥手。

"谢谢你。"我透过窗户对他说。他笑了笑，点点头。我往前开着，振作起来，对事情的态度也变了。通过后视镜，我看到他抬起手问候所有路过的司机。

——詹尼·艾薇

A Shining Star in the Midst of Darkness
黑暗中闪烁的星辰

If I could reach up and hold a star for every time you've made me smile, the entire evening sky would be in the palm of my hand.

—Author Unknown

There are certain things that occur in our lifetime that are forever etched in our memories, and we can recall them as vividly as if they happened yesterday. May 29, 2009 is the date that I replay over and over in my mind because it was the day that we were told that my beloved niece, Cassy, was terminal and that her time remaining with us was limited.

"Three months at best," they said, and they would be dedicating their efforts to "keeping her comfortable" and "pain-free." I remember looking over at my sister, Cathy, and watching her face as the devastating news settled in and our fourteen-month journey suddenly veered off to an unwanted destination.

Cassy was diagnosed with Ewing Sarcoma, a form of bone cancer, when she was just eleven years

Chapter 4 Role Models
第四部分　榜样

old and she handled every surgery, treatment, and medical procedure with grace, bravery and a positive attitude that touched everyone who knew her. The roller coaster that our family rode during this time was exactly that, with highs and lows that kept us reeling with emotions that are hard to describe. There were many lessons learned as we tried to cope with the numerous doctor's appointments and hospital stays, while trying to maintain some level of normalcy within our lives. Cassy and our family worked very hard to keep this monster disease at bay, and no one would ever deny our tenacity and dedication to this cause.

When we were faced with the daunting task of telling Cassy the terrible news, we sat as a family and explained to her that treatments were being discontinued, and we were going to focus on helping her attain any wishes that she might have over the next several months.

Once again, we were amazed by Cassy's positive attitude and her acceptance of this unfair fate. She made a "list" of things that she wanted to do and places she wanted to go and our family set out on the mission of working through her wishes.

Her requests were so typical of a teenager that they made us smile when we read them. They were things that people take for granted, and yet they were incredibly important to Cassy.

She wanted to go to high school for a day, get a tattoo, get her belly button pierced, learn to drive, go on a trip with her family, go to her eighth-grade graduation (even though she was only in seventh grade), go to Prince Edward Island, and have a eleven birthday party with a Hawaiian luau theme. Well, over the next six weeks, Cassy did most of the things on her list… and we have lots of pictures that chronicle this last chapter in her life. It was a very special time for all of us, and we are thankful for those memories.

Cassy turned eleven on July 8, 2009 and I remember struggling with what to buy her for her birthday and wondered… what do you buy a young girl who is not going to be with us very long? I decided to "name a star" in Cassy's name and I took the documentation up to the hospital on her birthday. Cassy was thrilled with the thought of having this special star named in her honour. She had lots of questions about where it was and how we would be able to find it. She found some solace in knowing we would have an ongoing connection with her, and we in turn, found some sense of peace in having this special symbol of our beloved angel.

When Cassy took a turn for the worse four days later, the family traveled to the hospital in the middle of the night to pay vigil with her as she made the difficult transition from this world to the next. My thoughts that evening drifted back to the night when she was born eleven years earlier and I was called to the hospital to help coach my sister through the birth. I was the first one to hold her when she entered this world, and now I was watching her take her last breath.

It can be difficult to look back at Cassy's challenging journey, and think that there could be anything positive about it, but despite the heartaches and tears, there were definitely some life lessons learned. Our family learned the true value of friendship, community support and the love of family. We learned not to take the small things in life for granted, and that perhaps we should all be a bit more spontaneous. We learned that you can influence people and leave an imprint on their heart, even if you are only here for a short while, and that memories provide us with the ongoing strength to keep going even when we don't feel like it.

Today we continue to cope with the loss of our precious Cassy, but we know her spirit is strong and her presence is felt daily through the subtle messages that she sends our way. We look up to the heavens and smile when we see the sparkling stars that have become our symbol of faith and hope.

She was and always will be our "shining star in the midst of darkness."

~Debbie Roloson

你总是让我情不自禁地微笑，如果每次微笑我都伸手摘一颗星星，那么整个夜空都在我的手掌之中了。

——逸名

有些事，我们会终生难忘。当我们回忆起来的时候，那些事好像发生在昨天。2009 年 5 月 29 日，是我经常回忆起的日子，因为那天，我们知道我挚爱的外甥女卡西到了癌症晚期，她和我们在一起的时间很有限了。

医生说"最多还有三个月"，他们会尽力"让她舒服些""没有痛苦"。我记得在听到这灾难性的消息时，我看着我姐姐凯茜，注视着她的脸，我们十四个月的旅程突然转向了令人意想不到的结局。

卡西被确诊患上了尤文氏肉瘤，那是一种骨癌。她只有十一岁，但她在做手术、接受治疗时表现出来的勇敢和积极感动了认识她的每一个人。那段时间经历的突变，让我们心里五味杂陈，那种感觉很难表达。那期间，在协助医生的时候，在医院的时候，我们学到了很多东西。同时，我们试着维持生活的常态。家人和卡西尽全力控制这致命性的疾病，没人能否认我们的坚持和付出。

告诉卡西这个噩耗是个艰巨的任务。我们全家坐在一起，告诉她治疗可能会一直持续，我们会帮她在未来的几个月里完成所有的心愿。

卡西态度积极，她接受了命运的不公待遇，这让我们又一次感到惊讶。她列了个表，写出她想做的事、想去的地方，我们家人承担起了实现她愿望的使命。

她的愿望是典型的青少年的心愿，当我们读她的列表的时候，不禁笑了。那是些一般人觉得理所当然的事，而它们对卡西来说却特别重要。

她想去高中待一天、文身、穿肚脐环、学开车、和家人旅行、参加八年级毕业典礼（虽然她才上七年级）、去爱德华王子岛，以及办个十一岁生日宴会，以夏威夷宴会为主题。

六个星期里，卡西列表上的大部分心愿完成了，我们拍了很多照片来记录她生命的最后一段时间。这对我们来说是一段特别的时光，我们都感谢那段回忆。

卡西在 2009 年 7 月 8 日过十一岁生日。我记得我绞尽脑汁在想要给她什么生日礼物……要给这个即将离开我们的小女孩儿买点儿什么呢？我打算以卡西的名字"命名一颗星"，然后在生日那天把证明文件带到医院给她看。听到要以她的名字命名一颗星，卡西很兴奋。她问了很多问题，比如那颗星在哪里，我们怎么能找到它。当意识到我们还可以继续与她联系着，她感到些安慰。而这个代表我们挚爱天使的星星，也让我们感到一些平静。

四天后，卡西病情恶化了。我们在半夜去了医院，陪着她，因为她可能要离开人世了。我回想起十一年前她出生的时候，我当时被叫到医院帮我姐姐接生。在她出生的时候，我是第一个抱她的人，然而现在我却看到她奄奄一息。

　　我难以回顾卡西与病魔做斗争的富有挑战的路程，也难以想到什么积极的事。但是除了心碎和眼泪，我们的确学习了生命中的一课。我们知道了友谊的真谛，社区支持的可贵，家人的爱的重要。我们学会不要认为日常小事都是理所当然的，我们应该更主动点儿。我们学到你可以影响别人，让别人心里留下你的痕迹，即使相处的时间不长，回忆让我们有力量继续前行，虽然有时我们没有感觉到这种力量。

　　今天，我仍然为失去珍爱的卡西伤感，但我知道她的意志坚强，通过微妙的联系，我们可以感觉到她的存在。我抬头看着天，当我看着那闪闪的星星，看着那象征着我们信念和希望的星星，我笑了。

　　她曾经是，也永远是我们"黑暗中闪亮的星辰"。

——黛比·洛路逊

心灵鸡汤：
每一次跌倒，
都是最好的成长

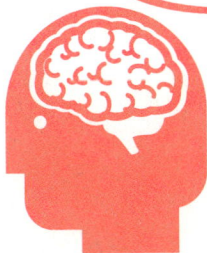

第五部分　细数幸福

Chapter 5
Counting Your Blessings

The hardest arithmetic to master is that which enables us to count our blessings.

— Eric Hoffer

··

最难掌握的算术便是学会细数我们的幸福。

——埃里克·霍夫

Counting Our Blessings
细数幸福

Why not learn to enjoy the little things—there are so many of them.

"We're not getting a paycheck this week."

I wasn't particularly alarmed by my husband's words. After all, he had gone without a salary in the past, and we had always made do. Mentally, I congratulated ourselves that we had no debt outside the mortgage on our home.

With two partners, my husband owned a small engineering firm. When times were tight, he and his partners went without paychecks, making certain their employees were paid. I was grateful to be married to such an honorable man.

Two weeks passed, then four, then six, all with no salary in sight. The bills arrived with depressing regularity, though, and we lived off our savings, a spotty food storage, and faith in the Lord.

The fall of 2008 marked an economic downturn for the entire country. Caught in the spiral, clients who had always paid on time in the past now failed to pay their bills.

Christmas approached and I wondered how we would find the means to buy even small presents. I didn't mention this to my husband, knowing he had worry enough on his mind. I searched bargain bins and put my creativity to work.

In the meantime, I joined freecycle.com, an international organization devoted to preventing more items from ending up in already overburdened landfills. As a freecycle member, I could post items online that I no longer needed or wanted and other members could respond. In the same way, I could answer others' posts if I saw something I needed.

Four weeks into our doing without a salary, I noticed two messages listing pantry items. I e-mailed back immediately, saying that my family could really use the food.

In freecycle, the first person to answer a listing is usually the one who receives it. When I noticed the time the listings were posted, my heart sank. Several hours had passed.

Surely the items had already been taken.

To my surprise and delight, both freecyclers e-mailed me, saying that the food was mine. They gave me their addresses, and we arranged a pick-up time.

I went through the boxes of food like a child opening presents on Christmas morning. Cans of vegetables. Potato flakes. A cake mix. Even fresh fruit. My husband, teenage daughter (the only child remaining at home), and I feasted that night!

A quick friendship developed between an older lady and myself. She gave me other foodstuffs when she had more than she needed. I drove her to various stores and did errands for her, as she was unable to drive. We sent each other inspirational messages and discovered we had much in common, including a deep faith in our Creator.

My membership in freecycle encouraged me to clean out clothes, books, and household goods that we no longer used. As I uncluttered my house, I felt as though I were also uncluttering my soul, ridding it of old grudges, resentments, and fears.

I wrote our four adult children, explaining our situation.

I also mentioned that we would be cutting back on Christmas presents that year and suggested they do the same. As a gentle hint, I told them that the best present they could give their father and me was to get out of debt.

In previous years, I had kept a gratitude journal. Every day I had recorded things, both large and small, for which I was grateful. As frequently happens with good habits, this one slipped away in the busy-ness of life. I revived it, listing five things every night as I wrote in my journal.

Small occurrences found their way into my gratitude journal. A shiny penny found during a walk. A letter from a friend. An unexpected phone call from a long-distance relative. A hug from my usually standoffish teenage daughter. The feeling of sunshine on my face.

Everyday things became a cause for rejoicing. When was the last time I had been thankful for a washing machine and dryer?

When had I last given thanks for friends who listened to my complaints without sharing their own? (Shamed, I resolved to mend that nasty habit.) When had I last thanked God for a strong body, even though it wasn't in the shape or condition I desired?

My priorities began to shift. I stopped thinking of what I didn't have and began to think more of what I did. At the same time, I looked around and realized that others were suffering as well. I took time to send notes to friends and church members who needed an extra dose of love. I prayed more and complained less. I counted my blessings.

Our financial situation hadn't changed, but my attitude had.

Nearly eight weeks had passed since my husband had received a paycheck and Christmas was upon us. I had managed to buy and make modest presents for family and friends. I refused to give in to the temptation to apologize for the humbleness of the gifts, knowing those who loved me would understand and accept my offerings.

One evening my husband returned home, a wide grin stretching across his face. "Money came in the mail." He went on to explain that one of his customers, also a victim of the slow economy, had sent a long overdue check.

We had gone nearly two months without a paycheck. Not only had we survived, we had thrived.

I took stock of our lives: we had friends, family, and faith. We were rich indeed.

—Jane McBride Choate

何不学习于细微处见快乐？——细微之事是如此繁多。

——逸名

"又是没有薪水的一个星期。"

我丈夫的话并未使我特别惊慌。毕竟，过去他也曾有拿不到工资的时候，但我们总能想出办法。而且我从心底庆幸除了房屋抵押贷款我们并无他债。

我的丈夫和两名合伙人共同经营一家小型工程公司。当世事艰难时，他和合伙人会牺牲自身利益来确保雇员们能够领到薪水。我感激上苍让我嫁给这么一个值得尊敬的男人。

两个星期过去了，四个星期过去了，六个星期过去了，领薪日还是遥遥无期。更令人倍感压力的是，账单却总是如期而至，我们靠积蓄，靠东拼西凑的食物和对上帝的信仰勉强维持生活。

2008年秋天大家见证了蔓延全国的经济衰退。

深陷于这种衰退，那些过去总是按时付款的客户现在也无力偿付。

圣诞节将至，我在考虑怎样才能买到哪怕只是一些小礼物。关于这点我并未向我的丈夫提及，因为我知道他早已忧心忡忡。我淘遍便宜货市场，将我的创造力充分发挥。

同时，我加入了自由循环网，一个致力于阻止更多的闲置物品沦为废弃物而增加已不堪重负的填埋场负担的国际组织。作为一名倡导循环利用的成员，我可以将不再需要或不再喜欢的物品条目挂到网上，这样其他成员就会予以回应。同样，若我看到自己需要的东西也可以回应他人的招贴。

在长达四个星期无薪水的艰难日子里，我注意到两条关于食品转让的信息。我迫不及待地回复了邮件，告诉他我的家庭确实能够用上这些食物。

在自由循环网，第一个回复招贴的人往往能够最终得到物品。当看清招贴发布的时间时，我的心沉了下去。离招贴发布已经过去数小时。

这些物品一定已被预订走了。出乎我意料又让我倍感欣喜的是，两个贴主都回复了我，告知我食物是我的了。他们给了我地址并且安排了取货时间。

我查看着这些箱箱罐罐，兴奋得像圣诞节早晨打开礼物的孩子一样。成罐的蔬菜、西红柿片，一个夹心蛋糕，甚至还有新鲜的水果。那天晚上，我的丈夫、我的小女儿（唯一还住在家里的孩子）和我大饱口福！

我和一位老妇人很快建立了友谊。当她有太多食品时会把多余的送给我，我则载她去逛各式各样的商店并帮她跑跑腿，因为她不能开车。我们互发勉励短信并且发现彼此有很多共同语言，包括对造物主的虔诚信仰。

加入自由循环网促使我清理了我们不再需要的衣物、图书及家居用品。整理房屋的同时，我感觉自己的精神也接受了洗礼，清除了宿怨、憎恶和恐惧。

我写信给我们四个已成年的孩子，向他们诉说我们的处境。

　　我也有提到那一年我们将大幅削减圣诞礼物并建议他们效仿我们。作为温情提示，我告诉他们能够给他们父亲和我最好的礼物就是还清债务。

　　前些年，我一直坚持写感恩日记。每天我都将自己所感恩的事情记录下来，无论大事还是小事。正如所有好习惯常常遭遇到的，这个习惯也在繁忙的生活中悄悄溜走。我重拾这个习惯，每天晚上都从感恩日记中挑选五件事列出来。

　　小事件也会在我的感恩日记中留下足迹——一枚散步时捡到的闪亮的硬币，一封朋友的来信，一通意料之外的远亲打来的电话，一个平日一贯冷漠的小女儿送出的拥抱，一份阳光映射脸颊的感受。

　　日常事物变成欢欣的缘由。我已记不得上一次为拥有一台洗衣机和脱水机而感恩是什么时候，记不得上一次为朋友倾听我抱怨而不提及他们的抱怨而感恩是什么时候（深感惭愧，我已下决心改正这令人讨厌的习惯），记不得上一次为上帝赐予我强健的身体，尽管并不是我渴望的体形或状态，而感恩是什么时候。

　　我思想的侧重点开始转换。我不再计较自己所缺失的而开始注重自己所做到的。同时，我推己及人，意识到他人同样也在承受苦难。我空出时间为特别需要关爱的朋友和教会同胞送去祝福。多一份祈祷，少一份抱怨，我细数自己拥有的幸福。

　　我们的经济情况未有好转，但我的态度转变了。

　　离我丈夫上一次领到工资已过去了近八个星期，圣诞节也已近在咫尺。我成功地为我的家人和朋友置办了合适的礼物。我拒绝成为诱惑的俘虏，没有为礼物的平庸而道歉，因为我知道爱我的人会理解并接受我的心意的。

　　一天傍晚，丈夫笑容满面地回到了家，说："汇款邮到了。"他继而解释道，有一个顾客，同样也是经济危机的受害者，寄来了拖欠已久的支票。

我们已经度过了近两个月的无薪之日。我们不仅生存下来，而且过得万分精彩。

我计算了一下我们的财富：我们有朋友、家庭，还有信仰。我们其实很富有。

——简·麦克布莱德·乔特

Getting Old Gratefully
心怀感恩至古稀

To be interested in the changing seasons is a happier state
of mind than to be hopelessly in love with spring.

—George Santayana

When I turned sixty-eight, old age seemed
to have arrived. Seventy loomed close, and felt
especially ominous, as my mother died at seventy-
two. My husband Tom, ever the optimist, reminded
me that my father lived to be ninety-four—also, that
I'm a lot more active and health-conscious than my
mother was. After all, we stretch every morning
before a breakfast of steel-cut oatmeal, take our
vitamins and supplements, get plenty of exercise, and
have meaningful days. Mine are filled with gardening
and writing, Tom's with singing, playing keyboard
and trumpet.

Still, sometimes it takes two of us to come
up with an acquaintance's name, or the title of a
movie we saw just yesterday! Once I could garden

Chapter 5 Counting Your Blessings
第五部分 细数幸福

nonstop for six hours, but now I need a break after two hours. Then there are those startling moments when I turn the corner in a store to face an unexpected mirror. Who is that old person in the glass?

It's no accident that the three light bulbs above the mirror in my bathroom are now fifteen watts. I like that soft glow. Besides, without my reading glasses I can't see the wrinkles, although it does seem that my eyes are shrinking. Is it time for an eyelift? In a heartbeat, dread of surgery overcomes vanity. Then I think to myself that I've simply got to find a way to accept old age with all its changes. I'm making the last years of my life miserable with worry!

When I started to worry about aging, I decided to get some help from my friends in the Golden Years Gardening Group. We meet once a month to talk about our gardens and anything else on our minds. We're all women over sixty with a common love for plants. I proposed that our next meeting topic be "The Positive Aspects of Aging."

I worried that no one would show up. Why on earth had I suggested this topic? It might be too serious, too fraught with anxiety. So what a relief that most everyone showed up.

Gail Austin started the Golden Years Gardening Group a year after her husband Ken died. She wanted more time to spend with friends, to enjoy life—to work less and play more. As she began simplifying her large, high-maintenance garden, Gail realized that many older gardeners were struggling with a similar process and could use a support group to help them accept life's changing circumstances. We would share the adventure of letting go of stressful work and learn to enjoy less complicated gardens.

That afternoon Gail suggested we go around the room and give each person her turn to speak about the benefits of aging, without any interruptions. She began with a key statement.

"I don't worry about the little things anymore," Gail said. "Forty was the beginning."

This theme—the perspective we gain after experiencing many of life's changes over time—came up repeatedly. Hazel, a recent member, put a similar idea in her own words.

"Resilience," she said. "Life experience has given me that." There was a moment of quiet in the room as we all absorbed the importance of Hazel's wisdom. By now, some of us were nodding our heads in agreement, smiling in recognition of this big advantage of growing old.

Next, Lisa announced another common thread.

"My grandchild," she said. "I understand now why my grandmother meant a lot to me. I understand the love she was giving to me and can transmit it to my granddaughter." Some of Lisa's grandmother's love came in the form of discipline. Now Lisa practices that same tough love with her granddaughter, helping her set boundaries.

Jepi added another layer to the topic of family connections.

"I have a new relationship with my dad, who's eighty-nine," she said. "He became a gardener in his late seventies." Now they share that passion and spend time together in the garden. Her dad is slow, but that's just fine. What's important is that they're growing closer.

Dru reminded us about the importance of a positive attitude.

"I'm a 'cup is half full' kind of person, not a 'cup is half empty,' and I'm lucky for that," she said.

Ann echoed Dru's affirmation, adding more details.

"The cup is full, a new day is always wonderful. I feel appreciation to be here," she said. Ann practices gratitude each evening, reviewing the gifts of the day before she goes to sleep.

Diane reminded us about financial independence.

"I feel lucky to have retirement income," she said. "Now it's fun to get up at 6 AM!"

Renee piggybacked on that idea:

"I finally have my independence," she said. "I get to decide what I want to do."

By this time, I was feeling pretty good about growing old. I hadn't prepared what I'd say, but when my turn came I knew just what it was. Without any rehearsing, I blurted it out.

"I'm so happy to have found love late in life," I said. "I met Tom when I was fifty-eight years old, and we married five years later. After twenty-three years of being divorced, falling in love with a wonderful man was a great gift of older age."

I put my arm around Diana, who sat next to me in the circle of friends. We'd been gardening friends for many years, way before Golden Gardeners had been formed.

"Diana here was my role model—she encouraged me not to give up, to keep searching until I found the right man," I said.

Diana smiled and explained to the group that it took her five marriages before she found a lasting love. Both of us married younger men who would have been out of the picture when we were in our twenties—actually they would have been in high school! As we get older, ten years difference in age doesn't matter.

I thought more about how getting older helps us love more deeply. Tom is there for me when I'm sick, just as much as when I'm healthy. A natural-born comedian, he keeps me laughing every day, the best tonic I know. When I was younger, I never would have considered a short, bald man who'd been married and divorced three times. But when I met Tom, all I could see was his beautiful smile, warm blue eyes, and loving heart. I gave him extra credit for continuing to marry; I'd met so many men who'd become embittered after even one divorce. Tom's hopefulness gave me courage to marry again.

Our group had helped me more than I'd imagined. Not only were my worries about growing older quieting down—I was actually thrilled to be in this stage of life, now that I saw the big picture. Best of all, our circle had grown closer after sharing these intimate details of our lives. I looked around at my friends with greater understanding, respect and love. How wonderful to be part of this gathering of wise women, all of us lending strength to each other on such an interesting journey.

—Barbara Blossom Ashmun

感悟四季变换是一种比无望地爱恋春天更愉悦的精神状态。

———乔治·桑塔亚那

　　过了六十八岁，古稀之年似乎已不期而至。七十岁可怕地逼近，想到我的母亲去世于七十二岁，我就感到万分沮丧。我的丈夫汤姆，一向积极乐观，提醒我我的父亲享年九十四岁——而且我比母亲更爱运动也更注重养生。毕竟我们每天早餐都会喝打磨的燕麦粉，在这之前我们会舒展一下筋骨。我们摄取维生素及其他补品，做大量的运动，充实地度过每一天。平时我主要是打理打理花圃、写写东西，汤姆则唱唱歌、弹弹电子琴、吹吹小号。

　　然而有时候我们两个人冥思苦想半天，才能想起昨天刚见过的友人的名字或刚看过的电影名称！以前我可以一口气在花圃干活六小时，现在却隔两小时就需要休息一下。如今转过街角的商店撞到一面镜子时，我会吓一跳：镜子里的老妇是谁啊？

　　目前位于我浴室镜子上方的三个灯都是十五瓦特，这并非偶然。我喜欢那柔和的光线，这样，如果不戴上老花镜我就不会看到自己的皱纹。但是，看上去我的眼部皮肤在变松弛，难道我该去做眼部提拉了吗？经过一番思想斗争，对手术的恐惧还是打败了我的虚荣心。于是我对自己说，我只是需要找到一个接受老年变化的出口，否则这样下去我只会在担忧中度过自己的暮年。

当我开始害怕变老，我决定向"流金岁月园艺协会"的朋友求助。我们每月会见一次面谈谈各自的花圃及其他关心的话题。我们都是年过六十又对花木有着共同喜好的妇人。我提议我们下次聚会的主题为"迟暮的朝阳面"。

我担心无人参加。我是着了什么魔提出这么个主题？这个话题可能太过严肃，太过阴郁。所以当看到大部分人都出现的时候我着实松了口气。

盖尔·奥斯汀在她丈夫去世一年后成立了流金岁月园艺协会。她希望能有更多的时间和朋友们聚在一起，一起享受生活——少一份劳作，多一份欢愉。当盖尔开始整理自己难以打理的大花圃时，她意识到许多老年园艺爱好者也在相似的过程中挣扎，他们同样需要群体的帮助来接受生活境况的变化。我们可以共享抛开工作压力的冒险乐趣并学会从日益规整的花圃中体验快乐。

那天下午盖尔建议我们围成一圈，让每个人都来谈谈变老的积极意义而不去打断。她首先做了关键陈词。

"我不再为琐事而烦恼了，"盖尔说，"四十岁是一个转折点。"

这个主题——在我们历经岁月变迁、体味过百态人生后获得的感悟——一遍又一遍地获得共鸣。最近加入的成员黑兹尔也用自己的话提出了相似的观点。

"坚忍，"她说，"生活阅历教我学会坚忍。"

房间里沉静了片刻，我们所有人都沉浸在黑兹尔的智慧之言中。当时，有的人点头表示赞成，为认识到年长的这一大优势而露出微笑。

接下来，莉萨发表了又一个引发共鸣的观点。

"我的孙女，"她说，"我现在明白了为什么我的祖母对我至关重要，我理解了她所给我的爱并将爱继续传递给我的孙女。"莉萨祖母所给的爱有些是以规则的形式展现出来的。如今莉萨在孙女身上践行着同样严苛的爱，为她设立规范。

关于家庭关系的话题，杰皮补充了几句。

"我和我八十九岁高龄的父亲有一种新的相处模式，"她说，"他在接近八十岁的时候成了一名园艺爱好者。"现在他们共享那份从事园艺工作的热忱并一起在花园里劳作。她的父亲动作迟缓，但是这并不碍事。重要的是他们的关系日益紧密起来。

德鲁提醒了我们积极态度的重要性。

"我是'杯子有一半是满的'型的人，而非'杯子有一半是空的'型，我为此感到庆幸。"她说。

安响应了德鲁的发言并补充了更多的细节。

"对于从满溢面来看杯子的人来说，新的一天总是无限精彩。我很感激自己在这儿。"她说。安每天晚上都会记录感恩，在睡觉前回顾一下今天得到的恩赐。

戴安娜让我们注意到经济独立的重要性。

"我很庆幸自己有退休金，"她说，"现在每天六点起床非常愉快！"

雷内支持这个观点。

"我终于取得了独立，"她说，"我能决定自己想要做什么。"

通过这次讨论，变老带给我非常美妙的感觉。我并未事先准备发言，但轮到我的时候我很清楚自己要说什么。没有彩排，我脱口而出。

"我为在晚年找到真爱而感到无比幸福。"我说，"我在五十八岁那年遇到了汤姆，我们五年之后喜结连理。在离婚二十三年后，和一个出色的男人坠入爱河是我晚年得到的巨大恩赐。"

我搂住戴安娜的肩膀，在这圈朋友中她就坐在我的旁边。我们在流金岁月园艺协会成立之前就是共同爱好园艺的朋友，我们的友谊已有些年头了。

"在这里戴安娜是我的榜样——她鼓励我不要放弃，坚持寻找直到找到对的人。"我说。

戴安娜微笑着向大家解释她经历了五段婚姻才找到持久的爱。我们俩都嫁给了比自己年龄小的男人，他们是我们在二十多岁时根本不会遇到的——实际上当时他们还在读高中呢！当我们年龄大些了，十岁的年龄差距便不再是问题。

关于年龄越大越有益于我们深入去爱彼此我想了很多。无论我生病还是健康，汤姆都在我身边陪伴我。他是一个天生的喜剧演员，是我认识的最令人愉快的人，每天都逗得我笑意连连。在我年轻时，根本不会去考虑一个又矮又秃顶且离过三次婚的男人。但是当遇到汤姆，我能看到的只有他俊朗的微笑、饱含暖意的蓝色眼睛和一颗炙热的心。我格外信任他，决定再次结婚。我遇到过那么多离过一次婚就一蹶不振的男人，汤姆的信心给了我再次嫁人的勇气。

我们协会对我的帮助超出了我的想象。不仅平复了我对变老的担忧，而且让我切切实实地为踏入生命的这一阶段而兴奋不已，现在我看到了壮阔的前景。最值得庆贺的是，在共享了彼此生命的诸多私密细节后，我们协会成员之间的关系变得越来越紧密。我环视周围的朋友，心中充满更多的理解、尊重和喜爱之情。能够加入这些智者的聚会是多么美妙的事啊。在如此有趣的生命旅程阶段我们互相扶持，给予彼此力量。

——芭芭拉·布洛瑟姆·阿什曼

Shiny Nickels
闪亮的五分镍币

I don't think of all the misery but of the beauty that still remains.

——Anne Frank

She had no business being so cheerful. All over the country people were out of work, losing homes, and being pushed into social services or the streets. Young people in the college classes I taught were cynical and apathetic. Why study hard when there'd be no jobs? Was I teaching skills and work ethics that might be meaningless? Was I encouraging false hope?

Yet each day in the front row forty-five-year-old Betty smiled eagerly. She was a big woman draped in shapeless sweatshirts and baggy jeans, her gray hair hung straight to her shoulders, and she shuffled with the painful effort of someone with arthritis. How could she compete in today's dog-eat-dog job market? If anyone should be sour, it was

Betty. But her homework was always done thoroughly, and she waited for class to begin like a horse fidgeting at the starting gate.

It wasn't just that she earned straight A's, jumped into every discussion, and did extra research. She accepted no cynicism or apathy. One time we discussed a story about a man who freed a bird from a zoo hunter's live trap so it could rejoin its mate that hovered in the sky overhead. Betty sighed, "I'm glad somebody does things like that. It's beautiful!"

A young man scoffed. "What's one bird more or less? It would've lived longer in captivity. Besides, they'll just catch another one. Do you know how much money people make capturing rare birds?"

Betty smiled. "That's true. But what counts is the moment when the birds meet again in the sky. Picture that and forget the rest. It doesn't matter if hunters catch another one, if the birds die, or if the world explodes. You have to live for those shining moments or why live? Life is full of loss and death. That's not news. You young people think the world is falling apart, but it's not. I know what real disaster is. My husband died last year. My daughter has kidney disease. We have no health insurance or income." The young man's face reddened. Betty smiled. "No, don't feel bad. How could you know? It's all right. Just because bad stuff happens doesn't make life bad. It should teach us to love what's good now. Don't wait for money and success to light up your life. You've got to grab the little shiny moments that come to all of us while they're here."

Yes, I thought. That's what I ought to be telling my students—and myself.

A week later I saw someone bending deep into a trash bin in the student union. It was common these days for homeless men to comb the college trash for beverage cans redeemable for five cents each. But when this person straightened up with two cans, it was Betty. I hesitated to greet her. Being caught raiding the trash by her professor might be embarrassing. Heck, it embarrassed me. As I tried to slip by, she noticed me, and her face brightened. "Professor!"

"Hello."

"I collect cans between classes. It's my bus fare! It's amazing what people throw away, even in times like this." She dropped the cans into a bag. "Actually, it's wonderful. I come to college each day with an empty purse. Not a cent sometimes! But I always find enough cans for bus fare and sometimes lunch too. They're waiting for me every day."

"Suppose you can't find enough?"

She laughed and shrugged. "I could hike home if I had to, I guess. But they just keep coming. What a person needs is usually there if you search hard." I told her that if she ever fell short, to stop by my office. She smiled. "See? Now I have bus fare insurance!"

I drew her aside from the streaming crowd. "You know, what you said in class last week really hit those young people hard. They've been writing about it. You made them see things differently. Me too," I admitted.

"I'm glad. Maybe even suffering can do some good."

"I'm so sorry about your husband."

"Oh, I won't lie. For a long time I was broken without him. Broken in pieces. And it's been horrible trying to survive. He died two months before qualifying for his pension and of course the health insurance expired when we needed it most. I'm lucky I still have him to hang onto."

"What do you mean?"

She smiled. "I love him so much, just like always. Every night I think about how we'd lie in bed and read and talk, sometimes until 3 AM. We owned a rickety old house, but we had dreams. Oh, such shiny dreams! You can't ever take that away from a person who wants to hold onto it. I'm alone in an apartment now, but we're still in love and married. It's just that he's dead.

We'll meet again someday, just like the birds in the story."

"What will you do about your daughter?"

"The doctor says her kidneys might last another five years. I'd give her one of mine, but we don't match. We'll just have to see what happens. I can't control what fate brings. I can only control how I respond to it. So why choose misery? Isn't it wonderful enough just to have lived? To have felt and seen and tasted life? Bill and I made sure our daughter did that. She won't die without having lived."

I suggested several agencies that might help with her daughter's medical bills. "Oh, I know them," she said. "We're working on that. And here I am at my age starting college to get a decent job!" She laughed. "Bill would love that! Those young people don't think jobs are out there. But you can find one if you look hard and aren't afraid to get dirty. There's a job out there that I'll find." She shook her bag so the cans rattled. "These aren't garbage. They're not recyclable aluminum. They're shiny nickels."

—Garrett Bauman

我不会去想所有的苦难而只看到仍然存在的美好。

——安妮·弗兰克

她没有事业值得她如此开朗。全国人民都在失业，大家流离失所，被迫接受社会救助或在大街上流浪。我所任教的大学课堂上的年轻人个个愤世嫉俗、麻木不仁。既然找不到工作何必还要用功读书？我在教授的技巧和职业道德是有意义的吗？我是不是在鼓励虚假的希望？

然而前排四十五岁的贝蒂却天天笑意盈盈。她是个很结实的女人，穿着肥大变形的套衫和宽松下垂的牛仔裤，灰白的头发散落在肩上，并且正举步维艰地和关节炎做斗争。她怎能应对如今人吃人般竞争激烈的人才市场？如果有人有难言之隐，那应该是贝蒂。但她总是毫无疏漏地完成作业，等待上课就像在起跑线前即刻待发的马。

她不仅一路得 A（优秀），参与每一场讨论和做额外的研究，而且她从不抱怨，从不会表现出冷漠。有次我们讨论一个故事，故事是关于有人将一只鸟从动物园猎手的圈套中解救，这样鸟儿就可以和在上空盘旋的伴侣团聚了。贝蒂听后感叹道："听到有人能做出这样的举动我很高兴。这太美了！"

一个年轻人不屑道："一只鸟儿有什么值得大惊小怪的？它若被捕捉到，活的时间会更长。而且，人们还会再去捕捉一只。你知道捕捉一只稀有品种的鸟儿需要耗费多少钱吗？"

贝蒂笑道："你说得对。但是真正重要的是鸟儿们在空中团聚的那一刻。我们只须铭记那一刻，无须在意其他的。假如猎手捕获另外一只鸟，鸟儿最终死去或是世界爆炸，那都没关系。你应该为那些闪光的瞬间而活，否则我们何必活在这个世界上？生命充满了缺失和死亡。这并不新鲜。你们这些年轻人以为世界正在分崩离析，但并非如此。我知道什么是真正的灾难，我丈夫去年去世了，我女儿身患肾病，我们没有医疗保险也没有收入。"

那个年轻人的脸变红了。贝蒂继续笑道："不，不要感到内疚。你怎么会知道呢？我没关系。仅仅因为坏事情的发生并不能让人生变得糟糕，它教会我们应该珍惜眼前美好的事物。不要等待金钱和成功来点亮你的人生，你应该趁那些闪光时刻来到的时候抓住它们。"

有道理，我想。我应该将这些讲给我的学生——还有我自己。

一个星期后，我看到学生中有个人深深地弯着腰埋头在一个垃圾桶中。这在这些日子是很常见的，经常有流浪汉搜寻学校的垃圾桶翻找可回收的饮料罐，每个饮料罐可换取五分钱。但当这个人拿着两个饮料罐站起来的时候，我却犹豫着要不要打招呼，那是贝蒂。被自己的教授发现在翻垃圾也许并不是件光彩的事。糟糕，这让我很尴尬。就在我试图溜走的时候，她看到了我，面露喜色地叫道："教授！"

"你好。"

"我在班级的垃圾桶中翻找饮料罐，它们是我的公交车费！即使在这样的时期，人们扔掉的东西也让人倍感惊讶。"她将瓶瓶罐罐扔进一个袋子里。"事实上，它们棒极了。我每天都是口袋空空地来上学。有时连一个硬币都没有！但我总能捡到足够的饮料罐来付公交车费，有时还够支付一顿午饭。它们每天都等着我来捡。"

"那若是你捡不到足够的饮料罐呢？"

她笑着耸了耸肩："我想，如果是这样，那我不得不走回家吧。但是它们天天都会有，我们所需要的只是努力搜寻。"我告诉她如果她什么时候手头拮据了，可以来我的办公室找我帮忙。她微笑道："看到了吗？现在我有公交车费保险了！"

我穿过熙熙攘攘的人群走近她。"你知道吗？上个星期你在教室里说的话确实深深地触动了那些年轻人，他们已经在写那件事了。你让他们从另一个视角来看待问题。我也是。"我承认道。

"我很高兴能有所帮助。也许灾难也会产生积极的影响吧。"

"关于你丈夫，我很难过。"

"噢，我不会讲谎话，失去他后很长一段时间我都很悲痛，悲恸欲绝。而且尝试活下去是很困难的。他在还有两个月就可以领退休金的时候去世了，于是自然地，在我们最需要的时候，健康保险到期了。但我很庆幸自己仍然有他陪伴。"

"这怎么讲？"

她笑道："像往常一样，我深爱着他。我夜夜回想我们躺在床上一起阅读聊天的情景，有时候我们会聊到三点钟。我们只有一幢简陋的旧房子，但是我们有梦想。噢，那么美妙的梦想！只要一个人想要坚持梦想，你就无法将它夺走。现在我独自住在公寓里，但我们仍然相爱，我们仍然是夫妻。他只是暂时离开了，我们终有一天会再次相遇的，就像故事中的鸟儿一样。"

"关于你女儿你打算怎么办？"

"医生说她的肾可能还能维持五年。我愿意把我的一个肾给她，只是我们的肾并不匹配，只能静观其变。我无法左右命运的安排，只能选择怎么去应对它。所以为何要选择悲伤？能够活着，能够感觉，能够欣赏和品味生活不就是最大的仁慈了吗？贝尔和我相信我们的女儿会这样做。在没有认真活过之前她是不会离开的。"

我建议了几个可能会帮助解决她女儿医药费的机构。"噢，我知道这些机构，"她说，"我们正在做这些事。而且为了得到一份体面的工作，这个年纪的我开始在这儿上大学！"她笑了："贝尔会喜欢我这样做的！那些年轻人不认为工作就在那里。但如果你努力寻找并且不怕脏是可以找到的。我会找到一份工作的。"她晃了晃她的袋子，罐子哗啦哗啦作响。"这不是垃圾，也不是可循环利用的铝，这是闪亮的五分镍币。"

——加勒特·鲍曼

Power Out

停电

My riches consist not in the extent of my possessions, but in the fewness of my wants.

—J. Brotherton

I awoke to a silent chill. In my cottage, no clocks blinked, no refrigerator hummed. In this rural Oregon coast area, power pauses are frequent: a minute, an hour, sometimes three. Then, eventually there's that cascade of welcome sound—buzz, blink, hum and whirr—as radio, refrigerator, clock, computer, TV, heater and answering machine snap back to life.

I've made it through numerous power failures. No light, no heat, no sound—all that I can handle. But I can't function without morning coffee. I could have built a fire on the stone patio outside my back door and heated water. But it was pouring rain. I could have hiked up the hill to my neighbor's, to see if Jenn had coffee perking on her camp stove. But wind whipped through tree branches. At least the phone was working.

I telephoned my boss. "It's going to be a long time before the lines are repaired," she said. "Hunker down. Work's cancelled. There's emergency food and shelter in town at the Methodist Church." Groping in the dim morning light, I excavated a lantern and my down sleeping bag from the back of my closet. I set the lantern on the kitchen counter, reread the instructions, struck a match and lit the mantle.

Blessings to Coleman for inventing this marvel. The metal top heated quickly. Maybe coffee was possible after all. But what balances on a conical lantern lid? I attempted to heat water by balancing a thick-bottomed saucepan, then discovered a tomato sauce can from my recycling bin worked best. After rinsing and filling the can with clean water, I put on potholder mitts and steadied the tin with two plastic chopsticks. Soon a mini-cup of instant coffee steamed fragrantly. Four tins later, I'd enjoyed a jolt of caffeine and even had a half-cup of hot water for a spit bath. I relished the simple pleasure of a warm washrag on my face. It would ready me to cope with the powerless day.

I put on an old feather parka and sheepskin booties. Gathering several books from my bedside stand, I zipped up the parka, tied the hood tight and crawled into my sleeping bag. I adjusted the lantern and snuggled in to read. Descriptive passages from *Under the Tuscan Sun* transported me to sunny Cortona with Frances Mayes while outside my window the thermometer read thirty-four degrees. Poorly insulated, my old cottage was chilly and damp. Turning pages, my fingertips grew numb. I wiggled out of my down bag to search for wool gloves. I was mentally listing friends with wood stoves, yet I relished the thought of some solitude. Then my neighbor Jenn drove up. "I'm going to my boyfriend's," she said, poking her head inside my door.

"That's seventy miles and mud slides along the road." I was concerned.

"Lucky man has power. Lucky me. You're welcome to stay in my house,

use the wood stove, except I'm out of wood. Keep company with my Lab and kitty. They'll keep you warm."

Walking back toward her vehicle, she added, "Oh, there's brandy left from the party. Help yourself to anything." My vision of a warm wood stove was about to become a reality.

I assumed there would be no problem finding wood. We live in a forest. Branches and twigs litter the ground. I scoured the yard, gullies and roadside, but found only water-soaked wood. Chopping branches kept me sweating for hours.

That night the temperature plummeted to well below freezing. With a barely smoldering fire, I needed multiple layers of clothing and three sleeping bags to keep me warm. The cat and dog curled up with me. We survived. The next day was much like the first: hunting for wood, chopping branches, feeding the fire torn cardboard and scrunched up newspapers—anything to get the wet wood to burn. Outside the window, fir trees thrashed in the wind. While I watched the storm, the aroma of spicy lentil soup simmering on the stove wafted in the air.

On the third morning without electricity, I was desperate for dry wood that could fit into the stove without hours of chopping. I walked back to my cottage and hunted in closets, in cupboards and under the bed for wooden objects to burn. I scanned the walls, shelves and tables. In desperation I grabbed the engraved plaques from Toastmasters, the wooden clock my ex-husband had made, a redwood jewelry box, garage sale picture frames waiting for family photos, knickknack shelves that needed glue.

At first, it seemed like a crime to burn my teakwood tongs and salad bowls, but I rarely used them. Torching Grandma's rolling pin struck me as taboo, but it was moldy and missing one handle. I wrestled with the idea of burning my walnut bookshelf. No way! Instead, I stacked wet branches on

Jenn's porch, getting them out of the rain, then sawed them into stove lengths and brought them in to dry near the fire. Who knew how long the power would be out?

I'd always intended to purge my cottage. Now, desperation pushed me past intention into action. For each wooden item, I quizzed myself: "Do I love this? Do I need this?" Soon objects were heaped by the door: the driftwood lamp, the myrtle wood breadbox, the dilapidated three-legged plant stand. As I whacked each item apart with a hammer, I began to feel a sense of inner strength. I hauled the wooden pieces up to Jenn's house. After I shoved the forlorn keepsakes and family artifacts into the wood stove, I realized the power outage had filled me with intent and courage—a ritual release of my past.

While the crackling fire in the stove cranked out heat, I peeled off parka, sweater and turtleneck, rocked in an overstuffed easy chair and sipped apricot brandy, while snuggling with the pets. A pot of Swiss fondue bubbled on the stove and my cup steamed with hot coffee. Looking around, I appreciated Jenn's simple décor and reflected on how her energetic spirit seemed rarely weighted down. I picked up my pen and wrote Jenn a thank-you poem and decided that next Christmas I'd tell her boyfriend to buy her a mini chain saw.

Having to survive without electricity for eighty-four hours I developed a new appreciation for light, heat and an electric stove. I was also grateful for the experience. I'd burned relics that had cluttered my life. Thanks to the blackout, to Jenn, and to fire, the great purifier, I felt empowered and warm all over. My possessions were fewer, my blessings greater.

—Shinan Barclay

我富有不是因为我拥有的多，而是在于我计较的少。

——J.布拉泽顿

　　我醒来时，周围一片冷飕飕的静寂。我的小屋里，没有时钟的嘀嗒声，也没有冰箱在嗡嗡作响。在这片俄勒冈的边缘海岸带，停电并不新鲜，有时是一分钟，有时是一小时甚至三小时。然后，令人欢欣的声音终于喷涌而来——嗡嗡声、啪嗒声、嘀嗒声和呼呼声——收音机、冰箱、时钟、电脑、电视机、加热器和答录机迅速恢复运转。

　　我已经历过不计其数的电源故障。没有灯光、没有热度也没有声音——这些我都可以应付，但是早晨不喝咖啡却是万万不行的。我本可以在后门外的石台上生火烧水，但是外面暴雨如注。我本可以上山去求助邻居珍，看看她屋里的火炉上有没有咖啡在煮，但是屋外风在呼啸着抽动树枝。至少电话还可以用。

　　我打电话给我的上司。"电线修好还需要很长一段时间，"她说，"不要慌张，工作取消了，在镇上的卫理公会教堂有应急食物和庇护所。"借着朦胧的晨光，我摸索着从衣橱的里层找出提灯和羽绒睡袋。我将提灯放在厨房的柜台上，重新阅读了说明书，划了一根火柴点亮了纱罩。

感谢科尔曼的这一伟大发明，金属顶部迅速热了起来，也许我终究能喝上咖啡的。但是用什么放在上面才能和圆锥形的提灯盖吻合呢？我首先尝试架上一个厚底的平底锅来烧水，后来从我的回收物储备箱中发现了一个番茄酱罐，适合用来烧水。

我将罐子洗过后倒入清水，然后戴上隔热手套用两根塑料筷子将其固定，很快一小杯速溶咖啡就散发出了诱人的香气。四罐下肚后，我享受着咖啡因带来的清醒，甚至还烧了半杯热水用来稍做梳洗。我很享受湿热的毛巾轻抚脸颊的简单乐趣，它让我为接下来停电的日子做好准备。

我穿上我的旧毛皮大衣和羊皮靴，从床头柜拿了几本书，拉上大衣、系紧风帽后爬进了睡袋。调整了一下提灯，靠近它，我开始阅读。《托斯卡纳艳阳下》中的描写让我和弗朗西斯·梅斯一起感受托斯卡纳的明媚阳光，而当时温度计显示窗外是三十四华氏度。我的旧屋舍没有很好的防护设施，又阴又冷。翻着翻着，我的手指僵硬起来。我扭动着爬出羽绒睡袋，去找羊毛手套。我在脑海中搜寻着有柴炉的朋友，还有一些享受独处的乐趣。这时我的邻居珍开车过来了，"我要去我男朋友家看看。"她边说边将头探进门里来。

我不无担心地说："那儿离这儿有七十英里，路面泥泞，湿滑不堪啊。"

"受上帝庇护的人是充满力量的，我是上帝的孩子。欢迎你来我家共享柴炉，只是我家的木柴烧完了。有我的猎犬和小猫和你做伴，它们会让你温暖的。"

说完她返回停车处，边走边补充了一句："噢，还有派对剩下来的白兰地。请一切随意。"我对一个温暖柴炉的渴望即将成真了。

我本以为找木柴是毫不费力的，因为我们住在森林中，地上铺满了枯枝落叶。寻遍院落、沟渠和路边，我能发现的只有被雨水浸透的木柴。数小时的砍柴让我汗流不止。

那夜温度直降至冰点以下。仅靠不温不火的炉火是不行的，我需要多穿几层衣服和用三个睡袋来保暖。珍的猫和狗在我身边蜷缩成一团，我们熬过了那一夜。接下来的一天跟第一天非常相似：找木柴、劈柴，撕纸板、将报纸揉成团，来维持火苗——只要能让湿木柴燃烧起来的物品我都会拿来用。窗外的杉树枝在风中瑟缩。就在我目光停留在窗外暴风雨时，炉上辛辣扁豆汤煨出的香气在空气中弥散开来。

在断电的第三个早晨，我已不抱希望能找到不需要劈上几小时就能填到火炉中去的干木柴了。我走回自己家，在衣橱、碗橱中和床底下寻找能烧的木制品，我扫视墙壁、书架和桌子。绝望中，我一把抓起雕刻着演讲词的饰板、前夫制作的木钟、红木首饰盒、旧货市场淘来的用来放家庭照片的相框和需要涂胶的小饰品架。

刚开始，烧掉柚木火钳和沙拉碗让我充满犯罪感，但我很少使用它们。点燃祖母留下的擀面杖就像大不敬冲击着我的心灵，但它已经发了霉且掉了一个把手。我内心激烈挣扎着要不要烧掉我的胡桃木书架。不可以！取而代之，我将湿树枝整齐堆放在珍的门廊里，让它们避免再次淋湿，然后根据火炉尺寸将其锯成合适的长短，拿进屋里放在炉边烘烤。谁又能知道要停电多长时间呢？

我一直想清理一下自己的房子。现在，绝望促使我将计划付诸行动。面对每一个木制品，我都扪心自问："我喜欢它吗？我需要它吗？"很快物品都堆积在门边：浮木台灯，香桃木面包盒，残缺的三腿花草台架。当我将这些物品用锤子逐一敲击时，我开始感受到一种来自心底深处的力量。我将这些木片运到了珍的家中。将这些孤独的纪念品和家庭装饰品推到了柴炉后，我意识到断电后的经历给了我满足感和勇气——一种告别过去的仪式上的释放。

伴着噼啪作响的炉火带来的热量，我脱下了毛皮大衣、毛衣和高领毛衫，陪伴着依偎在旁的小宠物，在舒软的安乐椅中晃动着，小酌杏色的白兰地。一小壶瑞士干酪在火炉上呼呼冒泡，杯中的咖啡热气腾腾。环顾四周，我欣赏着珍家里的简单装饰，一下子明白了为何她精力充沛，极少沮丧。我提笔为珍写了一首感谢诗，同时决定下个圣诞节提醒她的男友为她买一把迷你链锯。

在度过了八十四小时的无电时光后，我对光、热和电炉产生了一种新的感恩之情，我也很感激这段经历，我烧掉了生活中杂乱的遗留物。感谢停电，感谢珍，感谢火——伟大的净化器，我感觉周身重新充满力量，无限温暖。财物变少了，我却更加幸福了。

——世南·巴克利

One Hundred Blessings
一百个赐福

If you count all your assets, you always show a profit.
—Robert Quillen

One day, while I was going through tough times, I read a book that challenged me to stop feeling sorry for myself and instead, list one hundred blessings in my life. Since I was wallowing in my dark mood it seemed like an impossible task. But as soon as I began to randomly write down the positive things in my life, I was amazed how quickly one hundred blessings spilled onto the page. Soon my furrowed brow disappeared and I began to smile.

Afterwards, when I read though my long list of blessings I realized… I could easily add a hundred more.

Life is good.

100 Blessings

1. Being alive

2. Being healthy

3. Being able to exercise

4. Being an American

5. Having enough money

6. Husband Jim

7. Married for 47 years

8. Daughter Betsy

9. Daughter Lori

10. Son Steve

11. Grandchild Rachel

12. Grandchild Adam

13. Grandchild Kyle

14. Grandchild Sarah

15. Grandchild Emma

16. Grandchild Amy

17. Grandchild Anna

18. Grandchild Ava

19. Grandchild Andrew

20. Son-in-law Geoff

21. Son-in-law Matt

22. Daughter-in-law Stephanie

23. Writers

24. Writing group

25. Writing talent

26. *Chicken Soup for the Soul* books

27. Editors publishing me

28. Beautiful home

29. Courtyard

30. Decorating talent

31. Waterfront view

32. Dolphin encounters

33. Little boat

34. My car

35. Music

36. Flowers

37. Good food

38. Sale of farm

39. Memories

40. Computer

41. Cousin Lyz

42. Clothes

43. Parties

44. Good books

45. Backrubs

46. Holidays

47. Good teeth

48. Shopping bargains

49. Laughter

50. Hanging out with my kids

51. My kitchen

52. My laundry room

53. Antiques

54. Christmas trees

55. Freedom

56. Mild climate

57. Coconut palms

58. Healing

59. Travel

60. Kindness from others

61. Stimulating conversations

62. Walks in the neighborhood

63. Sunrises and sunsets

64. Birds at birdfeeder

65. Deck

66. Comfortable bed

67. Antique bedstead

68. Fireplace

69. Education

70. Retired from teaching

71. Interesting TV

72. Peaceful beach

73. Good tenants in our rentals

74. Family adventures

75. Church

76. Safety from harm

77. Comfort

78. Quiet neighborhood

79. New job in retirement

80. Beauty of nature

81. Precious moments

82. Glad I lived this long

83. Special friendships

84. Free time

85. Gardening

86. People who respond to me

87. A good doctor

88. A future

89. Smiles from others

90. Forgiveness

91. Praise

92. A teaching career

93. No major disasters in life

94. Free of cancer

95. A good night's sleep

96. Relationship with God/Christ

97. Two *Bible* studies

98. Electricity

99. Air conditioning

100. That I have 100 things to be grateful for

—Miriam Hill

清算自己的财富，你总会有所收获。

——罗伯特·奎伦

　　一天，正身处困境的我在读了一本书后促使自己停下来，不再自哀自怜，取而代之，我逐一列出我生命中的一百个赐福。鉴于彼时我正沉溺于自己的暗淡情绪中，这看上去是一个不可能完成的任务。然而一动笔开始随意写下自己生活中的积极面，我就惊讶于一百个赐福喷涌到纸面的速度。很快，我紧锁的眉头舒展开了，我笑了起来。

　　随后，当我通读自己长长的赐福列单时我意识到……我可以很轻松地再加上一百条。

　　生活是美好的。

　　一百个赐福

　　1. 活着

　　2. 身体健康

　　3. 能够锻炼

　　4. 是一个美国人

　　5. 有足够的金钱

　　6. 丈夫是吉姆

　　7. 已婚四十七年

8．有女儿贝琪

9．有女儿洛丽

10．有儿子史蒂夫

11．有外孙女雷切尔

12．有外孙亚当

13．有外孙凯尔

14．有外孙女萨拉

15．有外孙女埃玛

16．有外孙女埃米

17．有外孙女安娜

18．有孙子阿瓦

19．有孙子安德鲁

20．有女婿杰弗

21．有女婿麦特

22．有儿媳妇斯蒂芬妮

23．是作家

24．是作家协会成员

25．有写作天赋

26．为《心灵鸡汤》系列励志书籍撰稿

27．编辑们帮助出版我的文章

28．家园美丽

29．有庭院

30．有装饰天赋

31．看得到海滨风光

32．邂逅过海豚

33. 拥有一条小船

34. 有车

35. 喜欢音乐

36. 喜欢花草

37. 有美食享用

38. 销售农产品

39. 拥有回忆

40. 有电脑

41. 有堂兄莱兹

42. 有衣服穿

43. 有派对参加

44. 有好书读

45. 有备份

46. 有假期

47. 牙齿健康

48. 购物会砍价

49. 爱笑

50. 和孩子们打成一片

51. 厨房合心意

52. 洗衣间合心意

53. 有珍藏的古董

54. 有圣诞树

55. 享有自由

56. 气候温和

57. 有椰树

58. 分歧消除

59. 可以到处走走

60. 被友善相待

61. 能够推动谈话

62. 邻里关系和睦

63. 看得到日出日落

64. 有鸟儿喂养

65. 拥有甲板

66. 床很舒服

67. 有古董床架

68. 有壁炉

69. 受过教育

70. 从教职岗位退休

71. 有感兴趣的电视节目

72. 有安宁的海滩

73. 有好的租客

74. 喜欢家庭冒险

75. 可以去教堂

76. 远离伤害，享有安全

77. 生活舒适

78. 邻里环境安静

79. 退休后有份新工作

80. 大自然充满魅力

81. 有珍惜的瞬间

82. 感恩活到这么久

83. 有特别的友谊

84. 有闲暇时间

85. 享受园艺工作

86. 有给予我回应的人

87. 有优秀的医生

88. 拥有未来

89. 来自他人的微笑

90. 对人宽容

91. 善于赞赏他人

92. 有一份育人事业

93. 生命中没有重大疾病

94. 未患癌症

95. 夜晚睡眠质量高

96. 信仰上帝和基督

97. 从事两项有关《圣经》的研究工作

98. 有电

99. 有空调

100. 有一百件事情值得我感恩

——米丽亚姆·希尔

316_

Death Star
死亡之星

If the skies fall, one may hope to catch larks.

—Francis Rabelais

The Ides of March is layoff notice day. As a teacher and the teachers' union representative, it is a day I dread. It is the day the victims get their notice. The meetings are brief and wretched. It is hard to shake the gloom.

After the painful meeting, I rounded a corner to return to my classroom and bumped into a former student's father. His daughter had been in my class the previous year. Three months earlier, he had been shot by a gang member—a fourteen-year-old who had been in my fifth grade class. A boy who had written to me twice from prison, most recently that Friday. It was jarring to see the man stand a foot in front of me and know that at home I had two letters from the student who had shot him.

What do you say to someone who's been shot?

Chicken Soup for the Soul 每天读一篇美丽英文
心灵鸡汤 每一次跌倒，都是最好的成长

I opened with, "So, I heard you had some troubles."

The man lifted his draped black jacket and showed a bandaged shoulder, "Got shot, lucky to be here."

"What did you get hit with… a 22, a 38?"

"25 caliber."

"Good luck. Got to go."

I left and shook my head in disbelief. It was turning out to be a dark and very strange day. Layoff notices, I get a letter from a teenage shooter and then I see the victim. What else would go wrong?

I later ate lunch off campus with a fellow teacher and when we crossed the road a car screeched to a stop. Someone lowered the passenger window and a face beamed at me. "Hey, Mr. Karrer. I got it. I got it two weeks ago!"

The boy in the car, Zavier, was my former student. He'd been on dialysis for most of his twelve years, slept at death's door, and had lucked out finally getting a kidney transplant two weeks ago. His mom, the driver, said, "Show him."

Zavier opened the door, climbed out, and lifted up his shirt.

A nasty, six-inch horizontal scar started near his belly button, then made a vertical ninety degree upward turn for another six inches.

"Best scar I've ever seen," I said.

His mom, still sitting in the driver's seat, held up a huge plastic container filled with prescription drugs. "He needs thirty pills a day for the rest of his life."

The boy stepped closer and gave me a hug. He beamed and I couldn't help but notice his red cheeks and healthy skin. Last year he held his head low, his skin was gun-barrel blue, and he grimaced most of the day.

He stepped back in the car. "You got a second chance kiddo," I said.

"Same exact thing I told him," his mom said. "We didn't think he'd make it past last year and now he's twelve."

"Yeah and remember I almost killed him too."

We were all quiet for a second. THAT had been scary.

***

Last year, in the teachers' lounge, a fellow teacher had asked, "Mr. Karrer, would you like some star fruit for your kids?"

She smiled and sliced pieces of fruit one-tenth of an inch thick and tossed them into a huge green, plastic container.

"Sure. Where are they from? So I can tell the kids."

"Taiwan."

"Okay." Taiwan?

I gave a piece to each kid but the supposed Taiwanese origin bugged me. I booted up the computer to Google star fruit.

"Star Fruit—Carambola

Originally from Sri Lanka… blah blah blah…

IMPORTANT NOTE:

Star fruit causes several symptoms in patients with chronic renal failure or end-stage renal disease. The symptoms include insomnia, intractable hiccups, agitation, muscle weakness, confusion, consciousness disturbances of various degrees, seizures, and cardio-respiratory arrest. Because no effective treatment is currently available, patients must be warned not to ingest star fruit, even in small amounts."

I stared at Zavier Mendoza. Renal failure meant failing kidneys. I stood and looked at Zavier. He caught me, smiled and licked his fingers.

"Zavier." I tried to remain calm, "Where… is your star fruit?"

He smiled and pointed at his stomach. I turned pale.

"Zavier. You and I need to go to the office, now!"

We made it to the office. He sat and I shut the door behind him. I cornered a secretary. "Get the principal ASAP."

Long and short of it, we called Stanford—the kidney center where Zavier went every single week—and they said they didn't know about star fruit, but watch the kid like a hawk, and they'd call back in a minute. In less than one minute Stanford called back. "You taught us something today. Star fruit can kill him. We have a helicopter on the ready. Keep an eye on the kid. We're in the air if he starts hiccupping. Can we land in the school ground if we need to?"

Zavier Mendoza never hiccupped. The helicopter never needed to come. He was fine. He came to school the next day with a big, fat grin on his mug. But I didn't sleep too well. Apparently there are different kinds of star fruit. That had been a year ago.

***

Zavier put on his seatbelt and looked at me. "Mr. Karrer? You know when we went up to the office last year cuz of the fruit? I never seen you run so fast. Even when we did laps."

I shook my head. "Well, promise me no more star fruit for you—EVER!"

"Duh… Mr. Karrer. Duh…. Cuz YOU might get a heart attack and you'll need the chopper to Stanford."

We all laughed. They waved and I did the same.

Some terrible days can end very, very well.

—Paul H. Karrer

如果天空塌下来，我们仍可寄希望于捕获几只云雀。

——弗朗西斯·拉伯雷

3月15日是发布解雇人员名单的日子。作为一名教师和教协代表，这是一个我惧怕的日子，这是一个受害者面对布告的日子。会议简短，气氛凝重，我无法摆脱沮丧的情绪。令人心碎的会议结束后，我转身返回教室，途中突然碰到了去年曾就读于我们班级的一个女学生的父亲。三个月前，他被一名歹徒——一个十四岁的学生射伤，这个学生五年级时是我的学生，那个星期五前后他刚从狱中给我写了两封信。面对站在我面前仅一尺之隔的这个男人，想着家里尚存着的那个射伤他的学生的两封信，我不由得心跳加速。

你们都和被射伤的人说什么呢？我开口道："那个，我听说你碰到了些麻烦。"

面前的男人掀开他披着的黑夹克，露出绑着绷带的肩膀，说："被枪击中了，很幸运还能站在这儿。"

"你是被多大口径的枪射中的……二十二还是三十八？"

"二十五口径的。"

"祝您好运。我得走了。"

我难以置信地摇着头走开了。这是一个黑暗阴沉又非常离奇的日子。先是解雇通告，我收到了一个少年枪击犯的来信，之后又碰到了受害者本人。还有什么会这么离奇？

之后，我和一个同事一起到校外吃午餐，当我们过马路时一辆车急刹车停了下来。乘客座的车窗打开，一张脸出现在我面前："你好，卡勒尔先生。我得到了，两个星期前我得到了！"

车里的男孩儿，扎维尔，是我之前的学生。十二年来他的大部分时间都在做透析，在死亡之门前徘徊，他终于幸运地在两个星期前做了肾脏移植手术。他母亲坐在驾驶座上，说道："给老师看看。"

扎维尔打开车门爬出来，把衬衣掀上去。

一道可怕的六英寸长的疤痕从肚脐旁延展开来，然后垂直向上还有另外一道六英寸长的疤痕。

"这是有史以来我见过的最美的疤痕。"我说。

他妈妈仍然坐在驾驶座上，举起一个巨大的装满处方药的塑料容器，"他的余生每天都需要吃三十粒药。"

男孩儿走近我，给我一个拥抱。他面带微笑，我不禁注意到他红润的面庞和健康的肤色。去年他一直低着头，他的皮肤呈枪管青色，一天中大部分时间面部都痛苦地扭曲着。

他退回车中。"你获得了重生，孩子。"我说道。

"我正是这样跟他说的。"他妈妈说道，"我们以为他活不过去年，现在他都已经十二岁了。"

"是啊，记得我也几乎把他毁了。"

我们都沉默了一下。那是非常可怕的往事。

去年，在教师休息室，一个同事问我："卡勒尔先生，你想为你的学生们分点儿杨桃吗？"

她笑着将杨桃切成十分之一英寸厚的片状，然后将它们放进一个很大的绿色塑料容器里。

"当然。这是从哪里运过来的？我可以告诉我的学生。"

"从台湾。"

"好的。"台湾？我给每个孩子分了一片杨桃，但台湾是原产地的假设却让我将信将疑。我打开电脑搜索"杨桃"。

"杨桃——又称五敛子，原产地斯里兰卡……

"注意：

"慢性肾功能衰竭或末期肾脏疾病患者食用杨桃会引发一些症状。这些症状包括失眠、顽固性呃逆、躁动、肌肉无力、迷糊、不同程度的意识障碍、癫痫和心肺功能骤停。鉴于目前尚没有治疗的有效措施，病人必须警惕切勿食用杨桃，即使少量也不行。"

我盯着扎维尔·门多萨。肾功能衰竭意思是肾脏衰弱。我站着看着扎维尔。他发现我在看他，微笑着舔了舔手指。

"扎维尔，"我努力保持镇定，"你的杨桃……到哪儿去了？"

他笑着指了指肚子。我脸色煞白。

"扎维尔，你跟我去办公室，现在就去！"

我们终于到了办公室，他坐下来，我在他身后关上了门。我走投无路求救秘书："赶快把校长找来。"

在短暂的煎熬等待后，我们给斯坦福大学——扎维尔每个星期都要去的肾病研究中心打去电话——得到的答复是他们不熟悉杨桃，但要我们好好看护这个孩子，他们会很快打回来。

不到一分钟，斯坦福那边就回了电话："你们今天教会我们一些知识，杨桃对他是致命的。我们有一架直升飞机随时待命，好好看护这个孩子，只要他一出现打嗝儿症状我们马上就起飞，如果需要，我们可以在学校的场地降落吗？"

扎维尔·门多萨一直没有打嗝儿，直升飞机也没有飞过来，他很好。第二天他带着一个大杯子来学校，杯子上有灿烂的笑容，但我却没能睡好。很显然杨桃分很多种。那已经是一年前的事情了。

扎维尔系上安全带然后看着我："卡勒尔先生？你还记得去年我们因为杨桃去办公室的时候吗？我从来没见你跑得那么快，即使在我们赛跑时也没有那么快。"

我摇了摇头："那么，答应我不要再吃杨桃了——永远都不要！"

"嗯……卡勒尔先生。嗯……也许有一天你心脏病发作会需要那架直升机带你去斯坦福大学的。"

我们都笑了起来，挥手告别。

有些糟糕的日子结局却可以非常美好。

——保罗·H. 卡勒尔

From Nuisance to Blessing
从讨厌到喜欢

A dog is one of the remaining reasons why some people can be persuaded to go for a walk.

—O.A. Battista

From the first, I thought of him privately as Natty the Nuisance. My husband had picked up the puppy as a freebie from the Flour Mill, a local feed and hardware store where people bring unwanted litters. He'd been advertised as a Great Pyrenees mix, but he looked more like a Heinz 57 to me.

"Look, isn't he a lively one?"

Ken set the black ball of fur on the floor and our usually aloof adult female Akita bounded over to nuzzle him. She immediately flopped on the floor and rolled over on her back so that he could pounce on her belly and gnaw on her ankle.

"I just know this mutt will be a great companion for her," Ken said. "She's been lonely."

I just stared at the rollicking seven-week-old pup. That's just what I needed… another creature to pick up after, and a shaggy one, too. What a nuisance!

Besides the dogs, three cats also shared our house. I liked animals in theory, but Ken had been ailing for years, so feeding, grooming, walking and cleaning up after all of them fell on me.

I muttered through the weeks of mopping up messes until Natty was housebroken. I grumbled until he finally learned to lap water out of a bowl without tipping it over. He sensed I was not his fondest fan, and spent most of his time curled up in Ken's lap. When he got too big for that, he settled for resting his nose on Ken's knee as my ailing husband idled away his days watching reruns of *Gunsmoke and Cheyenne*. Whenever I walked into the living room, Natty would cast me a mournful glance, and then bound over to Ken's recliner to snag some petting.

The only time Natty ever came near me was when I ran a comb through our Akita's coat or cuddled a cat. Then he'd scamper over and nose my hand away from the other pet. If I ignored him and continued to groom or caress, he'd whine and whimper, and then poke my hand again, harder. A total nuisance, I'd say to myself, the world's biggest pest.

"I've never seen an animal that craved so much attention," I'd complain.

"Oh, he's just a puppy," Ken would say. "He'll outgrow it."

But he never did. Then last spring my husband died. In the days that followed, Natty's neediness quadrupled. He'd avoided me before, but now he wouldn't let me out of his sight. He'd track me from room to room, and if I settled down to read or to work on the computer, he'd immediately sidle up and start nudging my arm.

I felt sorry for him. Ken had been his constant companion. I know dogs mourn loss just as we humans do. Nonetheless, I didn't appreciate the annoying interruptions. I wondered vaguely if I should find another home for him, one where he could get all the attention he hungered for... maybe a family with children to play with. I had my Akita as a guard dog, so I couldn't figure out what purpose Natty really served.

Nearing his sixth birthday, which should be middle age for a dog of his size, Natty suddenly seemed to be sliding into an early senescence. I noticed that he spent most of his time in the backyard just lazing on the grass, watching the birds and occasionally barking as a truck passed the house. Where he used to shoot back and forth from the patio to the apple tree, now, if he even bothered to get up, he'd plod slowly across the lawn.

Kind of like me, I thought. But I'm well into my seventies and this dog was far too young to have severe arthritis as I do.

When I took Natty in for his annual checkup and shots, the vet didn't pull punches.

"No arthritis. He's pretty healthy. But he's overweight, and should lose around twenty-five pounds. I know it's hard, but see if you can walk him more."

I sighed. I needed to lose twenty-five pounds, too. I'd packed on weight during my husband's decline. In grief, I'd comforted myself with creamy casseroles and carrot cake. And though I lived on a country loop frequented by walkers, joggers and bikers, I found endless excuses to avoid walking that mile-long course myself. It was too hot. It was too cold. I was too tired. I was too old.

Twice daily I'd been taking the leashed Akita for a brief stroll up and down in front of my property, with Natty trotting along beside us. But I hadn't walked the mutt around the loop since his puppyhood.

The next morning I dragged out Natty's old leash. While I snapped it onto his collar he thudded his tail against the front door. At least one of us was excited. I put on my jacket and mittens and the two of us set out.

To my surprise, Natty confidently lead the way, keeping a steady pace, not stopping to sniff at every twig the way his Akita sister does. He marched ahead, tugging me in his wake, not even pausing when neighbor dogs scrambled to the front of their owner's property to growl their territorial rights.

To my surprise, I enjoyed breathing in the scent of lilacs on the fresh spring air, feeling my heart beat a little faster from the mild exercise, even running my fingers through Natty's coarse fur when I reached down to pat him in approval when he heeled rather than strained to chase a passing car.

The next day we did it again. Then again. Soon we settled into a routine. If I grow too engrossed in catching up on my e-mail correspondence, around 10 AM Natty will be at my side, shoving his snout under my arm. Or if I become too distracted by household chores, he'll plant himself by the front door and rumble until I remember it's time for our walk.

Nowadays I see Natty as a blessing rather than a nuisance. Though the Akita remains my bodyguard, my elegant and diligent protector, scruffy Natty has become my personal untrained therapy dog. Together we're striding into shape.

He's nudged me into a new lease on life.

—Terri Elders

狗是仅剩的能够促使一些人去散散步的原因之一。

——O.A. 巴蒂斯塔

　　从一开始，我就私自认定他是讨厌的纳蒂。
这只宠物是我丈夫从磨坊免费认领的，那是当地
的一个饲料和五金店，聚集了人们拿来的不需要
的东西。宣传说他是大白熊狗，但对我来说他看
上去更像只杂种狗。

　　"看，他不是很活泼吗？"

　　肯把这黑茸茸的一团毛球放在地板上，我们
一向冷漠的青年母狗秋田突然跃过去，用鼻子蹭
他。然后她直接躺在地板上，背朝下翻过身来，
任纳蒂趴在她的腹部啃她的爪子。

　　"我就知道这个小家伙会是秋田很好的伴
儿，"肯说，"她太孤独了。"

　　我只是盯着这个快活的七个星期大的小幼
崽。这只是我需要照顾的……又一个动物，又是
毛茸茸的。多讨厌！

　　除了狗，我家还有三只猫。理论上来讲我是
喜欢动物的，但肯已经病了好些年，所以给他们
喂食、梳洗、带他们散步以及清理的工作都落在

了我的身上。

在纳蒂被驯服前，要为他清理粪便的这些日子，我一直很不满。直到他终于学会不打翻碗就能从里面喝到水我才不再抱怨。他觉出来我不喜欢他，于是大部分时间都蜷缩在肯的腿上。当他太大了不适合再那样做时，他就在我生病的丈夫靠看《硝烟和夏安族》的回放打发时光时坐下来把鼻子靠在肯的膝盖上。每当我走进客厅，纳蒂总会报以幽怨的眼神，然后跳上肯的躺椅去索取些许抚摸。

纳蒂唯一靠近我就是在我为秋田梳毛或抱起小猫的时候。然后他就会跑过来用鼻子蹭我的手让我从其他宠物身上挪开。如果我忽视他继续梳理或抚摸，他就会呜咽哀嚎，继而更用力地再次拨拉我的手。真是讨厌至极，我在心里想，世界上最让人讨厌的东西莫过于此了。

"我从来没见过有哪个动物这么爱抢风头。"我会抱怨道。

"噢，他只是只小狗嘛，"肯会说，"他长大后不会再这样的。"

但是他却从未改变。去年春天我丈夫去世了。接下来的几天里，纳蒂的需求更是变本加厉。以前都是躲着我，现在却时刻关注我的行踪。他跟着我从一个房间到另一个房间，如果我坐下来读书或者用电脑工作，他就马上挨近，开始轻推我的胳膊。

我可怜他，肯曾是他最忠实的伙伴。我知道动物和人一样会因失去真爱而悲伤。尽管如此，我仍不喜欢这种烦人的打扰。我隐约琢磨着是不是应该为他再找个家，一个能够给他他所渴望的所有关爱的家……也许找一个有孩子可以一块儿玩耍的家。我已有秋田来看家，所以我想不出纳蒂能有什么用。

六岁生日临近，这应该算是他这种体型的狗的中年了。纳蒂看上去一下子衰老了，过早地衰老。我注意到他大部分时间都只是躺在后院的草坪上看着鸟儿，偶尔当有卡车经过时叫两声。他以前常常在庭院和苹果树间来回飞奔，现在即使不情愿地站起来，也只是沉重缓慢地穿过草坪。

有点儿像我了，我想。但是我已年过七旬，这只狗太年轻了，不可能像我一样被严重的关节炎缠身。

当我带着纳蒂接受一年一次的检查并注射疫苗时，他都没有反抗。

"没得关节炎，他很健康，但他超重了，应该减掉大约二十五磅的重量。我知道这很难，但这得看你能不能多遛遛他。"

我叹了口气，我也需要减掉二十五磅，在丈夫生病的日子里我体重骤长。悲痛中，我暴食油腻的焙盘炖菜和胡萝卜蛋糕来缓解情绪。尽管我所在的环形区域常见步行者、慢跑者和自行车手，我却有无穷的借口来逃避走那一英里长的路线——天太热了，天太冷了，我太累了，我太老了……诸如此类。

我曾一天两次牵着秋田在房前上坡下坡简单地散散步，纳蒂在我们旁边慢跑。但自从纳蒂的青春期脾气上来后我再也没带他绕环形道走过。第二天早上我拉出纳蒂的旧皮带，当我将皮带套系到他项圈上的时候，他把尾巴啪地甩到了前门上。

至少我们当中有一个是兴奋的。我穿上夹克，戴上手套，我们两个出发了。

让我惊讶的是，纳蒂自信满满地带路，节奏平稳，没有像他的姐姐秋田一样遇到东西就停下来嗅上一番。他一路前行，拉着我，让我随着他的行迹走，甚至在邻居家狗疯了似的在门前狂吠着宣告领土权时也毫不停顿。

让我惊讶的是，我喜欢呼吸春天清新空气中弥漫的丁香的香气，喜欢自己心跳因适量的运动而加速的感觉。甚至喜欢手指穿过纳蒂粗糙的皮毛，那是我蹲下拍拍他作为对他跟在一辆过路车后而没有逞能追车的肯定。

第二天我们像前一天一样继续锻炼，接着是第三次，很快我们就固定下一条路线。如果我太聚精会神于赶着回复邮件，早上十点左右纳蒂就会出现在我身旁，用鼻子推我的胳膊。或者如果我因家庭杂事太过分心，他就会靠在前门上不停哼叫，直到我记起到我们散步的时间了。

现在我对纳蒂是喜爱而不再讨厌。尽管秋田仍是我的保镖，我优雅而聪明的守护者，邋遢的纳蒂却已成为我专属的未经训练的狗医生，我们一起大踏步恢复体形。

他将我推向了生活的新篇章。

——特里·埃尔德斯

Living in Barbie's Dream House
住在芭比梦之屋

The man who has no inner-life is a slave to his surroundings.
—Henri Frederic Amiel

Years before treading the murky waters of our dismal American economy, my husband and I challenged ourselves to seek the positive side of a simplified lifestyle. With eyes wide open we made a conscious choice to live within our means rather than kill ourselves living beyond them. Simplifying in many ways means doing without. For us the bottom line translates to a positive outcome though I must admit, it's not all sunshine and rainbows.

The house we've lived in for the past twenty years is a pretty good example of real estate with no bells or whistles. Most people refer to it as quaint, but frankly I've seen phone booths with more square footage than our living room. One or two things out of place in this small house and all of a sudden it looks as if I haven't done any housework since the

Reagan Administration.

If you're trying to picture our humble abode, it's not exactly Barbie's Dream House. It's probably the same size, but I imagine Barbie has better plumbing. We don't let it bother us. I'm confident it's only through the Grace of God that we enjoy indoor plumbing in the first place. So what if it's not possible to take a shower and run the dishwasher at the same time without risking a scalded appendage or two? Maybe the guy who invented paper plates suffered from the same problem, and look what it did for him!

Our "Graceland" was built 140 years ago on ground originally used to stable horses. About 141 years ago the horses left town, and I know why. The draft that blows through our living room in the winter could knock a Clydesdale off its feet. I'm the only person I know who dresses according to the wind chill factor—in the living room. As you might have guessed, I've amassed quite an extensive sweater collection, and there are days when I wear them all at the same time. If it's cold enough outside, I end up looking like the Michelin Man. But, it beats having to work sixty hours a week just to afford the mortgage payment on one of those houses with the newfangled, double-paned, insulated, energy-friendly windows I keep hearing about.

Over the past twenty years we have discovered what makes a house comfortable and it has nothing to do with acreage, inground pools, or multi-car garages. We have none of the above, unless you count the moat around the sump pump as an inground pool of water. Yet, people often remark about the cozy and inviting atmosphere that flourishes here. A home is comfortable and inviting when the occupants are relaxed and content. It's just that simple.

We don't watch our DVDs on a TV the size of a roadside billboard. Of course, we don't have a room large enough to accommodate one of those things anyway, but we do sit down together every night and relish each other's company over a home-cooked meal. Neither one of us is ever in a rush to get out the door to a second job.

On Sundays we savor a pot of coffee and the Sunday paper. We read it all afternoon if the mood strikes us. Well, the truth be told, it is a bit of a squeeze finding a spot on our downsized coffee table for the coffee pot and that big fat newspaper, especially if the idea of bagels and cream cheese enters the picture. Somehow we juggle things and make do.

We make no pretense of striving for the good life. We enjoy the good life every day. Free from the financial burden of keeping up with everyone else allows us time for laughter and fun. I imagine it's not easy to relax by the pool when you are robbing Peter to pay the pool man.

The price paid in time alone (not to mention stress and aggravation) to support state-of-the-art home theaters, flashy cars, and overpriced real estate, along with countless other so-called amenities is staggering. Without a doubt it quells the occasional twinge of envy I have over the luxuries of others. Our luxury is having no worries about how to pay for big-ticket toys.

We spend a great deal of time at home, cramped quarters, drafty rooms and all. I don't mind a bit when we are snuggled together on the couch under a cozy afghan enjoying an old movie, or out on the side porch sipping iced tea and basking in the beauty of a summer sunset.

Oh, we occasionally grumble about how grand it would be if we could take a shower and run the dishwasher at the same time, but we get over it.

Especially when we consider that at the close of last year we made our final mortgage payment on this little house, many years in advance of the scheduled payoff date. I'm positive we were not expecting this outcome when we made our decision to live a simplified life. It just turned out to be one of the perks.

—Annmarie B. Tait

没有内心生活的人是周围环境的奴隶。

——亨利·弗雷德里克·埃米尔

　　在涉足美国萧条经济污水的几年之前，丈夫和我就挑战自我，寻找简单生活方式的积极面。我们睁大双眼做了一个理智的选择，那就是按照力所能及的方式去生活而不是追求力所不能及的去自我毁灭。简化从很多方面意味着将就。对我们来说，最低标准也能转化成积极结果，尽管我必须承认，并不都是阳光和彩虹。

　　过去二十年我们住的屋子就是没有铃声、汽笛声的房产的佳例。大多数人称其为古色古香，但是坦白讲我见过很多电话亭都比我们客厅的面积大。在这个小屋子里如果有一两件东西乱了，猛然看上去就像我从里根执政时代就没有做过任何打扫一样。

　　如果你正尝试着想象我们的陋室，它并不完全像芭比的梦之屋。可能面积是一样的，但我想芭比有更好的管道装置。我们并不受它影响。首先我相信只有承蒙神恩我们才能够享受室内管道。那么即使如果同时洗澡和洗碗就可能烫坏一两个附属物又有什么关系呢？也许发明纸盘的人也遭遇了同样问题，但是看看这为他带来了什么！

我们的"雅苑"建于一百四十年前，这片土地本来是用来养马的。大约一百四十一年前马儿们离开了小镇，我知道其中缘由。冬天吹过我们客厅的劲风足以将强健的挽马击倒。我是我所知道的唯一一个在客厅中根据风寒因素来穿衣的人。你可能已经猜到了，我攒了大量的毛衣，有些日子我会同时把它们穿在身上。如果室外够冷，我看起来就像米其林先生（身体肥胖穿着臃肿的人）。但是，我不断听说，有人为了支付那些设计新颖、绝缘隔热、环境友好的双层玻璃窗而贷款，一星期必须工作六十小时以上。

在过去的二十年中我们已经发现是什么让房屋变得舒适，和面积、室内水池或多车车库无关，这些我们都没有，除非把污水泵附近的小水沟算作室内水池。然而，人们却经常谈论这里洋溢着的舒适诱人的气氛。只有当居住者放松且满足的时候一个家才会舒适诱人。就是这么简单。

我们不用街旁广告牌那么大的电视来看光碟。当然，不管怎么说，我们也没有房间大到能装得下那种东西，但是我们确实每天晚上都坐在一起陪伴着彼此共享家常便饭。我们两个人都不曾匆匆忙忙出门去找过第二份工作。

星期日我们会品一壶咖啡，读一读当天的报纸，如果兴致来了我们会读上一下午。其实说实话，在我们精简的咖啡桌上为咖啡壶和那份大报纸找个地方着实有些困难，更不用提再考虑加上面包圈和奶油干酪了。但我们总能想方设法变戏法似的完成任务。

我们从不伪装去争取好生活，我们每天都在享受好生活。没有跟他人攀比的经济压力让我们有时间来笑来闹。我想当你靠拆东墙补西墙来支付水池工工钱的时候是很难享受在游泳池中放松的乐趣的。

　　单是及时支付账单这一项（更不用提压力和恼怒），来维持最新式的家庭影院、花里胡哨的汽车和昂贵的房产，还有不计其数其他的所谓的享受品就足以令人咋舌。虽然我偶尔也需要克服因嫉妒别人的奢华生活带来的刺痛感。我们的奢华就是不必担心怎样去支付昂贵的大物件。

　　我们花大量的时间在家，在狭窄的住处、有穿堂风的房间待着。我丝毫不介意我们依偎在铺着舒软阿富汗毛毯的沙发上一起看部老电影，或是去走廊旁呷一口冰茶，沐浴在美丽的夏日余晖下。

　　哦，我们偶尔也会抱怨一下如果能同时洗澡和洗碗该多好，但我们已经克服了，尤其是当我们想到在去年年底我们已经比计划日期提前好多年付完了我们这套小房子的按揭贷款时。我很确信在我们决定简单生活时并没想到这个结果。它只是我们的额外收获之一。

——安玛丽·B. 泰特

Pressed, Stressed and Blessed
从紧迫的压力中感到幸福

There are no menial jobs, only menial attitudes.

—William J. Bennett, The Book of Virtues

I once saw a bumper sticker that read, "Too blessed to be stressed." I snorted, "Yeah, right. It's more like 'too stressed to be blessed.'" I was fifty-eight and heading to a job interview that paid a whopping eight dollars an hour and involved some lifting, mail sorting and conveyor work. I had planned to be semi-retired by this time, living off the benefits of a lovely investment—one that had unexpectedly gone south along with our economy. I had to give up health insurance and my body was beginning to tell me things I did not want to hear. I wallowed in my own pity party, remembering nostalgically how I once co-owned an export business that paid well, afforded me good vacations, international travel and a primo health insurance policy.

My body protested loudly for the first couple of months on the job and I was known to spit out an occasional expletive under my breath when a fifty-pound bag of mail got the best of me. I was determined to show the owner that this "old broad" could perform. I did everything and anything, usually before I was asked. This behavior sparked the "youngsters" on board to up their performance levels and the operations of the plant actually improved. My rah-rah attitude and outward appearance of boundless energy came at a price. I came home exhausted, whining and moaning for Bengay. My husband would disappear when he heard my car in the driveway. But eventually a transformation took place. My quads and biceps toned up and those flabby thingies on the backs of my upper arms disappeared. I lost weight and my back toughened up once I taught myself how to bend at the knees. And that blessed, sweaty little job not only helped pay bills but brought me at least two life-changing opportunities simply from chatting with clients who came by to drop off their orders.

The first was a writing contract that I landed from one of the clients who hired us to print and mail her marketing brochures. I noticed the text was a bit weak and unappealing from my point of view. I decided to approach her when she came by. After admiring her artwork I gulped down my fear and offered her a couple of suggestions to make the text "pop" a bit. She looked at me and asked, "What do you do here?" I stammered, "Well, I work here part-time doing this and that, but I also write." She gave me what I thought was an odd look and left. She must have thought I was an idiot, a presumptuous one at best. I was immediately immersed in self-doubt wondering if I had overstepped my bounds. Would I be fired? About a month later she came back in to talk to me personally. She told me she was impressed with my ideas and asked if I would consider doing some independent work helping with the text of her website and her bio. And I could work from my computer at home. Wow! I was being paid to write something and my hourly rate just tripled. Was it my imagination or did my body suddenly feel more energized and less tired?

The second opportunity came from the owner herself. Noting how much I took on and the way I worked with some of the clients, she nominated me to join an organization called Women of the Year in our community. She added, "It's a year-long commitment and you will meet some wonderful people." She was right. I did meet a woman who told me about a national organization called eWomen Network. I thought the initial fee a bit pricey, but within the first year I had ten new clients. It was at one of these eWomen Network monthly events that I spoke to the featured speaker, LeAnn Thieman, a wonderful, vibrant woman who was a nurse earlier in her career but is now a professional writer and public speaker. She also co-authors books for *Chicken Soup for the Soul*. "I love those books!" I gushed. I asked her if anyone could submit a story. She in turn asked me, "Do you have a story?" I responded yes and she told me how to go online and find instructions for making a submission. To my surprise and joy, my story was later accepted and published. Who would have thought that my personal experience with hot flashes would become a story that someone else might find interesting enough to publish?

Eventually, I quit my job sorting mail and lifting bags. The owner offered me a fifty-pound mailbag when I left, joking, "Here, I don't want you to get out of shape." I grinned at her but declined. I did thank her for the opportunity of working for her. It had been a blessing in disguise.

Today, as I sit here typing, my fountain bubbling in the background, my legs pumping away at the portable pedal cycle (much better than the mailbag) beneath my desk, I am smiling. Hindsight is an amazing tool to rethink my abundant blessings and how they came to be. Yes, I admit I feel pressed at times about a deadline or finances. Yes, I sometimes allow myself to worry about something that, in the long term, is not worth the effort. And we all know that worrying puts deep creases into the face right between the eyes, something I definitely do not need. If I am going to have lines in my face let them be from smiling in joy and gratitude. My husband says those lines are kind of cute. Does he know what to say, or what? Oh yes, indeed, I am blessed—too blessed to be stressed.

—Linda L. Leary

工作不分贵贱，态度决定一切。

————威廉 J. 贝内特，《关于美德》

    我曾在保险杠上看到一张招贴是这样说的："太幸福而不觉得有压力。"我嗤之以鼻："嗯，是的。更像是'太压抑而感觉不到幸福'。"五十八岁的我正要去参加一个工作面试，工资高达每小时八美元，包括一些搬运、整理邮件和运送工作。我本计划到这个年龄就退休了，靠一项明智投资的利润来生活——而计划却始料未及地随着我们的经济一起破灭了。我不得不放弃医疗保险，而我的身体已开始发出一些我并不想听的信号。我沉浸在自己的遗憾派对中，怀念自己也曾是一家利润丰厚的出口公司的合伙人，能支付愉快的假期、国外旅行和一流的健康保险的费用。

    在刚开始工作的两个星期里，我的身体严重抗议，偶尔五十磅重的邮袋会让我忍不住悄悄吐脏话。我下定决心做给老板看：这个"老家伙"也可以很出色。常常在被要求前我就会做好每一件事，不论什么事都做。这种行为激发了周围的"年轻人"提高工作水平，而且公司的实际运作效率也提高了。我卖力的态度和活力无限的表现也是需要付出代价的。回到家我已筋疲力尽，会跟本葛发牢骚。我丈夫听到我的车驶进车道就会躲起来。但是终于还是有了改变。

我的股四头肌和肱二头肌更强壮了，上臂后面那些松弛的赘肉也不见了。我体重减轻了，而且有次我试着弯膝时背部也可以挺起来了。更幸运的是，稍显吃力的工作不仅帮我支付了账单，而且给我带来了至少两次改变人生的机会，这都只是靠与来下订单的顾客交流得到的。

第一次是我接手来自一位顾客的书面合同，她雇我们为其印刷邮递市场宣传小册。在我眼里，册子的文字不够出色且不够吸引人。在赞美了其插图后，我克服胆怯向她提出两条建议来让文本"出彩"一点儿。她看着我问道："你在这儿是做什么的？"我结结巴巴地说道："我在这儿做兼职，打打杂，但我也从事写作。"她向我投来我认为怪异的目光然后离开了。她一定认为我是傻瓜，最多也不过是个自大狂。我一下子陷入了自我质疑，怀疑自己越界了。我会不会被开除？大约一个月后她返回来单独找我谈话。她说我的建议让她印象深刻，她问我能否考虑做一些独立工作，帮她处理网站文本及产品介绍，而且我可以在家用电脑工作。哇！我可以写东西赚钱了，而且我每小时的工资都成现在的三倍了。这是幻觉吗？我的身体突然感觉变得更加强健而不那么疲惫了。

第二个机会来自老板本人。注意到我承担的工作量及我与一些客户交流的方式后，她推荐我加入我们社区一个叫"妇女年"的组织。

她补充道："协议是一年，你将见到一些很棒的人。"她是对的，我确实遇到一个人告诉了我一个叫"妇女网"的国际组织。我觉得入会费有点儿高，但在第一年中我就得到了十个新客户。就是在一次妇女网每月例行的活动中，我和一位很杰出的发言者——利安·蒂曼交谈过。她是一个优秀且充满活力的女人，早前是护士，现在已是一位专业作家和大众演讲家。她也是《心灵鸡汤》系列丛书的合著者之一。"我很喜欢那套书！"我脱口而出。我问她是不是任何人都可以投递故事。她反问我："你有故事吗？"我回答说有。然后她告诉我怎么上网去找投递的相关要求。意料之外却又让我无限欣喜的是，我的故事随后就被采纳并发表了。谁会料到我更年期的个人经历会写成故事，而且他人会觉得足够有趣值得发表呢？

最终我辞掉了整理邮件和提包的工作。离开时老板给我一个五十磅重的邮包开玩笑道："我不想你的身材再走样！"我冲她笑了笑但是拒绝了。我确实感谢她给了我为她工作的机会。这是一份被掩饰了的幸福。

今天，当我坐在这儿敲字，背景中的喷泉在突突冒泡，桌下我的腿在便携式踏板（比邮包好多了）上活动着，我在微笑。后见之明是神奇的助推器，助我重新想想自己丰厚的祝福及它们的来历。是的，我承认有时面对截止日期或经济问题我会感到压力；是的，有时我会放任自己去担心一些长远看来根本不值得担心的事情。我们都知道担忧会在我们两眼之间留下深深的褶皱，这是我决不想要的。如果我的脸上注定要留下线条，那就让它们是开心和感激的微笑留下的吧。丈夫说那些线条有几分可爱。他知道在说什么，它又会是什么呢？噢，的确是的，我很幸福——太幸福而不觉得有压力。

——琳达·L.利里

Meet Our Authors
见见我们的作者

Jack Canfield is the co-creator of the *Chicken Soup for the Soul* series, which *Time* magazine has called "the publishing phenomenon of the decade." Jack is also the coauthor of many other bestselling books.

Jack is the CEO of the Canfield Training Group in Santa Barbara, California, and founder of the Foundation for Self-Esteem in Culver City, California. He has conducted intensive personal and professional development seminars on the principles of success for more than a million people in twenty-three countries, has spoken to hundreds of thousands of people at more than 1,000 corporations, universities, professional conferences and conventions, and has been seen by millions more on national television shows.

Jack has received many awards and honors, including three honorary doctorates and a Guinness World Records Certificate for having seven books from the *Chicken Soup for the Soul* series appearing on the *New York Times* bestseller list on May 24, 1998.

You can reach Jack at www.jackcanfield.com.

杰克·坎菲尔德是《心灵鸡汤》系列丛书的策划人之一，该系列曾被《时代周刊》赞为"十年来出版界的神话"。杰克同时也是其他很多畅销书的合著者。

杰克是加州圣塔芭芭拉市坎菲尔德集团的总裁，加州卡尔弗市自尊基金会的创始人。他给二十三个国家超过一百万人就成功原则举办过多次有关个人和职业发展的研讨会，在一千多个企业、大学、专业会议和大会对成千上万人做过演讲，在全国电视节目上的出色表现更是让数百万人一睹风采。

杰克曾获多项奖项和荣誉：他曾获得三个名誉博士学位，也曾因七本《心灵鸡汤》系列丛书同时荣登《纽约时报》1998年5月24日畅销书名单而获得国际吉尼斯世界纪录证书。

杰克的网址：www.jackcanfield.com。

Mark Victor Hansen is the co-founder of *Chicken Soup for the Soul*, along with Jack Canfield. He is a sought-after keynote speaker, bestselling author, and marketing maven. Mark's powerful messages of possibility, opportunity, and action have created powerful change in thousands of organizations and millions of individuals worldwide.

Mark is a prolific writer with many bestselling books in addition to the *Chicken Soup for the Soul* series. Mark has had a profound influence in the field of human potential through his library of audios, videos, and articles in the areas of big thinking, sales achievement, wealth building, publishing success, and personal and professional development. He is also the founder of the MEGA Seminar Series.

Mark has received numerous awards that honor his entrepreneurial spirit, philanthropic heart, and business acumen. He is a lifetime member of the Horatio Alger Association of Distinguished Americans.

You can reach Mark at www.markvictorhansen.com.

马克·维克托·汉森和杰克·坎菲尔德一起成立了《心灵鸡汤》编辑部。他是位广受欢迎的演讲者、畅销书作家及销售专家。马克强有力地向世人传达了关于可能性、机会和行动的信息，为全世界成千上万个机构以及数百万人带来了巨大的改变。

马克著作颇丰，除了《心灵鸡汤》系列外，他还著有许多畅销书。马克在人类智慧、销售成就、财富积累、出版奇迹和个人与职业发展方面著书立说，通过音频、视频和文章在人类潜力领域带来了巨大影响。他同时也是米加研讨会系列的创立者。

马克荣获多项大奖，表彰他的企业家精神、慈善之心以及商业头脑。他是霍雷肖·阿尔杰杰出美国人协会的终身成员。

马克的网址：www.markvictorhansen.com。

Amy Newmark is the publisher and editor-in-chief of *Chicken Soup for the Soul*, after a 30-year career as a writer, speaker, financial analyst, and business executive in the worlds of finance and telecommunications. Amy is a magna cum laude graduate of Harvard College, where she majored in Portuguese, minored in French, and traveled extensively. She and her husband have four grown children.

After a long career writing books on telecommunications, voluminous financial reports, business plans, and corporate press releases, *Chicken Soup for the Soul* is a breath of fresh air for Amy. She has fallen in love with *Chicken Soup for the Soul* and its life-changing books, and really enjoys putting these books together for *Chicken Soup*'s wonderful readers. She has co-authored more than two dozen *Chicken Soup for the Soul* books and has edited another two dozen.

You can reach Amy through the webmaster@chickensoupforthesoul.com.

艾米·纽马克是《心灵鸡汤》系列的出版者和主编，之前的三十年间，她是位作家、演说家、财政分析家以及财政和电信领域的商业行政主管。艾米是哈佛大学的优等毕业生，主修葡萄牙语，辅修法语，游历甚广。艾米与丈夫一起抚养了四个孩子，他们皆已长大成人。

艾米曾长期为电信学撰写书籍，也写了大量财务报告、商业计划和企业新闻稿。对艾米而言，《心灵鸡汤》系列像是一丝新鲜空气。她爱上了《心灵鸡汤》编辑部，很喜爱这改变人生的书籍，也以编辑这些书奉献给《心灵鸡汤》的读者为乐。她是三十多本《心灵鸡汤》的编者之一，还编辑了三十多本其他的书籍。

艾米的邮箱：webmaster@chickensoupforthesoul.com。

About Deborah Norville
德博拉·诺维尔简介

Bestselling author Deborah Norville credits many of the successes in her life to a positive mental attitude. The anchor of *Inside Edition*, the nation's top-rated syndicated news magazine, the journalist is a two-time Emmy winner.

Deborah is also the author of a half-dozen books including the *New York Times* bestseller, *Thank You Power: Making the Science of Gratitude Work for You. Thank You Power* brought together for the first time the growing body of academic research proving the benefits of gratitude. Similarly, *The Power of Respect* presented research detailing the benefits of respectful behavior with real life stories.

A lifelong seamstress and crafter, Deborah

recently introduced *The Deborah Norville Collection*, a line of fine hand yarns for knitting and crochet, available at craft stores nationwide.

Deborah Norville is a summa cum laude (4.0) graduate of the University of Georgia. She is married and the mother of three.

Deborah can be reached via her website www.DeborahNorville. com.

畅销书作者德波拉·诺维尔将人生中的多数成功归因于积极的心态。德波拉曾两次获得艾美奖，是国家顶级电视节目《新闻内幕》的节目主播。

德波拉还是几本《纽约时报》畅销书的作者，其中包括《谢谢你力量：让感谢的学问为你所用》。《谢谢你力量》首次用渐渐发展的学术研究证实感谢的益处。同时，《尊敬的力量》用研究向我们具体展示了真实故事中尊重行为的益处。

除此之外，德波拉还是女裁缝和手工艺人，她最近引进了德波拉·诺维尔系列，即可用来编织和钩边的精细手工纱线，在全国各地的手工店都有出售。

德波拉·诺维尔是佐治亚大学的优等毕业生，已婚，并育有三个孩子。

德波拉的网址：www.DeborahNorville.com。

Thank You
感谢词

We owe huge thanks to all of our contributors. We know that you pour your hearts and souls into the thousands of stories and poems that you share with us, and ultimately with each other. We appreciate your willingness to open up your lives to other *Chicken Soup for the Soul* readers.

We can only publish a small percentage of the stories that are submitted, but we read every single one and even the ones that do not appear in the book have an influence on us and on the final manuscript.

We want to thank *Chicken Soup for the Soul* editor Kristiana Glavin for reading every one of the thousands of stories that were submitted for this book, and narrowing down the candidates for final selection, as well as for her assistance with

Thank You
感谢词

the final manuscript and proofreading. We also want to thank our assistant publisher, D'ette Corona, who works closely with all the contributors, and our editor and webmaster Barbara LoMonaco for their expert editorial, proofreading, and organizational assistance.

We owe a very special thanks to our creative director and book producer, Brian Taylor at Pneuma Books, for his brilliant vision for our covers and interiors. Finally, none of this would be possible without the business and creative leadership of our CEO, Bill Rouhana, and our president, Bob Jacobs.

我们非常感谢所有投稿的人。我们明白，你们与我们、与大家分享的这成千上万篇故事和诗歌中有你们的心血。为了帮助别人，无论是多么痛苦的经历或是多么私人的故事，你们都愿意将自己的人生经历与《心灵鸡汤》读者分享，这让我们十分感激。

我们只能刊登一小部分收到的故事，但我们读过每一篇投稿，那些未能刊登在书中的故事也对我们和这本书的终稿都有很大影响。

我们想要对《心灵鸡汤》的编辑克里斯蒂娜·格拉文表示感谢，她阅读这本书里数千份来稿中的每一篇，缩小候选篇目范围，并帮助确定终稿及校对工作。我们还要感谢出版助理蒂戴特·科罗娜，她与所有的投稿人密切沟通，还有我们的编辑及网络管理员芭芭拉·罗莫娜卡，感谢他们专业的编辑、校对及组织协调工作。

我们还要特别感谢我们的创意总监和本书制作者，费尤玛出版社的布莱恩·泰勒，他对封面和本书内部的设计可谓别出心裁。最后，感谢我们的首席执行官比尔·洛哈纳和总裁鲍勃·雅各布，若没有他们的前瞻领导和商业眼光，就不会有这本书。

Chicken Soup for the Soul
Improving Your Life Every Day
《心灵鸡汤》
每天改善你的生活

Real people sharing real stories—for 17 years. Now, *Chicken Soup for the Soul* has gone beyond the bookstore to become a world leader in life improvement. Through books, movies, DVDs, online resources and other partnerships, we bring hope, courage, inspiration and love to hundreds of millions of people around the world. *Chicken Soup for the Soul*'s writers and readers belong to a one-of-a-kind global community, sharing advice, support, guidance, comfort, and knowledge.

Chicken Soup for the Soul stories have been translated into more than forty languages and can be found in more than one hundred countries. Every day, millions of people experience a *Chicken Soup for the Soul* story in a book, magazine, newspaper or online. As we share our life experiences through these stories, we offer hope, comfort and inspiration to one another. The stories travel from person to person, and from country to country, helping to improve lives everywhere.

真实的人物分享真实的故事——这么做已经十八年了。现在,《心灵鸡汤》已经不仅仅是书店里的一本书了,而是全世界致力于改变人生的领袖。通过书籍、电影、光盘、网上资源和其他方式,我们将希望、勇气、灵感和爱带给世界各地数不清的人们。《心灵鸡汤》的作者和读者是世界上独一无二的,他们分享建议,互相帮助,为彼此提供指引、慰藉和知识。

《心灵鸡汤》系列故事已经被译成四十多种语言,可以在一百多个国家读到它。每天,数百万人通过书籍、杂志、报纸或网络资源感受《心灵鸡汤》的魅力。我们通过这些故事分享人生经历,为彼此提供希望、慰藉和灵感。这些故事在人们之间传递,在国家之间交流,帮助世界各地的人们拥有更美好的生活。

Share with Us
与我们一同分享

We all have had *Chicken Soup for the Soul* moments in our lives. If you would like to share your story or poem with millions of people around the world, go to chickensoup.com and click on "Submit Your Story." You may be able to help another reader, and become a published author at the same time. Some of our past contributors have launched writing and speaking careers from the publication of their stories in our books!

Our submission volume has been increasing steadily—the quality and quantity of your submissions has been fabulous. We only accept story submissions via our website. They are no longer accepted via mail or fax.

To contact us regarding other matters,

Share with Us
与我们一同分享

please send us an e-mail through webmaster@chickensoupforthesoul.
com, or fax or write us at:

Chicken Soup for the Soul

P.O. Box 700

Cos Cob, CT 06807-0700

Fax: 203-861-7194

One more note from your friends at *Chicken Soup for the Soul*:
Occasionally, we receive an unsolicited book manuscript from one of
our readers, and we would like to respectfully inform you that we do
not accept unsolicited manuscripts and we must discard the ones that
appear.

　　我们人生中都有可以写进《心灵鸡汤》的时刻。如果你愿意与我们
以及世界各地数百万人分享你的故事或诗歌，请登录 chickensoup.com，
点击 "Submit Your Story"（提交故事）按钮。你或许可以帮助一位读者，
同时可以出版你的作品。之前一些投稿人就从在我们的书籍上刊登故事
开始，走上了写作和演讲之路！

　　我们的投稿量与日俱增——大家的投稿质量和数量都非常高。我们
只接受网站投稿。通过信箱或传真投稿将无法接收。

　　若需就其他事宜联系我们，请给我们发邮件至 webmaster@
chickensoupforthesoul.com，或者给以下地址发传真或写信：

心灵鸡汤编辑部 700 信箱

康涅狄格州，科斯科布（Cos Cob）

邮编：06807-0700

传真：203-861-7194

　　《心灵鸡汤》编辑部的朋友们注：有时我们会收到读者未经联系、擅自寄来的书稿，我们敬告您，我们不能接收此类书稿，收到后不得不将之丢弃。

（全书完）